Material Contradictions in Mao's China

Material Contradictions in Mao's China

Edited by

JENNIFER ALTEHENGER

and

DENISE Y. HO

UNIVERSITY OF WASHINGTON PRESS

Seattle

This book is published with the assistance of grants from the China Studies Program at the Henry M. Jackson School of International Studies at the University of Washington, the Frederick W. Hilles Publication Fund at Yale University's Whitney Humanities Center, and the Chiang Ching-Kuo Foundation for International Scholarly Exchange.

Copyright © 2022 by the University of Washington Press

Composed in Minion Pro, typeface designed by Robert Slimbach

All rights reserved. No part of this publication may be reproduced or transmitted in any form or by any means, electronic or mechanical, including photocopy, recording, or any information storage or retrieval system, without permission in writing from the publisher.

UNIVERSITY OF WASHINGTON PRESS
uwapress.uw.edu

LIBRARY OF CONGRESS CATALOGING-IN-PUBLICATION DATA
Names: Altehenger, Jennifer, editor. | Ho, Denise Y., 1978– editor.
Title: Material contradictions in Mao's China / edited by Jennifer Altehenger and Denise Y. Ho.
Description: Seattle : University of Washington Press, 2022.
Identifiers: LCCN 2022015137 (print) | LCCN 2022015138 (ebook) | ISBN 9780295750842 (hardcover) | ISBN 9780295750859 (paperback) | ISBN 9780295750866 (ebook)
Subjects: LCSH: China—Civilization—1949–1976 | Material culture—China | Communism and culture—China | Consumption (Economics)—China
Classification: LCC DS777.6 .M365 2022 (print) | LCC DS777.6 (ebook) | DDC 951.05—dc23/eng/20221003
LC record available at https://lccn.loc.gov/2022015137
LC ebook record available at https://lccn.loc.gov/2022015138

♾ This paper meets the requirements of ANSI/NISO Z39.48-1992 (Permanence of Paper).

CONTENTS

Acknowledgments vii

Introduction: Making Revolution Material 1
    Jennifer Altehenger and Denise Y. Ho

1   Bamboo Objects and Socialist Construction   20
    Jennifer Altehenger

2   The Brick   40
    Cole Roskam

3   Design and Handicraft   63
    Christine I. Ho

4   Dance Props and the Rural Imaginary   84
    Emily Wilcox

5   Mobile Projectionists and the Things They Carried   102
    Jie Li

6   Outside Objects and Material Propaganda   125
    Denise Y. Ho

7   The Problematics of Plenty   146
    Laurence Coderre

8   Nationalizing Food Provision in Beijing   161
    Madeleine Yue Dong

9   One Country, Two Material Cultures   183
    Jacob Eyferth

10 The Makings of China's Cold War Motor City   200
   Covell F. Meyskens

Afterword: Material Culture and the Socialist Uncanny in Mao's China   219
   Jonathan Bach

Chinese Character Glossary   233

Selected Bibliography   235

List of Contributors   241

Index   243

ACKNOWLEDGMENTS

IN THE AGE OF THE GLOBAL PANDEMIC THAT BEGAN IN THE WINTER of 2019–20, when the bodily reality of disease has made our interactions long-distance and virtual, we are doubly grateful for the network of scholars who have come together to make this book. This volume developed out of conversations that began in Shanghai in 2014, when we discussed the idea of connecting historians and others interested in the material culture of the Mao era. In 2015, we organized a panel at the Association of Asian Studies annual meeting, and the insightful comments from our discussant, art historian Alfreda Murck, as well as the enthusiastic response of our audience convinced us to continue the collaboration.

We were very fortunate to receive funding to organize a small exploratory workshop, which took place at King's College London in December 2016. We thank the British Academy and the Leverhulme Trust for the financial support they provided as part of the Small Grant (SG152539), and the King's History Department for hosting the workshop and providing administrative support throughout. We are grateful to Toby Lincoln, Weilin Pan, and Peidong Sun for sharing their research at the workshop and to our discussants Harriet Evans, Anne Gerritsen, Mary Ginsberg, Anke Hein, Michael Schoenhals, Sarah Teasley, and Helen Wang for thoughtful comments that helped us work out what we were trying to do. Cai Chen cheerfully supported us during the two days of the workshop and looked after everyone.

In September of 2018, the first drafts of the papers that became this volume's chapters were presented in New Haven, at the first conference in a series of two entitled "Material Culture and Mao's China," generously sponsored by the Whitney and Betty MacMillan Center for International and Area Studies at Yale. We extend our gratitude to the MacMillan Center's Council for East Asian Studies, especially Richard Sosa and Injoong Kim, for supporting this project throughout, and Elise Antel for organizing the two-day conference. We are also grateful to Sarah Anne Carter for providing a keynote address and leading us in the study of objects we brought to the conference, as well as to our discussants: Ned Cooke, Jonathan Bach, Hanchao Lu, and Dorothy Ko. Yale colleagues Ned Cooke and Deborah Davis attended all of the sessions and continued to provide feedback as this volume took shape. Jonathan Bach not only enlivened our conference with his perspective on Germany and experience in China, he also graciously agreed to write the afterword for this book.

Thanks to generous support from the Arts and Humanities Research Council (AH/R000174/1), we were able to work through revised drafts at our second conference at King's College London in May 2019. It was a rare pleasure to be able to meet twice in person to reflect on our papers as they developed. Paul Betts gave an inspiring keynote lecture that connected the history of material culture in European state socialism to our explorations of Mao-era China. Several colleagues, some of whom had already participated in the 2016 workshop, then generously provided feedback to authors in small discussion groups on the first day of the conference and helped us work through the volume overall on the second. These colleagues included Craig Clunas, David Edgerton, Harriet Evans, Anne Gerritsen, Michael Schoenhals, Sarah Teasley, and Helen Wang. Katrin Heilmann expertly helped organize the conference and ensured its success; we could not have done without her.

In the process of completing this book, we thank the two anonymous reviewers for their feedback and Lorri Hagman and Jennifer Comeau at the University of Washington Press for their stewardship. Also at the UW Press, Chad Attenborough coordinated the images and Richard Isaac provided expert copyediting. We are indebted to Charlotte Cotter at the Fairbank Center Collection of the H. C. Fung Library, Harvard University, who served as editor and project manager, helping us assemble multiple drafts of the manuscript, correspond with authors, and compile images. In the last stages, Cynthia Col prepared the index. We are happy to acknowledge the support of the Council for East Asian Studies at Yale University and the China Studies Program at the Henry M. Jackson School of International Studies at the University of Washington in the production of this book. In addition, the Frederick W. Hilles Publication Fund at Yale University's Whitney Humanities Center and the Chiang Ching-kuo Foundation for International Scholarly Exchange contributed to the final publication expenses.

Lastly, we wish to thank those individuals whose contributions to this book defy easy categorization. Over the course of the pandemic, frontline workers, caregivers, and schoolteachers enabled our labor and that of our contributors. We also wish to recognize Shirley Smith, who was at each and every meeting, reminding us of how much our families support us in both life and work.

Material Contradictions in Mao's China

INTRODUCTION

Making Revolution Material

JENNIFER ALTEHENGER AND DENISE Y. HO

ON NOVEMBER 16, 1973, WANG ZHENHUA AND LI SHUZHEN PUT their thumbprints one after another on a three-page handwritten document that served as their divorce papers. They also attached an appendix, a divided inventory of their household possessions. The fifty-three-year-old husband kept a small metal bedframe, a square wooden table, a fruit bowl, two washbasins, two woks, and a metal thermos, among other items. His wife, age forty-four, retained a large wooden bed, a wooden armoire, a red vase, a fruit bowl, two woks, and two thermoses, as well as other everyday goods. Each kept their own watch, and their one bicycle was left to the wife. This couple's divorce contract, itself an ephemeral and material trace of a two-decade marriage, provides a glimpse into the material conditions of an ordinary family, two workers with five children in the northern Chinese city of Tianjin. Their possessions were primarily everyday objects of use. Rather than purchasing them, Wang and Li had received them from their respective work units.[1] They were made of seemingly simple materials, like the wood of the furniture, the iron of the woks and a stove, and the aluminum of the kettles and pots. And yet in an era of scarcity, it would not have been simple to replace such daily-use items, to say nothing of the valuables: the watches and the bicycle.

China's Mao period, an era that began with the founding of the People's Republic of China (PRC) in 1949 and ended with the death of Mao Zedong in 1976, is an overlooked chapter in the history of material culture and materiality in China. Literature on the late imperial era of the eighteenth and nineteenth century and the Republican period (1912–49) has examined the relationship between materiality and modernity, from the rise of consumer culture to the objects such as porcelain and silk that circulated with increasing globalization after the founding of the Qing dynasty in 1644.[2] Histories of material life during the Republican period—a time shaped by revolution and war—have shown how some aspects of consumption were modernized while other traditions persisted across political ruptures, and how material conditions differed for urban and rural people.[3] On the other side of the Mao years, social scientists have long examined the rise of markets in the post-Mao era of reform, suggesting that state policies and individual initiative ushered in newfound consumer practices along with China's economic miracle.[4] By contrast, the Mao period—rightly framed as a time of scarcity—initially appears to have had little material culture to speak of, or its consumer products are seen as Maoist kitsch, basic daily necessities inscribed with propaganda.

But having had fewer commodities does not mean there was a lack of material culture. As the chapters in this book demonstrate, people attributed great meaning to materials and objects, often precisely because they were rare and difficult to obtain. This volume focuses on things like the contents of Mr. Wang and Ms. Li's two-room apartment in order to study how they were produced, how they circulated, and how they were used. Attention to the material landscape of the Mao era provides a new way of studying the Chinese Communist Party's (CCP) project of socialist construction as well as how Chinese socialism was experienced in everyday life. In recent years, scholars of the Mao era have provided rich insights into its social, cultural, political, and economic history. They have looked at different social groups and regions, at high politics and local experiences, and at the intended and unintended consequences of CCP governance.[5] Thus the work of PRC history has illuminated the lives of people like Wang Zhenhua and Li Shuzhen: we better understand the relationship between Tianjin and its surrounding countryside, the work unit system that governed life in Wang's factory and at Li's stadium, and the Cultural Revolution (1966–76) revolutionary committees that ultimately mediated their divorce. Yet their household possessions allow us to ask other questions: How were these items obtained, and what did it mean to own and use them? How did the family do their cooking and divide their domestic labor? How did Wang and Li view the items distributed by the work unit, and in what ways was frugality political? Potential answers offer glimpses into how people experienced socialist China, from how they navigated the system daily to how they aspired to a better material future.

In addition to filling a gap in the history of twentieth-century China, this book offers the case of socialist China to the global history of materiality. By drawing connections between Mao-era China and the wider world, our authors challenge perceptions that China was a complete autarky or that its connections were only among the socialist bloc. Beyond tangible objects and material exchanges, chapters demonstrate that the ideology of material things in China was linked to debates elsewhere, from the way an object reflects social relations to the role of the commodity in capitalist and socialist systems.

The material culture of China's Mao era was multifaceted and marked by tensions between materials and makers, people and objects, abundance and scarcity, ideology and practice, and more. As an entrée into these themes, we propose the idea of "material contradictions." In 1937, the year the Second Sino-Japanese War broke out, Mao Zedong wrote an essay entitled *On Contradiction* (Maodun lun) in which he outlined "materialist dialectics" and called for the study of things and their relationships, from atoms to social classes. Only in the contradiction, Mao explained, would there be development.[6] The essays in this volume focus on material life during the first three decades of the PRC, excavating objects and the historical contexts in which they were created, to show how tensions materialized, how objects made and mediated relationships, and how people conceived of themselves and their role in "New China" in material terms. Writing in 1992, historian Michael Schoenhals explained what it was to "do things with words in Chinese politics."[7] Over the following two decades, scholars explored the multiple ways in which words had power in the Chinese revolution, from the training of cadres and students to their role in mobilizing the masses. This book uses material culture, materiality, and material life to show what it was to do things with *things* in Chinese politics. Recalling the famine that followed China's Great Leap Forward (1958–62), for example, words could be manipulated to make hunger a crime, but material reality—privation followed by the bodies of excess mortality—remained. The challenge of resolving material contradictions underscores that objects could have power beyond words.

MATERIAL CONDITIONS IN THE EARLY PRC

When the People's Republic of China was established in 1949, the leaders of the Chinese Communist Party faced the task of rebuilding a country that had been torn by decades of civil conflict, economic devastation, the Japanese invasion, and natural disaster. In contrast to the preceding Nationalist regime, the CCP's revolution gained traction in the countryside, and in these base areas the party had already engaged in land reform, redistributing property from landlords to peasants. As the countryside was taken over by the People's Liberation Army (PLA), village governments were established and the economy began to recover: rural markets returned and livelihoods improved.[8] Upon entering cities, the CCP faced capital flight and labor unrest, and declared new urban policies to promote production and economic prosperity.[9] Its task of governance included the creation of a centralized bureaucracy that was led by the party, staffed by cadres, and reached the grassroots, from urban neighborhoods to rural villages. Party and state institutions, whether highly visible or in the background, shaped the material conditions that we examine.

Historians often periodize the Mao era by identifying two stages: the initial transitional years, called "New Democracy," followed by what some scholars describe as "high socialism," or the time between agricultural collectivization and industrial nationalization until the end of the Mao era.[10] In China, a division is made between the first seventeen years, or 1949–66, and what is officially called the "ten years of turmoil" of the Cultural Revolution (1966–76). No matter how the Mao era is periodized, it was marked by episodic and often violent mass campaigns: land reform, campaigns against counterrevolutionaries, the Three-Antis and Five-Antis Campaigns (1951–52), Socialist Transformation (1956), the Anti-Rightist Movement (1957), the Great Leap Forward (and its devastating famine), and the Cultural Revolution. While much scholarship has been devoted to these political movements, recent work has urged us to look beyond what historian Gail Hershatter calls "campaign time" to understand everyday lived experience.[11]

Material concerns animated both "campaign time" and domestic time, as well as time otherwise away from campaigns. Our volume's focus on material culture and materiality connects the temporalities and spaces of life during and away from campaigns. While mass campaigns were seldom central to the case studies explored in this book, they were always part of the larger context. Indeed, mass campaigns were ideological movements with everyday material consequences. In some cases, the link between campaigns and everyday life was explicit: land reform, the Five-Antis, socialist transformation, and agricultural collectivization transferred property from peasants to the collective, from the bourgeoisie to the state. Sometimes, campaigns led to indirect changes in individual material circumstance. For instance, the campaign against counterrevolutionaries included the creation of a household registration system (*hukou*), which facilitated the ration system for foodstuffs and other consumer goods. Campaigns that attacked those with bad class labels—or threatened to relabel people—could result in the immediate confiscation of personal property and a long-term drop in family welfare, with opportunities for education, work, and housing sharply restricted. Perhaps the most dramatic example of the material effects of a mass campaign is the Great Leap Forward, itself an agricultural and industrial drive that resulted in the largest man-made famine in history, with an estimated death toll of more than thirty million.

What were the material conditions faced by the average person living in Mao's China? Much of the answer to that question depends on where the person lived: in a city or in the countryside. In the early 1950s, people had to register their households as urban or rural, and one's status as a nonagricultural or agricultural household determined access to both public goods and consumer products. Those with urban household registration could use ration coupons to buy staple foods like grain and oil, as well as rare consumer purchases like a bicycle. In addition, many city residents were organized into work units (*danwei*) like a school or a factory, and it was through work units that they were assigned housing and accessed other public goods, such as education and health care. By contrast, most rural residents became part of agricultural collectives, and their labor was calculated in work points that were exchanged for grain. The urban-rural divide was so strong that what one ate and what one wore could be more dependent on household registration than on class label.[12]

The urban-rural divide, in other words, was material. In Chinese, a shorthand for one's basic necessities is the four-character phrase *yi shi zhu xing*: clothing, food, housing, and transportation. Comparing clothing and food in their urban and rural contexts illustrates the contrast. For example, in Tianjin and its surrounding countryside, throughout the 1950s the average Hebei grain consumption was 80.2% of Tianjin's.[13] This urban-rural gap was even more pronounced with other foods like cooking oil or pork, and rural bodies were also clothed differently than urban ones. Urban people often wore newer and trim-fitting clothing, while rural people wore old clothing made from homespun cotton.[14] Such differences were exacerbated during times of famine. In Shanghai in 1960, district party committees reported a widespread shortage of grain, as the supply could not fulfill the individual ration of 23.6 *jin*, or 14.6 kilograms, per month.[15] Meanwhile, peasants in rural Shaanxi received grain allocations of 15–20 *jin*, or 9–12 kilograms per month, eating cornmeal gruel and sweet potatoes before turning in desperation to food substitutes such as leaves, bark, and clay.[16] Though the Chinese economy recovered from the "three hard years" of famine, persistent privation created an imperative to make do, from local materials and as part of everyday practice.

The material conditions of Mao's China also existed in regional and international contexts. For example, geographic regions within China were encouraged to become self-sufficient. In fact, the ideal of autarchy applied to all of China, and after 1949, international trade networks became more restricted. In the 1950s, China's model was the Soviet Union, and in addition to adopting its economic system, the Soviet Union served as a source of advisors, machinery, and technological knowledge. China was integrated into a socialist world economy, conducting trade agreements that stretched from Eastern Europe to North Korea and North Vietnam.[17] After the Sino-Soviet split in the early 1960s, as the chapters in our volume show, China's international relations continued to influence people's everyday lives, from screenings of foreign films to food shortages exacerbated by the export of grain. China's socialist experiment was part of a global system.

MATERIAL CULTURE AND MATERIALITY

From theory to practice, materials and objects had a role to play in revolutionary social transformation. For Marx, the investigation of human society begins with its material conditions, and the "mode of production of material life conditions the social, political, and intellectual life process in general."[18] Thus in Marx's writings, things—made into products through human labor, and made into commodities through exchange—reflect the systems in which they were created and thereby change social relations.[19] Mao Zedong, too, was a materialist, arguing that dialectical materialism was both a way to understand the world and a tool to make proletarian revolution. Writing in 1938, Mao described the history of human production in which "man came into contact with surrounding nature, acted upon nature, and created things to eat, to live in, and to use, and adapted nature to the interests of man."[20] Indeed, the idea that man could conquer nature undergirded the ambitious projects of the Mao era, from the construction of bridges and reservoirs to experiments in agriculture and production.

While the average Chinese person may not have described their environment in materialist terms, these ideas were foundational to the political, social, cultural, and economic world they lived in. From different disciplinary perspectives, the chapters in our volume examine the role that people and objects played in making the Maoist world in theory and practice. The two interlinked concepts of "material culture" and "materiality" are central. Both have been extensively discussed in anthropology, cultural and visual studies, history, and philosophy, and both are productive in the analysis of Mao-era

China. We take "material culture" to consist of objects that are made and used, and which can provide a "window into social relations, economics, religion, politics and technology," as well as into practices of consumption and commodity circulations.[21] The concept of "materiality," meanwhile, allows us not merely to see material properties but, as anthropological research has suggested, to trace the "mutually constitutive interactions that take place between material objects, people, bodies, and cognition."[22] As historians Anne Gerritsen and Giorgio Riello write, objects are "part of the affective, social, cultural and economic relationships that form our lives,"[23] and the perspective of materiality opens up ways to explore processes of embodiment, sensorial experiences, the (re)configuration of social relations, and the mediation and re-mediation of knowledge.[24] According to anthropologist Daniel Miller, objects are important "not because they are evident and physically constrain or enable" but rather because "the less we are aware of them, the more powerfully they can determine our expectations by setting the scene and ensuring normative behavior."[25] This approach seems particularly fruitful given the Marxist and Maoist emphasis on the connection between people and things, and the belief in the power of material conditions to determine and alter social relations, people's interactions with the world, and regimes of inequality and oppression.

A focus on material culture and materiality can teach us about the experience of socialism in the People's Republic, a moment of "radical transformation of systems of production, distribution, and consumption" in which materials and objects changed meaning and acquired new significance.[26] We understand socialist China in a number of ways. First, we define socialist China as a period its leaders referred to as "socialist construction" (*shehuizhuyi jianshe*), which was marked by centralized rule by the Chinese Communist Party, collective ownership, and a command economy. The goal of socialist construction was to transform society and reconfigure social relations through the triumvirate of Marxism, Leninism, and Mao Zedong Thought and eventually reach the utopia of communism, a state which Friedrich Engels once described as the commodity-free world governed by an "administration of things." This process of socialist construction was understood to be gradual, an intermediary stage in China's long revolution. Following Laurence Coderre's work in the field of Chinese cultural studies and her reading of materiality in Maoist China, we take seriously the aim to work toward socialist transformation and its material dimensions during all phases of the Mao era.[27] Second, while the debate over whether China was socialist is beyond the scope of our volume, we underscore the ideals of socialism as part of everyday lived experience: Chinese state media and cultural production—for both foreign and domestic audiences—hailed the achievements of socialism; ordinary people like Mr. Wang and Ms. Li hewed to its virtues, like austerity and collectivism. Different groups—including party theorists, officials, intellectuals, economists, and others—fervently and repeatedly debated what socialism truly was and how it could be reached, while many people associated the experience of life during the Mao era with "socialism," even if their experiences often diverged substantially from its theories. What socialism was, then, becomes as much a matter of ideology and thought as of experience, sensation, feeling, and perception.

The historical case studies in this volume investigate the plurality and uneven texture of Chinese socialist experiences. One way to do so is by focusing on the material contradictions, that is, the tensions inherent in and expressed through material culture and materiality during the Mao era. Such tensions included those between consumerist and productivist, domestic and foreign, egalitarian and unequal, preservation and development, official and unofficial economies, old and new, public and private, and urban and rural. These categories and binaries were not natural—they were used to conceptualize social relations and lived environments at the time, and many of them were contested. This makes them analytically useful. These material contradictions reveal socialist China in all of its complexity and diversity, at a time when many workers lived in austerity while magazines and films promoted plenty, when most villagers had little access to commodities while some urbanites could purchase imported goods, and when performers could be at once urban while embodying the rural. These contradictions persisted and in some cases were exacerbated, their tensions unresolved. Contradictions, true to form, engendered more contradiction.

Centered on the relationship between objects and people, our volume brings China into the scholarly debates about the social, cultural, political, and economic history of material culture and materiality across different countries during the twentieth century and especially following World War II. Material culture, design, and consumption in particular have long been crucial to understanding historical developments in countries with a capitalist economic system.[28] These histories have revealed the dynamics behind the European "postwar economic miracle," for example, and the making of consumer societies. Scholars of the "socialist world," meanwhile, have demonstrated that material lives were equally important, though often in different ways, in countries governed by a communist party.[29] They have illustrated the manifold debates surrounding how to define and meet needs (rather than desires), the complexity of economic planning and associated challenges of storage and shortages, and the ways in which ordinary people navigated the networks of material provision to which they had access, often resorting to making things themselves at home. In addition to highlighting the detailed aspects of material life in these different countries, such studies have shown that material culture and materiality are part of a global history in which political systems are one of several considerations.

Far from a replica of the Soviet Union, the case of socialist China has much to contribute to this material turn in contemporary history. To be sure, the model of the Soviet Union always loomed large, whether it was China emulating its mentor in the 1950s or contending with its competitor after the Sino-Soviet split. Yet as the chapters in this volume show, China in the Mao era followed a unique trajectory, with both material and ideological consequences. For instance, in the case of the brick and its role in construction, China was unable to match the production of capitalist countries or the Soviet Union, so architectural theorists had to aspire to the age of steel while contending with the limitations of manufacturing brick in China's vast countryside. Another example of divergence is the way in which rural people in China were excluded from the commodity economy, while simultaneously being cast in a commodity relation with urban industry. The fact that socialist China increasingly styled itself as the leader of world revolution—projecting displays of productivist plenty despite famine—makes our analysis of its material reality all the more imperative. The material conditions of Mao-era China—products, in turn, of its diversity, geography, and historical legacies—heightened the contradictions of its socialist experiment.

FROM MATERIALS TO OBJECTS

Materials were elementary to socialist construction and to people's sensorial experiences of striving for its achievement. Industry, handicraft, and agriculture all relied on materials, including oil, coal, timber, bamboo, steel, aluminum, copper, enamel, glass, concrete, clay, mud, cotton, and silk. Materials were the basis of production and were needed to make objects that in turn could facilitate more production, such as agricultural and artisanal tools or industrial machinery. However, many materials considered central to socialist construction, such as timber, were either naturally scarce or became scarce due to heavy demand. How to obtain and efficiently use materials was a constant problem. As owners of the means of production, Mao wrote in his 1937 *On Practice* (Shijian lun), China's "masses" had to engage in material production.³⁰ This meant that each citizen was responsible for working with and making the most of materials, while exercising frugality; it was a skill to be acquired through practice, but it could only be carried out successfully in the larger collective. The conviction that individuals could achieve the extraordinary if propelled to experiment and work in the collective, and that they could discover new ways of dealing with materials, guided the entire Mao period. This conviction resulted in plenty of failure, as in the example of backyard steel furnaces that produced unusable chunks of melted metal. Yet it could also result in remarkable achievements, as in the example of grassroots agricultural science.³¹

How did the party-state embed materials in the larger socialist imaginary? Few of the materials central to "New China"—from making objects of use to building large housing projects—were new. They had been in use for decades and sometimes centuries.³² State authorities, as the first two chapters illustrate, therefore tried to imbue familiar materials with new meanings and to promote new narratives of the connection between humans, labor, and materials. Chapter 1 explores this process with the example of bamboo objects. Unlike other materials, bamboo was a local material with a long history. After 1949, state media publicized narratives that recounted how local artisans, craft collectives, and smaller factories, supported by the party-state, developed innovative methods of processing ordinary bamboo. Using these methods, bamboo furniture, tools, and other objects would become more affordable and could in time be produced in large quantities. These narratives suggested that liberating artisans and others, and empowering them through the collective, would allow them to unlock the full potential of bamboo to meet the needs of the "laboring masses." This socialist materiality was made up of a network of liberated humans, innovative materials, and high-quality objects now available to the "masses" at large. Yet, such narratives were often also marked by contradictions: handicraft proved difficult to mechanize, and people continued to associate bamboo objects with scarcity rather than abundance.

A material could therefore at once signify development and a lack thereof. China's built environment showcases the extent to which materials determined the process and progress of "socialist construction." While steel and concrete may be the best-known building materials, bricks, the subject of chapter 2, were the most ubiquitous. From the 1950s and well into the Reform Era, bricks materialized socialist modernity. Made locally from mud or clay, bricks were both material and object. To make them, people required some knowledge of the material and production processes but not advanced and specialist expertise. Different localities circulated brickmaking recipes, especially during the Great Leap Forward. Bricks thus became popular not because they were an ideal building material but because they could be made widely available. Because "brick's ontological profile is one generally defined by a modesty imposed by constraints," its preponderance in socialist China's built environment came to signify advances made in construction as well as material constraints.

Design played a formative role in determining the significance and use of materials. This was the case globally during the mid-twentieth century, including in China. Chapter 3 explores discussions about how to create design and design pedagogy for socialist China. Like their contemporaries in other socialist countries, Chinese intellectuals who were later affiliated with the Central Academy of Craft and Design, established in Beijing in 1956, debated what the socialist object in China should be and how it should look. In their opinion, Chinese socialist design was intricately bound up with folk-national handicraft. Craft was to be an expression of party-enabled nation-building and national identity, linking design, makers, their materials and skills, and building on the legacies of pre-revolutionary China's laboring masses. "Hand-derived design knowledge" was to be integrated into the mass manufacture of light industrial goods. Yet, such plans proved difficult to enact once state collectivization and centralization of the handicraft industry obliterated exactly those traditions of folk-national handicraft that many intellectuals had envisaged as the essence of socialist material culture.

OBJECTS AS MEDIATORS

Objects occupied a particular place in communist theory and praxis. Objects themselves were deemed to reflect the class conditions under which they were created. Hence, during China's Mao period, personal possessions became imbued with class. For example, a painting was defined by a retroactive class category applied to an elite artist, and a wedding ring was categorized according to the way it was purchased. If the ring was purchased with the product of the owner's own labor, it was legitimate; if it was bought with money gained by exploitation, it could be confiscated during moments like the Cultural Revolution.[33] In addition, objects had a role to play in political consciousness. In *On Practice*, Mao further justified engagement with material production in that knowledge was based on practice. At a fundamental level, "man's knowledge depends mainly on his activity in material production," and it is through production that people understand human, social, and class relationships. In addition, Mao distinguished between perception and cognition; one has to perceive physical things before understanding their "essence and internal relations," a dialectical process that was to lead from perceptual knowledge to rational knowledge.[34]

The idea of learning by doing was thus central to Mao-era politics. Political cadres formed work teams to study local conditions, intellectuals and officials were sent to the countryside to learn from the peasants, and students were required to labor as part of their education. This principle of practice animated the dancers in Mao-era performances (chapter 4). For the generation of choreographers and dancers who came of age in the 1950s, material objects allowed urban performers to embody rural life. Dance props—from fans and scarves to tea baskets and water buckets—were an inseparable part of Chinese dance and an extension of the dancer's body rather than an accessory. These objects served as mediators, between dancers and life in the countryside, between urban and rural performers who learned from each other, and between dancers and the characters they portrayed on stage. Dancers represented new conceptions of materiality in socialism, performing and embodying the connection between bodies and objects, people and things.

A close connection between objects and bodies was also crucial to other kinds of cultural work, such as film, designed to render socialist ideals more tangible and relatable to everyday life. Film projection from the 1950s to the 1980s relied on the "material infrastructure of cinema," a network that extended the showing of films from several hundred movie theaters to some 162,000 teams of mobile film projectionists who traveled around the country to show films outdoors (chapter 5). Archival sources and oral histories document the mobile film projectionists who carried and operated the objects required for cinema—generators, projectors, screens, and films—as well as bamboo clappers and lantern slides, using them to become performers in their own right. Mobile film projectionists were acutely tuned to the material condition of their equipment: machines needed to be protected and maintained, the films themselves had to be preserved in order to function, and their own voices and hands were used to enliven the show. Mao-era cinema was a "physical and spirit medium," one dependent on materiality and one that transmitted propaganda to mobilize the masses.

Like dancers, film projectionists enlivened the tools of their trade, mediating between objects and bodies, performers and audiences, urban and rural. They illustrate how materiality can enable us to see propaganda work as more than text and discourse. That objects did not just represent but materialized reconfigured social relations is highlighted in chapter 6 on "outside objects" that were carried or mailed from Hong Kong and Macau to mainland China. Despite the border controls established after 1949, members of the diaspora continued to visit relatives in the People's Republic and send two-pound "small packets" to their families. While individuals consistently dispatched outside objects—from used clothing and fabric to foodstuffs and medicine—the package phenomenon reached a height in the "three hard years" of famine, during which as many as two million parcels were sent a month. Thus "the Bamboo Curtain" was traversed by the Chinese diaspora as it offered material tokens of familial care, individual responses to social conditions, things rather than words, and packages from a world of seeming plenty in a time of scarcity. In the same way that the material technology of cinema mediated propaganda, mailed goods also transmitted messages—in this case, a material propaganda that ran contrary to that of the state.

BETWEEN ABUNDANCE AND SCARCITY

For many people, life during the Mao period was marked by a constant push and pull between promises of material abundance and everyday experiences of material shortages. "Abundance" and "scarcity" were not merely terms people used to express lived experience; they were also terms state media used to explain the historical path of progression toward communism. The CCP aspired to create a socialist state that would be able to provide adequately for everyone's needs. To achieve this goal, the population was to be mobilized to work toward increasing industrial and agricultural production. State media constantly emphasized the importance of "hard work and frugal living" (*jianku pusu*) while never failing to connect CCP rule, liberation, and—eventual—material improvements for everyone. This message, however, became more difficult to sustain over time. What constituted abundance and scarcity was also subject to constant debate and shifting interpretation as party officials, economists, and ordinary people defined "need" in different ways. During the early 1950s, shortages could still be presented as a result of almost two decades of war and revolution and as a necessary contribution to postwar reconstruction. People in China shared experiences with those living across Europe and the Soviet Union, where shortages and postwar austerity measures, such as rationing, were part of daily life.

Yet as the years went on, economic reconstruction in Europe progressed and de-Stalinization resulted in a comparatively more extensive socialist consumer culture in Eastern Europe and the Soviet Union and a reconceptualization of what constituted material needs and "the necessary" in state socialism, which led to a status quo better described as a "storage economy" rather than a "shortage economy."[35] Explanations for continued sacrifice in China lost much of their power as it became more evident that shortages were often man-made, a result of poor planning or unequal distribution. The plenty that some parts of Chinese society enjoyed, especially selected groups of urban residents, derived from the visible reality of imposing scarcity on others.

In response, the government amplified the message that the PRC was taking a separate road from all other countries, socialist and otherwise. According to the rationale, this road would prove to be the only one that could truly lead to communism, but it would also demand more sacrifices than any other government was willing to admit. Chapter 7 traces how the problem of plenty and need was theorized and then explained to a general audience. Earlier scholarship often mistakenly assumed that Mao Zedong Thought advocated a unique kind of socialist asceticism ("Maoist asceticism") as a means in itself. But party publications, statements of party policy, theoretical treatises, and cultural representations of plenty and scarcity reveal that discussions of and calls for frugal living served a larger goal that was the very opposite of asceticism. Cultural mediations of scarcity and abundance were guided by productivist convictions. For the CCP, these convictions and the practices of advocating continuous austerity—sometimes to an extreme extent and with disastrous consequences—were the stepping stone to eventual material abundance. This fact was obvious to many at the time, but it was later forgotten or reinterpreted to suit contemporary agendas.

Socialism as people experienced it in daily life, meanwhile, challenged political legitimacy. A constantly pressing question was when this material abundance would arrive and who would really get to benefit. People increasingly judged CCP governance not merely by what they heard and saw but what they could hold, feel, and even taste, as chapter 8's example of the Beijing food industry during the 1950s shows. Political change, policies, and economic planning transformed the "foodscape" of Beijing from vegetable vendors to restaurants. The city's famed culinary world underwent "socialist transformation" in the mid-1950s. Private commercial businesses, many of them small in size, merged into larger state-owned or joint state-private units. This "socialist transformation" changed urban citizens' experience of food, and, by extension, what they tasted. Some vegetables and products that had been widely available before 1949 could no longer be found, while the preference for faster-growing vegetables made bok choy and leafy greens ubiquitous. To those who had relished Beijing foods before "liberation," socialist rule was a step backward, subjecting residents to alternating phases of shortage and wasteful oversupply, to less choice, and to foodstuffs many considered less tasty. To those who had little before 1949, conversely, Beijing's new foodscape could represent an improvement. Either way, even with the restricted availability of goods, Chinese consumers, like their contemporaries in the Soviet Union and Eastern European countries, continued to have opinions about products and made choices where they could.[36]

Outside of urban China, things—in a literal and metaphorical sense—looked very different. Chapter 9 demonstrates why it is not helpful to think of a single material culture shared by all Chinese. Instead, there were at least two: rural and urban. In urban areas, the promotion of factory-made mass commodities like wristwatches, bicycles, and sewing machines reproduced not only a desire for prestigious brands but the social hierarchies that China's socialist experiment claimed to eliminate.[37] For those urban residents who consumed them, these commodities created an urban material culture that linked residents across China's different cities. China's rural material culture, by contrast, was made up of products "grown on local land and fashioned from local resources." The latter were "noncommodities" that were subject to allocation rather than currency-based transactions. Oral histories from villages in central Shaanxi show how people navigated this material culture in the essential areas of food, clothing, housing, fuel, and lighting. Reliance on noncommodities, undersupply, and systematic extraction from the countryside in favor of urban areas meant that rural residents developed an understanding of socialism and "the socialist world" distinct from their urban counterparts.

The scarcity of rural material culture was not just experienced by villagers. It was also part of the experience of industrialization in the countryside, as chapter 10's study of the Second Auto Works in rural Hubei demonstrates. After years of tension on the Sino-Soviet border, clashes broke out in 1969, and the threat of invasion led to the creation of "the Third Front," a campaign to build industrial bases deep in China's interior. The situation at the Second Auto Works shows how such geopolitical concerns shaped China's industrial landscape in rural areas, and how making do with China's material conditions directed production as well as everyday experience on the construction site. Memoirs and oral histories reveal the lived experience of a Third Front campaign through descriptions of spartan living conditions: sleeping on a wooden plank in a thatched hut, eating rice porridge with pickled vegetables, and having only a kerosene lamp for lighting. As in chapter 9's example of Shaanxi villagers, Third Front workers were pushed to the limits of their abilities, and their material resources were stretched extremely thin. Material culture became predominantly a product of substitutes and practices of making do with what was locally available. Unlike villagers, however, many of the urban workers sent to join the Third Front were less able or willing to deal with the austerity and sacrifice that this militarization of everyday life and "industrialization without urbanization" demanded.[38]

CONTENDING WITH MATERIAL CONTRADICTIONS

For Mao, material things were not simply products—they were productive. That is, objects had their own internal logic, and they also reflected other things in the world around them. In this volume, we invite our readers to reflect on China's recent past and to use materiality as lens into the history of the Mao period. We may not ever know much more about Mr. Wang and Ms. Li, the Tianjin couple who divorced in 1973. Yet the inventory of their material possessions provides a fleeting view into how their family came together, and how it came apart. We might guess, for example, that the few things not marked "distributed" were pieces from Wang and Li's families, items that were returned to their original owners after twenty years. And while Wang and Li were given separate financial responsibility for the upkeep of their two youngest daughters, the division of the beds and the woks—with Li keeping a large and small bed and the larger of the two iron woks—reveals that the two girls slept and ate with their mother. We know from the summary jointly issued by both revolutionary committees that new housing was too scarce to be ready immediately, so Mr. Wang and Ms. Li continued to live in the two-room apartment, divided into dual sides. Thus their material lives lingered even as their marriage came to an end, a contradiction of private life in a larger story of socialist China.

NOTES

1 Communist Chinese Political Movements, Box 15, Accession No. 2015, C24-33.07, Folder 129, Divorce Papers, 1970s, Hoover Institution Archives. (These names have been anonymized.)

2 These works include, to cite a small selection, Craig Clunas, *Superfluous Things: Material Culture and Social Status in Early Modern China* (Honolulu: Univeristy of Hawai'i Press, 1991); Timothy Brook, *The Confusions of Pleasure: Commerce and Culture in Ming China* (Berkeley: University of California Press, 1998); Anne Gerritsen, *The City*

of Blue and White: Chinese Porcelain and the Early Modern World (Cambridge: Cambridge University Press, 2020); Jonathan Schlesinger, *A World Trimmed with Fur: Wild Things, Pristine Places, and the Natural Fringes of Qing Rule* (Stanford, CA: Stanford University Press, 2017); and Tobie Meyer-Fong, *What Remains: Coming to Terms with Civil War in 19th Century China* (Stanford, CA: Stanford University Press, 2013), as well as Ko, *Social Life of Inkstones*.

3   Dikötter, *Things Modern*; Lu, *Beyond the Neon Lights*; Madeleine Yue Dong, *Republican Beijing: The City and Its Histories* (Berkeley: University of California Press, 2003); Goldstein and Dong, *Everyday Modernity in China*; Finnane, *Changing Clothes in China*; Joshua Goldstein, *The Remains of the Everyday: One Hundred Years of Recycling in Beijing* (Berkeley: University of California Press, 2020). For the political dimensions of these changes in China's cities, see, for example, David Strand, *Rickshaw Beijing: City, People, and Politics in the 1920s* (Berkeley: University of California Press, 1989).

4   See, for example, Davis, *Consumer Revolution*; or Charlotte Ikels, *The Return of the God of Wealth: The Transition to a Market Economy in Urban China* (Stanford, CA: Stanford University Press, 1996).

5   Pathbreaking volumes over the last fifteen years have conceptualized the study of the People's Republic as history. Such works include Joseph W. Esherick, Paul G. Pickowicz, and Andrew G. Walder, eds., *The Chinese Cultural Revolution as History* (Stanford, CA: Stanford University Press, 2006); Jeremy Brown and Paul G. Pickowicz, eds., *Dilemmas of Victory: The Early Years of the People's Republic of China* (Cambridge, MA: Harvard University Press, 2007); and Brown and Johnson, *Maoism at the Grassroots*. Similar volumes have been published in China and Hong Kong, such as Huadongshifandaxue Zhongguo Dangdaishi Yanjiu Zhongxin, *Zhongguo dangdaishi yanjiu*; and Xiong Jingming, Song Yongyi, and Yu Guoliang, eds., *Zhongwai xuezhe tan Wenge* [Chinese and foreign scholars discuss the Cultural Revolution] (Hong Kong: Chinese University of Hong Kong Press, 2018).

6   Mao Zedong, "On Contradiction" (August 1937), www.marxists.org/reference/archive/mao/selected-works/volume-1/mswv1_17.htm.

7   Schoenhals, *Doing Things with Words*.

8   Andrew G. Walder, *China under Mao: A Revolution Derailed* (Cambridge, MA: Harvard University Press, 2015), 53.

9   Brown and Pickowicz, *Dilemmas of Victory*; see especially chapters 2 and 3.

10 Brown and Johnson, *Maoism at the Grassroots*, 6.

11 Hershatter, *Gender of Memory*, 24–27.

12 Wemheuer, *Social History of Maoist China*, 25.

13 Jeremy Brown, *City Versus Countryside in Mao's China: Negotiating the Divide* (Cambridge: Cambridge University Press, 2012), 36.

14 Jeremy Brown, "Spatial Profiling: Seeing Rural and Urban in Mao's China," in *Visualizing Modern China: Image, History, and Memory, 1750–Present*, edited by James A. Cook, Joshua Goldstein, Matthew D. John, and Sigrid Schmalzer (Lanham, MD: Lexington Books, 2014), 203–18.

15 Feng Xiaocai, "Baowei 'shehuizhuyi jianshe de minggenzi': 1959-1961 nian Shanghai de liangshi jinzhang ji yingdui" [Protect the 'lifeblood of socialist construction': Responses to grain shortage in Shanghai, 1959–1961], *Xin shixue* 7 (2013): 223–53.

16 Hershatter, *Gender of Memory*, 255–56.
17 William C. Kirby, "China's Internationalization in the Early People's Republic: Dreams of a Socialist World Economy," in *The History of the PRC, 1949–1976*, edited by Julia Strauss (Cambridge: Cambridge University Press, 2007), 16–36.
18 Robert C. Tucker, ed., *The Marx-Engels Reader* (New York: W. W. Norton & Company, 1978), 4. This excerpt comes from the preface to *A Contribution to the Critique of Political Economy*, first published in 1859.
19 Karl Marx, *Selected Writings*, edited by Lawrence H. Simon (Indianapolis: Hackett, 1994), 220–30. This excerpt comes from *Capital*, vol. 1, ch. 1, "The Commodity."
20 Mao Zedong, "Dialectical Materialism" (April–June 1938) in *Selected Works of Mao Tse-tung*, www.marxists.org/reference/archive/mao/selected-works/volume-6/mswv6_30.htm.
21 "Material Culture" in Luis Vivanco, ed., *Oxford Dictionary of Cultural Anthropology* (Oxford: Oxford University Press, 2018). See also Kaori O'Connor, "Anthropology, Archaeology, History and the Material Culture of Lycra," in Gerritsen and Riello, *Writing Material Culture History*, 73–92, 80. These approaches overlap with the field of consumption studies but extend it in significant ways, seeing consumption as including not merely the acquisition but also the use and experience of things. Consumption, in other words, is taken as one of several perspectives on material culture and materiality.
22 "Materiality" in Vivanco, *Oxford Dictionary of Cultural Anthropology*.
23 "Introduction," in Gerritsen and Riello, *Writing Material Culture History*, 2.
24 On mediation and re-mediation, see Li, *Utopian Ruins*. For a detailed discussion of materiality in the Cultural Revolution and the role of objects and "things" at large, see Coderre, *Newborn Socialist Things*.
25 Daniel Miller, ed., *Materiality* (Durham: Duke University Press, 2005), 5.
26 Auslander, "Beyond Words," 1023.
27 Coderre, *Newborn Socialist Things*.
28 This literature is too numerous to list, but representative works that have informed our volume include Paul Betts, *The Authority of Everyday Objects: A Cultural History of West German Industrial Design* (Berkeley, CA: University of California Press, 2004); Victoria de Grazia, *Irresistible Empire: America's Advance through 20th-Century Europe* (Cambridge, MA: Harvard University Press, 2009); David F. Crew, *Consuming Germany in the Cold War: Leisure, Consumption and Culture* (Oxford: Berg, 2003); Frank Trentman, *Free Trade Nation: Commerce, Consumption and Civil Society in Modern Britain* (Oxford: Oxford University Press, 2008); and Frank Trentman, ed., *The Oxford Handbook of Consumption* (Oxford: Oxford University Press, 2012).
29 See, for example, Betts and Pence, *Socialist Modern*; Bren and Neuburger, *Communism Unwrapped*; the chapters on the GDR in Crew, *Consuming Germany in the Cold War*; Reid and Crowley, *Style and Socialism*; and Crowley and Reid, *Pleasures in Socialism*.
30 Mao Zedong, "On Practice: On the Relation Between Knowledge and Practice, Between Knowing and Doing" (July 1937), www.marxists.org/reference/archive/mao/selected-works/volume-1/mswv1_16.htm.
31 Schmalzer, *Red Revolution, Green Revolution*.
32 On the history of chemistry and chemical products, see James Reardon-Anderson, *The Study of Change: Chemistry in China, 1840–1949* (Cambridge: Cambridge University

Press, 1991). For a history of oil, petroleum, and other raw materials in China, see Kinzley, *Natural Resources*. The history of coal is traced in Shellen Xiao Wu, *Empires of Coal: Fueling China's Entry into the Modern World* (Stanford, CA: Stanford University Press, 2015).

33 Ho, *Curating Revolution*.
34 Mao Zedong, "On Practice."
35 Oushakine, "'Against the Cult of Things'"; Natalya Chernyshova, *Soviet Consumer Culture in the Brezhnev Era* (London: Routledge, 2013).
36 See, for instance, Chernyshova, *Soviet Consumer Culture*; Reid and Crowley, *Style and Socialism*; Bren and Neuburger, *Communism Unwrapped*.
37 Gerth, *Unending Capitalism*.
38 Hou, *Building for Oil*, 133.

1   BAMBOO OBJECTS AND SOCIALIST CONSTRUCTION

JENNIFER ALTEHENGER

THE HISTORY OF CHINA AND BAMBOO ARE INTERTWINED. CHINA has long been home to the largest variety of bamboo species and some of the world's most expansive bamboo forests. For centuries, bamboo has been a source of food, fuel, clothing, and housing and has been used to make objects, from the earliest bamboo strips to paper, pens, baskets, steamers, chopsticks, furniture, and all kinds of other items. Besides the fact that it grows locally, bamboo has several advantageous properties that have made it so useful over time. It grows more quickly than other kinds of timber; some species need only three to five years to mature, and trimmings can already be taken after the first year. Although vulnerable to insect infestation, it is nonetheless a sturdy material that is well suited to humid environments. While there are expensive rare species, many more common species are affordable, and some are very cheap. For all these reasons, the social life of bamboo has historically extended from the wealthy to the poor and from rural to urban; it was a material celebrated in poetry and art, and yet also decried as a symbol of precarity and destitution.[1]

If China and bamboo have traditionally been linked in the popular imagination, bamboo has told different stories about China over time. During the Mao era, it was used to narrate China's feudalist past, transitional present, and socialist future. After the People's Republic of China was established in late 1949, the Chinese Communist Party built a regime of "material governance" that pursued ambitious and rapid industrialization in the difficult conditions of postwar austerity inherited from decades of war.[2] As the latest heir to China's "material empire," with its resources of coal, oil, iron, minerals, timber, and cotton, the CCP's economic and social revolution had a clear aim: to make China's masses masters of their own society by way of making them owners of the means of production.[3] The means of production included China's resources as well as its people's long-established skills working with and maintaining these resources. Bamboo was part of this regime of material governance, and it had a specific role to play as resource and as material embodiment of the socialist revolution. The characteristics that had long made bamboo a popular material meant it was considered most suitable to a revolution that promised a future material plenty in which all people's needs would be provided for. Bamboo, then, seemed ideally placed to be an important part of China's socialist construction, that is, of the actual quotidian process by which China's people—now as their own masters—would work to make this better future a reality under party leadership.

Bamboo could depict socialist construction in numerous ways, in narratives about everything from food and nourishment to architecture to scaffolding used in construction to bamboo forests and their inhabitants. The example of everyday bamboo objects shows how writers, artists, artisans, and designers after 1949 explained the connection between raw material, handicraft skills, and humans as makers, users, and facilitators of knowledge about bamboo. As bamboo objects were familiar and had long been important to the daily lives of most people across China, they and their makers had to be reinterpreted as part of the socialist cultural imaginary.[4] Everyone was supposed to rediscover bamboo as a special material precisely because it was "Chinese," in the sense of being local and of the masses. It was predestined as a material for "massification" (*dazhonghua*)—in this case mass production— because of its historical association with rural life, hardship, and handicraft, not luxury and wealth. Accounts of bamboo objects and their makers told audiences not only that bamboo was a "means of production" but also what the transformation into conscious owners of this means of production looked like and entailed. When people learned about bamboo objects in socialist China, they learned about the potential of the "human-material"/"human-object" pairing in driving forward production and revolutionary progress.[5]

Bamboo was a particular kind of material and cultural connector: it was a "hinge material," and bamboo objects were "hinge objects." Material and objects linked selected aspects of China's past with a socialist future of collectively mass-produced objects for all. They also connected rural and urban, local and national, handicraft and industrial production. This distinguished bamboo from other materials, especially plastics and even steel. Both plastic (in the form of Bakelite) and steel had existed in Republican China, but in the PRC they were presented as new materials that connected only present and future.[6] The materials' past lives were of minor importance. Plastics in China thus functioned in a similar way to plastics in other socialist countries. In the German Democratic Republic, for example, a locally produced plastic called Plaste[7] was hailed as one of the major achievements of the new government and subsequently came to embody GDR socialism in the form of colorful plastic egg cups and the famous Trabant car.[8] Plaste told a story of East Germany as a new nation capable of producing affordable and at first seemingly endless supplies of materials. But when many plastics products turned out to be of lower quality or were only available to some, Plaste soon also told a story of "real existing socialism" and the GDR government's inability to deliver on many of its promises. Bamboo, too, was used to construct a positive account of the Chinese nation. It also encountered similar difficulties when narratives of bamboo plenty and Chinese people's experience of socialism failed to converge. In the case of a hinge material, however, such a failure led people to compare their daily lives not only with the promised socialist future but also with past experiences embodied in bamboo and bamboo objects, and to question the CCP's claim of having created a "new society."[9] Because they were made of a hinge material, bamboo objects were therefore powerful mediators of both liberation and the contradictions inherent to socialist construction.

LIBERATING PRODUCTIVE FORCES

During the 1950s, print and other media regularly discussed how bamboo might be useful in daily life. Magazines on arts and decor, such as the Central Academy of Craft and Design's *Decoration* (Zhuangshi), featured elaborate descriptions of bamboo-rich regions such as Sichuan or Fujian together with attractive photo spreads of bamboo goods and furniture.[10] One article, for instance, told readers about a Beijing comrade who had raved about Sichuan's "bamboo world," where "dwellings, desks and chairs, beds and bedding, and things for daily use are all made with bamboo." Regional experiences with this affordable material, in his opinion, had the potential to change the whole country.[11] Reportage in the *People's Daily* and other newspapers, too, encouraged people to pay more attention to bamboo, arguing that its natural properties would soon enable citizens across the country—not merely those living in bamboo-rich areas—to gain access to goods that everyone needed on a daily basis: bed frames, baskets, chopsticks, screens, sieves, and chairs.[12] Beyond the pages of magazines, people encountered examples of bamboo handicraft in exhibitions of timber, furniture, and objects of use in major cities across the country. In spaces dedicated to giving visitors a material sense of the country's socialist future, organizers and docents singled out items made of bamboo.[13]

Media agreed that bamboo objects were ideal agents of socialist construction because they could meet people's needs while being "practical, economical, and attractive" (*shiyong, jingji, meiguan*). Yet many people's experience of owning bamboo objects or working with bamboo was different. Because of existing shortages that predated the foundation of the People's Republic, bamboo for many symbolized necessity, not socialist plenty, and employing bamboo resources was a daily skill, not a socialist virtue. The CCP's policies after 1949 amplified this message of necessity. From the mid-1950s, the party had promoted self-reliance and called on people to maximize local resources to help socialist construction. Nothing, from waste to local resources such as grass, was too small or insignificant to utilize.[14] All resources, including bamboo, were in extreme demand and short supply, and people were exhorted to save. Designed to rapidly advance China toward socialism, the Great Leap Forward then exacerbated this situation: bamboo forests were cut down or cleared in many areas to provide material and free up land for other agricultural purposes. By the early 1960s, with resources depleted and state media continuously exhorting people to save, it was hard for many to see bamboo as anything other than a means to survive and make do.[15]

Writers were meant to resolve this apparent contradiction and explain that precisely because people had bamboo to cope with hardship, the material would eventually also facilitate socialist plenty. If hardship was the road toward plenty, it was paved with bamboo.[16] To make this message more relatable, accounts of bamboo connected the story of the material to that of labor models, the hardship they had endured, and their resulting achievements.[17] They were written to help readers see themselves not as objects but as agents of change, as owners of the means of production, to which bamboo and the skill of working with bamboo belonged. Zhang Shuiquan, a bamboo artisan from Hubei, was among the models selected to show how the party would help people transform themselves, maximize the potential of materials, and thus create new socialist objects and a new socialist life.[18]

Zhang Shuiquan was born in 1892 in Wuxue Town in Hubei's Guangji County. Coming of age in the waning Qing empire, Zhang learned the bamboo trade from his father, but he had a special talent: he could make affordable bamboo furniture that had the same skillful designs and was as long-lasting as expensive Ming dynasty (1368–1644)–style furniture made of precious woods. Ming designs during the 1950s were considered highly attractive and, unlike Qing (1644–1911) designs, which were often seen as foreign, they—like bamboo—were seen as local and Chinese. Zhang had devised a technique to prepare bamboo that ensured that his furniture would not deform or crack over time, both common problems of working with some of the more affordable species. One of Zhang's chairs won a prize at the Panama-Pacific International Exposition in San Francisco in 1915, and during the Second Sino-Japanese War (1937–45), his chairs and desks won prizes at the Tokyo and Osaka trade fairs.

After 1949, local CCP officials recognized the significance of Zhang's craft. In 1955, he joined the Wuxue Town bamboo goods cooperative.[19] This cooperative had started as a mutual aid team in 1952, producing mainly small objects such as egg baskets and fishing rods.[20] Once Zhang joined, the cooperative reorganized to focus on his furniture instead, making not only chairs and tables but also sofas, foldable furniture, and toys.[21] Zhang began to take in apprentices, and in 1956, he relocated to the city of Wuhan.[22] That same year, he was made a Hubei industry and agriculture labor model and exhibited his products in the Light Industry Hall's handicraft section of the Hubei Provincial Industry and Agricultural Exhibition in Wuchang.[23] In 1959, Zhang, who was then already in his late sixties, produced furniture for the Hubei Hall in Beijing's newly built Great Hall of the People.[24] His fame lasted beyond his death in 1962. The Wuxue factory became a provincial handicraft advanced work unit, receiving several thousand visiting cadres during the early 1960s.[25]

Zhang's trajectory was impressive, but to be of use to the socialist cultural imaginary, writers had to connect Zhang's skills to the transformative potential of socialism. In the late 1950s, his life was narrativized to tell a story of liberation, transformation, and individual ingenuity against all odds. It became the subject of a 1957 film, newspaper and magazine articles, and a 1958 comic book published by the Tianjin People's Arts Publishing House.[26] "Zhang the man" became "Zhang the model," whose life's accomplishment was the struggle to show the true merit of bamboo, China's homegrown material.[27]

In these accounts, Zhang and bamboo are subjects of CCP liberation, and agents of transformation themselves. The comic book opens with images and a description of Zhang living in impoverished circumstances, having to battle a series of obstacles that China's "old society" places in his way. He acquires skills to work with bamboo secretly, against the wishes of his patriarchal and imposing father. His work soon attracts official attention, and from then on, state power constantly prevents Zhang from making a living off bamboo because he is too good at what he does: Zhang's talent makes him a resource to be extracted.[28] Qing officials—representing the feudal state—take furniture pieces they like as tax payments. Later, Republican officials tell Zhang that one of his chairs—taken rather than purchased—has been successfully exhibited at the Panama-Pacific Exhibition. During the Second Sino-Japanese War, while Zhang's family are barely surviving, imperial Japanese officers take

FIGURE 1.1. Zhang Shuiquan teaching disciples in his new workshop after liberation. Shen Sha and Mo Shiguang, *Zhuqi mingjiang Zhang Shuiquan* (Tianjin: Tianjin Renmin Meishu Chubanshe, 1958), 64.

furniture without paying. They later return to hand him a prize certificate from fairs in Tokyo and Osaka. Zhang always gets the symbolic acknowledgment but none of the prize money, and thus his family lives in poverty.[29] To keep his family safe, he agrees to exhibit the despised certificate in his workshop. Then, in 1945, local military officials use the certificate to frame Zhang as a traitor, demanding free furniture as a bribe for them to keep quiet. Relief only comes after the CCP assumes power. Worried about the prizes his work obtained abroad, Zhang confesses to the party cadre when he comes to the workshop one day. Yet the cadre is kind, assuring him that there is no need to feel ashamed: the acknowledgment of his art won China international honor, and his skills can greatly benefit the masses.[30] At the end of the story, a grateful Zhang, who can now provide for his family, devotes all his energy to improving his skills, producing high-quality furniture pieces for everyone to buy, and training a new generation of disciples.[31]

This version of Zhang's life foregrounds the significance of materiality: the human's ability to use cheap local materials to created advanced objects.[32] The key to the story is not simply that Zhang can make furniture from this bamboo. His father and many others could do that. Rather, it is his ability to make beautiful furniture that is practical (*shiyong*), durable, and affordable.[33] Only objects that possessed these qualities had a genuine claim to addressing need and therefore also the necessary prerequisites to be suitable for mass production in state socialism. The ingenuity of folk (*minjian*) craft being able to identify and satisfy needs is signified in the visionary, partly self-trained craftsman becoming a furniture maker for the masses: in his hands, the locally available bamboo can be worked like precious wood, making it possible for everyone to obtain pieces of furniture previously reserved for the powerful and wealthy. Through individual hard study and experimentation, that is, the combination of theory and practice, Zhang unlocks the unexpected potential of the material. Simple bamboo transforms into a valuable material for the average person that can be used for mass production. In a second step, Zhang also facilitates a transformed aesthetic: successive images show ornamental but less intricately woven bamboo furniture. Simplicity is presented as beautiful and elegant, born of a practicality that requires less labor as well as economic and material resources, and that therefore is more befitting a "new era." And in a final step, Zhang can make this knowledge and technology accessible to others, as he is supported by the new party-state and is brought into the collective, where he can perfect his skills not in isolation but in exchange with others. Together, artisan and material can "serve the people" (*wei renmin fuwu*).[34]

As labor model, Zhang's life explained how revolutionary progress unfolded at the level of the individual and the community. The combined narrative—of his personal transformation into an accredited craftsman who is not exploited but can contribute to society, and of the transformation of bamboo into useful new bamboo objects—worked well to explain how ingenuity and perseverance would bring about a "new society." Yet there was also an inherent contradiction between man and model, city and countryside. The story celebrated the countryside as the source of advanced handicraft. The natural environment enabled Zhang to develop his technique and be ahead of his time. Yet, in actual life, Zhang's reward for his contributions was to leave the countryside. State patronage brought a monthly income of one hundred yuan, extra funds for his cooperative, an apartment in the city, and medical resources when he fell ill.[35] With a salary, Zhang could participate in the urban commodity culture, a privilege few rural inhabitants enjoyed.[36]

This suggested that being an accomplished rural artisan who could successfully manipulate a material was a path out of the countryside, and that this was desirable. Readers who knew the hardship of rural life would have readily agreed with this message. And it was reinforced by Zhang's first cohort of apprentices after 1955, which included urban youth assigned by the CCP to learn Zhang's carpentry skills. Working as an apprentice was tough, the work hours were long, and—at least in the eyes of urban youth—it was poorly paid. They soon returned to the city, replaced by rural apprentices who persevered.[37] For them, as for Zhang, the apprenticeship offered a better, urban future.[38] Not only did the contradiction between the idealized rural and the desirable urban remained unresolved, Zhang became a model of how to leave the rural behind.

FROM HANDICRAFT TO INDUSTRY

Zhang's furniture embodied the promise of objects for all, but also the CCP's continued reliance on handicraft to bring about revolutionary transformation. Translating handicraft into mass production was an important project, closely linked to the party's claim of imminent prosperity for all. Bamboo furniture produced in Zhang's workshop was everything that socialist furniture for the masses was meant to be: practical, versatile, and affordable, all qualities closely associated with the promise of industrialization and light industry production. Yet machines could not replicate his techniques or replace his tools. The furniture had to be manually made. And for as long as machines could not do the work, Zhang's embodied skills and knowledge could only be passed on through years of training apprentices. In other words, unless separated from the man, his techniques and achievements would not survive beyond his lifetime, and the quantity of furniture that could be produced was limited, as was its contribution to socialist construction.[39]

The demands of handicraft and light industry were therefore in tension, and the question was which techniques of folk craft could be adapted to industrial production. Many "arts and crafts workers" (*gongyi meishu gongzuozhe*) such as Zhang were invited to join regional research institutes. Zhang joined the South-Central Region's Bamboo Usage Research Committee (Zhongnan Zhucai Liyong Yanjiu Weiyuanhui), which brought together architects, engineers, designers, and wood and bamboo workers, among others. Committee members searched for methods to make ordinary bamboo more adaptable to mass production. This included solving problems such as how to make the material resistant to insects, and therefore more durable.[40] It also included working out which folk craft objects would lend themselves better than others to mechanized manufacturing processes and modular manufacturing in larger industrial units.

Projects to collectivize and mechanize bamboo furniture production were also underway in other parts of the country, including Fujian, a few hundred miles southeast of Hubei. Fujian was traditionally rich in bamboo, making its capital Fuzhou and surrounding counties a center of bamboo object manufacture. One smaller factory in particular, the Fuzhou Bamboo Craft Experimental Factory (Fuzhou Zhucai Gongyi Shiyanchang), became a model story, this time of collective research, design, and production. Set up in 1958 and active until 1969, the factory was a joint project of the Provincial Light Industry Bureau and the Arts and Crafts Bureau.[41] Its initial mission was to design and produce prototypes of cutting-edge bamboo furniture to be exhibited in the 1959 national arts and crafts exhibition in Beijing in celebration of the tenth anniversary of the People's Republic's founding. When it was set up, the factory had a small staff, including ten older Fuzhou bamboo artisans.[42] Two of its members, Lin Jianqing, a professor at Fujian Normal College, and Gao Yishui, an older bamboo master, left accounts that, read together with available archival documents, reveal how the collective was supposed to mobilize and enhance the individual and the material.

Lin, Gao, and their colleagues designed the factory as a space to pool and disseminate existing knowledge about bamboo work, and to create new knowledge and techniques through experiment, with the goal of making furniture designs that could be mass-produced. The factory brought together a younger generation of designers, older artisan masters, skilled industrial workers, and arts workers. Rather than focusing on their separate workflows, they contributed their respective skills to joint projects. Thus, theory and practice became linked in projects, rather than separated in distinct departments. In 1963, Gao attended the provincial artisan representatives' meeting to present the factory's work. In a longer speech, he outlined their work process and how it allowed factory members to reconsider established work modes both for their technical and political value. Gao explained that designers at the factory developed modern technical drawings for new furniture designs that could be replicated in other work units. They did so in close cooperation with artisans who immediately tested how a design could be produced in practice.[43] Workers constantly engaged in materials research, debating which of the many local variants of bamboo was most suited to manufacturing which part of an object. They also designed new tools and machinery. If a smaller team of designers, artisans, and skilled workers stumbled over a problem they could not solve, the factory would bring together everyone for what he called a "brainstorming conference." At such conferences, the team explained the problem, showing the prototype parts, and everyone present discussed possible solutions. Skilled workers and artisans learned to read technical blueprints and produce furniture according to them, while designers participated in hands-on production and benefited from artisans' extensive knowledge of the various properties of bamboo species.[44] This, as Lin later wrote, allowed "designers and construction workers" to have "a common language."[45]

Gao, the senior bamboo artisan, was a crucial facilitator between past and present, similar to Zhang Shuiquan. Lin's biography, meanwhile, underscored the importance of the committed, visionary amateur. A Fuzhou native, Lin was not a designer, artist, or skilled worker, but he spent his life reforming bamboo furniture. His approach to his craft exemplified the CCP's project of associating bamboo with socialism, and he recorded his experiences in several articles about Fujian and particularly Fuzhou's history of bamboo furniture.[46] Born in the first decade of the twentieth century, Lin graduated from Fujian No. 1 Teachers College and became a teacher at a primary school in Fuzhou. While growing up in the area, he wrote, bamboo and the city's natural environment had always fascinated him. In 1924, he cofounded the Fujian Natural Sciences Research Association, which collected bamboo samples from adjacent counties.[47] Lin brought his fascination with this material into his classroom, where he had students make their own bamboo items. Some of these items were accomplished, and one class won a national prize for a bookshelf design at an exhibition of middle and primary school manual work accomplishments in Nanjing in 1934.[48] Lin's approach had official approval and support. His school provided him with a workshop for experiments and teaching where, in addition to classes, he brought together artisans and carpentry teachers to try and reform the curriculum, as well as develop modernized furniture designs using new types of three-dimensional blueprints. According to him, he was driven by the realization that "the reform of bamboo furniture was necessary and possible."[49] Having edited one volume on bamboo furniture design, Lin was appointed to Fujian Normal College in 1942, where he drew more designs and edited books. Not content to focus on theory only, he began to produce furniture in collaboration with local artisans and sold it successfully on the local market into the early 1950s.

Lin's and Gao's experiences, and their advocacy for bringing together designers and artisans, aligned well with state design and craft agendas. The experimental factory exhibited its designs and products to great acclaim at the national arts and crafts exhibition in Beijing in 1959, thus succeeding in the task for which it was initially set up. Moreover, the designers and artisans and their material and objects received the highest mark of party validation during their visit to the capital. Impressed by the "new-style" bamboo furniture they presented, a "leading cadre" working in the National People's Congress (the source does not disclose his name) invited them to his office and commissioned them to produce one-seat bamboo armchairs (a one-seat "sofa chair" in Chinese) for Mao Zedong and Zhou Enlai. In order to see what dimensions the armchair should have, Lin and Gao were given the unusual honor of visiting Mao's and Zhou's quarters.[50]

Following this success, in 1960, the tenth issue of *Decoration* magazine was devoted entirely to Fujian and its rich bamboo resources, including a major spread promoting the factory and its furniture.[51] This gave Lin an opportunity to demonstrate how he and his colleagues had combined folk-art furniture designs with "new style" modern designs. In this article, Lin once more highlighted the agency of local artisans, explaining to a wider readership how they had helped him understand the differences between bamboo and wood. He designed a cabinet using spotted bamboo (*xiangfeizhu*) and initially calculated that it should be thirty centimeters deep. He then consulted one of his colleagues, a bamboo artisan, who advised that because bamboo was less dense than wood, a bamboo cabinet should be deeper in order to be as stable. Lin changed his measurements to thirty-five centimeters to ensure that his cabinet would stand securely on its own. As in the story of Zhang, Lin's account emphasized how, designed correctly and with an understanding of the material's properties, bamboo furniture could do everything that modern furniture was meant to do. It was easy to assemble, dismantle, and transport, and could be stackable and foldable, all properties described as serving the masses.

MEDIATING KNOWLEDGE

The accounts of Zhang Shuiquan, Gao Yishui, and Lin Jianqing narrativized how Chinese socialism facilitated novel modes of production that maximized the abilities of people and materials, fostered skills, and created as well as disseminated technical and design knowledge. In practice, such knowledge was shared among those involved in craft and bamboo work. Factory members in Fuzhou, for example, worked with members of their community in furniture and tool production. Extending beyond local contexts, practical knowledge about bamboo was also supposed to be made more accessible to the general population, so that they could appreciate not only bamboo's worth but also their role in creating the conditions for its success. Publishing houses assembled "how-to" manuals that taught readers of all ages how to cultivate and work with bamboo. Such manuals had already been popular during the Republican period, but production accelerated noticeably by the late 1950s as part of the CCP's belief that all scientific knowledge, including material sciences, could be made accessible and mediated.[52] Manuals became one element in a media landscape that included articles about bamboo objects in newspapers, internal compilations and reports on bamboo production across the country, and propaganda posters explaining why bamboo mattered and how to grow and protect it.[53]

There were different kinds of manuals, but most shared the same premise: the more people knew about bamboo, the more they might use material resources appropriately and effectively. In an ideal world, someone who had read about Zhang Shuiquan, the Fuzhou Experimental Factory, or other model stories, might look to a manual for more advice on how to emulate them. Three types of manuals exemplify how knowledge about bamboo was to be spread: cultivation and manufacturing guides; popular introductions to practicing bamboo craft; and illustrated generalist booklets that explained why bamboo was an important resource. In addition to mediating material knowledge and skills, manuals also allowed publishers to cast the material shortages readers might have experienced in daily life, and the party-state's call for austerity and thrift, not solely as a problem but as an opportunity for the discovery of overlooked local resources, and for local innovation in industrial and handicraft manufacturing techniques. Thrift and experimentation, readers learned, led to the unexpected and might offer solutions to a problem they had long been unable to solve.[54]

Readers, in other words, were extolled to use technical knowledge to emancipate themselves as owners of the means of production, much as Zhang had. Take the example of Wu Zhonglun's *How to Plant Bamboo* (Zenyang zhong maozhu), published by the China Forestry Publishing House in 1956. With six lessons and on only sixteen pages the manual was a handy guide for the aspiring bamboo worker. It was written for an audience with a medium level of literacy, used simplified sentence structures, and contained a few images, mainly of insects. The manual explained the basic types of bamboo species, when, how, and which types of bamboo to plant. It provided basic calculations of how much it would cost to plant a mu (ca. 1/6 of an acre) of bamboo, when and how much yield and income to expect. The manual also identified different plagues, how to deal with them, and how to prevent infestation.[55]

For readers wanting to work with and make things out of bamboo, there were manuals that encouraged amateur practice.[56] The ability to make one's own objects was an important skill, especially during times of shortage, which continued to be widespread. As in other socialist countries that experienced shortages of materials and goods, and production backlogs, these manuals encouraged people to make or re-make their own objects in order to take pressure off the market.[57] Bamboo was thought suitable because it was seen as comparatively easy to work with, familiar and affordable. A particular genre among these guides was toy-making. Besides being items to enjoy, toys were pedagogical tools, making their production useful for rearing the next generation.[58] Yang Qiyan and Liu Yousui's *Bamboo Animal Toys* (Zhuzhi dongwu wanju), published in 1957 and reprinted in 1960, for example, contained instructions for building 22 different kinds of animals, including a dragonfly, peacock, dog, rabbit, white crane, elephant, and tiger.[59]

The manual was meant to be educational as well as enjoyable. Its opening section on "general knowledge of bamboo artisanry" described tools, different types of bamboo, and how to work with the material.[60] There was one page for each animal, with half a page of text and half a page of blueprints (figure 1.2). Manuals such as these encouraged everyone to be a maker, emphasizing just how important it was for everyone, from a young age, to work with and experience materials. If everyone made objects themselves, everyone would contribute to building a socialist material culture, one self-made object at a time.

At the same time, implicitly contradicting this message, manuals often presumed a degree of material intuition and skill that challenged many readers. Although *Bamboo Animal Toys* was aimed at a young audience, it is striking how little explanation the volume contained and what elaborate skills it presumed readers had: the ability to magnify blueprints, to work with tools, and to cut fine shapes. Just like other attempts to mediate the embodied knowledge of practitioners through print media, *Bamboo Animal Toys* might have made some knowledge accessible, but it would not have unlocked bamboo craft for the complete beginner. Depending on the reader, manuals could therefore be encouragement or obstacle, and risked excluding some of the readers they had set out to reach.

Even readers who neither wished to cultivate bamboo nor make bamboo objects were to learn about bamboo and its significance in carrying China from a difficult past to a prosperous future. Publishers tried to cater to this

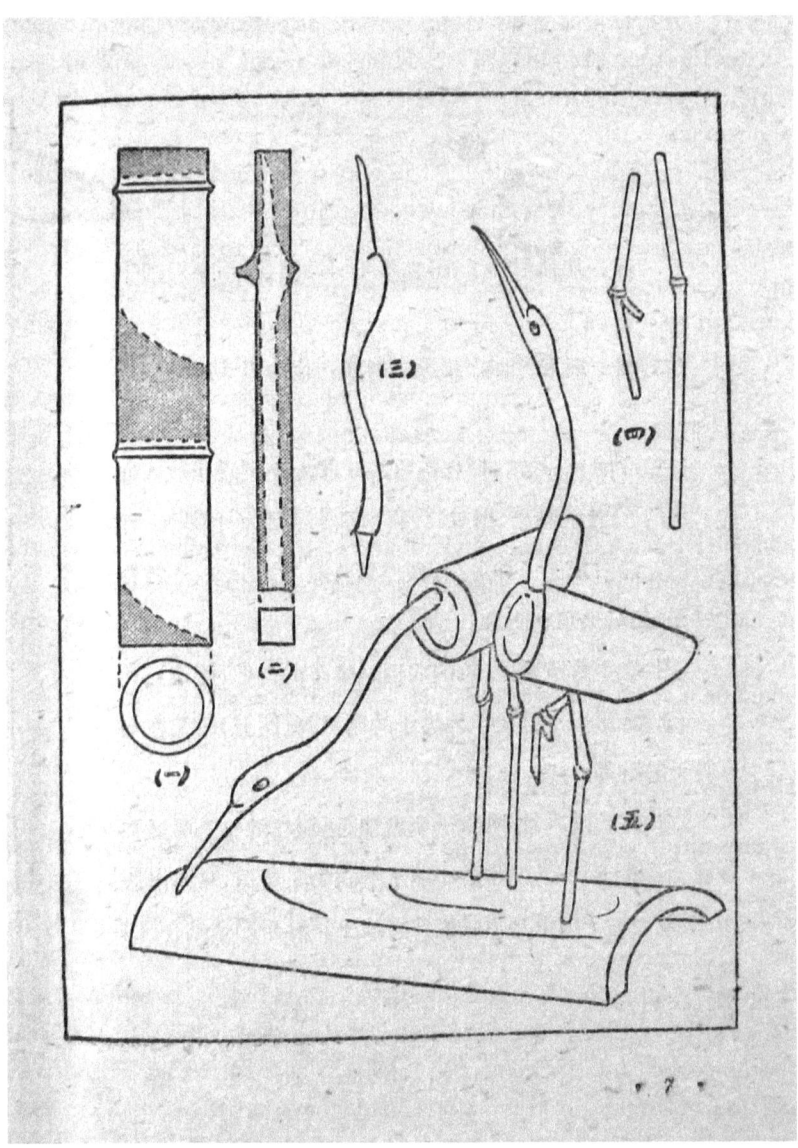

FIGURE 1.2. Drawing of a toy white crane made from bamboo. Yang Qiyan and Liu Yousu, eds., *Zhuzhi dongwu wanju* (Beijing: Shaonian Ertong Chubanshe, 1957), 7.

generalist audience with pocket-sized picture books that explained why bamboo had an important role to play in the politics, society, and culture of "New China." In October 1971, as the most intense phase of the Cultural Revolution came to a close, Shanghai People's Arts Publishing House published *Bamboo*, a booklet edited by the Shanghai Luwan District Workers

Literary and Artistic Creation Team.[61] A title-page summary informed readers that the booklet contained "scientific knowledge" about bamboo cultivation and work gained from the "experience of the masses."[62] In 54 photographs, one per page with two to three line captions each, the booklet then walked readers through the "bamboo world" in industry and agriculture as well as in people's daily lives: it explained that bamboo was one of China's traditional economic forests (*jingjilin*) and listed what all could be made of bamboo—as an industrial material, for paper production, for artificial fibers and textiles, in fishery, the manufacture of daily goods, ropes, artisanal products, and so on. Readers learned about different types of bamboo and these explanations were accompanied by close up photographic images of roots and fibers and photos of bamboo farmers working in the forests with their agricultural tools (which are also explained). Readers could discover more about pests and other dangers to bamboo cultivation, including how bamboo farmers prevented boars from eating the stems. On first glance, the booklet might have seemed like an interesting introduction to bamboo, but its underlying message was stronger: people as both makers and owners of the means of production should not merely be interested to know more about their country's resources. They had a responsibility to know.

MATERIALIZING SOCIALISM

In presenting bamboo as hinge material and bamboo objects as hinge objects, the party-state was able to construct an account about China's revolutionary progress, from the initial resilience of the few to the strength of the many. After 1949, those who owned bamboo objects of use were to see in them possibilities they had previously not recognized. Whoever purchased or otherwise obtained new bamboo objects was to see in them a sign of what revolutionary China could accomplish solely based on its local handicraft skills and materials. And those who made them were to see in their craft, skills, and technologies a contribution to the greater good. Folk craft and local materials were one of the keys to a socialist future.

The examples of bamboo and bamboo objects help explain how socialism was understood at the time. In and of itself, the material was not socialist. But objects made from bamboo were to embody socialism, that is, the understanding that they existed only because of the ingenuity of local people using local materials, and—under CCP patronage—then having the power to change social relations and the modes of production. This was a power that extended from individual to collective, and from those with bamboo skills to those without. The close connection between people, materials, and objects emphasized in all the examples symbolized a return to a focus on making, locality, use value, and the meaning that people—as makers and users—would derive from such objects. The stories of Zhang Shuiquan, the Fuzhou factory, and the materials produced to disseminate knowledge about bamboo were not designed to create consumers for commodities. They did not make sales pitches for goods one could find in stores.[63] Rather, they told narratives intended to empower audiences as users and makers of bamboo and bamboo goods in general, and to enable them to think about the significance of resources to their daily material life. In this way, socialism was not something unknown; it was hidden in objects that had always been present: simple furniture items, baskets, ropes, and steamers.[64]

If bamboo connected past and future, rural and urban, handicraft and industry, contradictions were inherent to these connections. Maximizing material resources was as important during times of material plenty as it was during times of scarcity. Similar strategies were used, for example, to advocate for bamboo during the late 1950s, at the height of the Great Leap Forward, when material provisions seemed (briefly) to be plentiful, as during the early 1960s, when shortages and starvation were widespread across the country, the command economy failed, and infrastructure collapsed. In other words, the skills and objects to ensure material plenty were the same as those to cope with hardship. This was at once a precondition for the hinge material to work as hinge, but it was also an impediment to it working successfully: it was both a signifier of plenty and of hardship, of experiences of making do and hopes for a better future, and of the continued significance of local handicraft and small stores despite dreams of mechanization, mass production, and consumption. The hinge could always work both ways, as a sign of the future or the past in the present, with both past and future in constant motion.

NOTES

1   For accounts on bamboo in China's food culture see Mark Swislocki, *Culinary Nostalgia: Regional Food Culture and the Urban Experience in Shanghai* (Stanford, CA: Stanford University Press, 2009), 52, 57, and 103. Bamboo as material for the construction of huts and as a material of scarcity is discussed in Lu, *Beyond the Neon Lights*, especially 119, 283, and 302. For a study of bamboo as a material for papermaking, see Eyferth, *Eating Rice from Bamboo Roots*. For an overview history of bamboo objects in China see Shen Min, *Bamboo in China: Arts, Crafts, and a Cultural History* (New York: Better Link Press, 2011).

2. I borrow the term *material governance* from Jacob Eyferth, "The Broken Link: Cotton Shortages and the Failure of Rural-Urban Integration in the PRC," an unpublished paper presented at the Association of Asian Studies annual meeting, 2018 (cited with permission).
3. Ko, *Social Life of Inkstones*, 15. For studies of these different materials see, for example, Eyferth, *Eating Rice from Bamboo Roots*; Kinzley, *Natural Resources and the New Frontier*; and Shellen Wu, *Empires of Coal: Fueling China's Entry into the Modern World Order* (Stanford, CA: Stanford University Press, 2015).
4. For a discussion on how to conceptualize the socialist cultural imaginary and its continued significance, see Cai Xiang, *Revolution and Its Narratives: China's Socialist Literary and Cultural Imaginaries, 1949-1966*, edited by Rebecca E. Karl and Xueping Zhong (Durham, NC: Duke University Press, 2016). Jonathan Bach discusses the question of appropriation in *What Remains*; see especially the introduction.
5. On the "human-object" pairing in mediating the rural through dance, see also chapter 4 of this volume. On the human-machine continuum in Mao Zedong Thought, see Tina Mai Chen, "Human-Machine Continuum."
6. On the history of the plastics and chemical industry in China, see James Reardon Anderson, *The Study of Change: Chemistry in China, 1840-1949* (Cambridge: Cambridge University Press, 2003). Dacron—the PRC's synthetic textile—is discussed in Antonia Finnane and Peidong Sun, "Textiles and Apparel in the Mao Years: Uniformity, Variety and the Limits of Autarchy," in *Fashion in Multiple Chinas: Chinese Styles in the Transglobal Landscape*, edited by Wessie Ling and Simona Segre-Reinach (London: I. B. Tauris, 2018), 15-43.
7. The term *Plaste* in German was a Cold War neologism, created to distinguish East German plastic from West German plastic (called Plastik).
8. Eli Rubin, "Plastics and Dictatorship in the German Democratic Republic: Towards an Economic, Consumer, Design and Cultural History," *Bulletin of the German Historical Institute* 38 (2006): 89-98, 89; and Rubin, *Synthetic Socialism*.
9. On objects distinguishing between but also connecting past and present, see Bach, *What Remains*; and also Jonathan Bach, Cristina Cuevas-Wolf, and Dani Kranz, "Objects," in *Ruptures in the Everyday: Views of Modern Germany from the Ground*, edited by Andrew S. Bergerson and Leonard Schmiedling (New York: Berghahn, 2017), 113-42. I am most grateful to Jonathan Bach for suggesting the term *hinge during our conference*.
10. An Ya, "Bianzhi," *Zhuangshi*, no. 3 (1959): 15-16; and Cao Hongchao, "Chuanxi minjian yishu - Chongqing zhu bian," *Zhuangshi*, no. 6 (1959): 38-39, 46.
11. Bao Zhi, "Zhu qi," *Zhuangshi*, no. 6 (1959): 46.
12. "Fengfu duocai de riyong zapin," *Renmin ribao*, June 14, 1959, 6.
13. Zhonghua Renmin Gongheguo Linye Bu Linchan Gongye Si, ed., *Zhongguo jiaju tuce* (Beijing: Zhongguo Linye Chubanshe, 1960); and Linyeguan, ed., *Linye jianshe de huihuang chengji* (Beijing: Zhongguo Linye Chubanshe, 1960).
14. Joshua Goldstein discusses this economy of reuse and recycling in Joshua Goldstein, *Remains of the Everyday: A Century of Recycling in Beijing* (Oakland: University of California Press, 2020), especially part 2.
15. "Guang zhong zhuzi jieyue yong zhu," *Renmin ribao*, April 25, 1963, 2.

16 See chapter 7 of this volume.
17 I therefore emphasize the role of extraordinary people but also model materials in the making of "labor model" narratives. The genesis of labor models is discussed in Nicola Spakowski, "Moving Labor Heroes Center Stage: (Labor) Heroism and the Reconfiguration of Social Relations in the Yan'an Period," *Journal of Chinese History* 5, no. 1 (January 2021): 83–106.
18 Fang Shengde, "Hubei Wuxue Zhang Shuiquan zhuyi yanjiu," *Huanggang shifan xuebao* 35, no. 4 (August 2015): 41–44. On the category of "new socialist things," see Coderre, *Newborn Socialist Things*.
19 "Hubei sheng zuxueshi zhuqi gongyi chang," in Xu Penghang, ed., *Zhongguo qiye dacidian: Hubei juan* (Beijing: Qixiang Chubanshe, 1993), 873.
20 "Gongye," in Hubei Sheng Wuxue Shi Difangzhi Bianzuan Weiyuanhui, ed., *Guangji xian zhi*, vol. 14 (Shanghai: Hanyu Dacidian Chubashe, 1994), 425.
21 "Shougong yiren zhizao de jingzhi mieqi," *Xinhuashe xinwen gao*, no. 2127, April 2, 1956, 6.
22 "Tezhong shougong yizhe de rongyu," *Xinhuashe xinwen gao*, no. 2359, November 22, 1956, 12.
23 "Hubei sheng gongnongye zhanlanhui jianlue jieshao," in Hubei Sheng Renmin Weiyuanhui Bangongting, ed., *Hubei sheng diyijie gongnongye laodong mofan daibiao dahui huikan* (1956), 173–74; see also Chen Rihong, "Hubei jindai shougong yiren yanjiu—yi zhuqi mingjiang Zhang Shuiquan weili," *Minyi*, no. 2 (2018).
24 "Hubei sheng gongnongye zhanlanhui jianlue jieshao," in Hubei Sheng Renmin Weiyuanhui Bangongting, ed., *Hubei sheng diyijie gongnongye laodong mofan daibiao dahui huikan* (1956), 173–74; see also Chen Rihong, "Hubei jindai shougong yiren yanjiu—yi zhuqi mingjiang Zhang Shuiquan weili," *Minyi*, no. 2 (2018): 6–11; and Yu Lizhu, ed., *Lishi de hui mou: Zhongguo canjia shibohui de gushi* (Beijing: Dongfang Chubanshe, 2009), 161.
25 "Gongye," 425.
26 Shen Sha and Mo Shiguang, *Zhuqi mingjiang Zhang Shuiquan* (Tianjin: Tianjin Renmin Meishu Chubanshe, 1958). Five thousand copies of the volume were reprinted in 2001.
27 I have adapted this distinction of "man" and "model" from Daniel Leese, "Mao the Man and Mao the Icon," in *A Critical Introduction to Mao*, edited by Timothy Cheek (Cambridge: Cambridge University Press, 2010), 219–39.
28 Shen and Mo, *Zhuqi mingjiang Zhang Shuiquan*, 10–22.
29 Shen and Mo, *Zhuqi mingjiang Zhang Shuiquan*, 47–48.
30 Shen and Mo, *Zhuqi mingjiang Zhang Shuiquan*, 56–58.
31 Shen and Mo, *Zhuqi mingjiang Zhang Shuiquan*, 62–64.
32 Cao Baoming, "Xi jian jueyi youren zhuan," *Renmin ribao*, August 4, 1962, 2; and Chen Rihong, "Hubei jindai shougong yiren yanjiu." See also chapter 4 of this volume.
33 This point is constantly repeated in all accounts, and also found its way into one of the most reliable academic treatments in Chinese, cf. Fang, "Hubei Wuxue Zhang Shuiquan zhuyi yanjiu," 44.
34 The idea of the Chinese artisan shares some similarities with the ideal of the American craftsman that Edward S. Cooke describes. Yet where the Anglo-American ideal sees

the individual craftsman working, to some extent, in isolation or in smaller groups, unperturbed by commercialization or the demands of mass production, the Chinese socialist artisan's ultimate purpose and fulfilment lies in working with the collective and for the masses, and in making his or her skill accessible such that it can aid mass production. "The Long Shadow of William Morris: Paradigmatic Problems of Twentieth-Century American Furniture," *American Furniture* (2003).

35 Fang, "Hubei Wuxue Zhang Shuiquan zhuyi yanjiu."
36 See chapter 9 of this volume.
37 Cao, "Xi jian jueyi youren zhuan."
38 Zhang Lang, "Hubei minjian gongyi meishu diaocha sanji," in Sun Changlin and Zhongguo Gongyi Meishu Xuehui Mingjian Gongyi Meishu Weiyuanhui, eds., *Mei de yuanquan: Zhongguo minjian gongyi meishu xueshu lunwenji* (Beijing: Zhongguo Lüyou Chubanshe, 1993), 337.
39 Eyferth, "Craft Knowledge."
40 "Zhongnanqu chengli zhucai liyong yanjiu weiyuanhui," *Xinhuashe xinwen gao*, no. 2309, October 3, 1956, 31.
41 Zhang Tianlu and Fuzhoushi Difangzhi Bianzuan Weiyuanhui, eds., *Fuzhou shi zhi*, vol. 4 (Beijing: Fangzhi Chubanshe, 2000), 151. I have not been able to find out why the factory closed.
42 Lin Jianqing, "Fujian zhucai jiaju de chuangxin he yanbian," in Zhongguo Renmin Zhengzhi Xieshang Huiyi Fujian Sheng Weiyuanhui Wenshi Ziliao Bianjishi, ed., *Fujian wenshi ziliao*, vol. 12 (Beijing: Zhongguo Wenshi Chubanshe, 1986): 163–70.
43 Fujian Provincial Archives, 186-3-706–120, Fujian Sheng Gongyi Meishu Yiren Daibiao Huiyi, "Guanyu chuangzuo xin de zhucai jiaju de tihui: Gao Yishui," August 29, 1963.
44 Fujian Provincial Archives, 186-3-706–120.
45 Lin, "Fujian zhucai jiaju de chuangxin he yanbian," 166.
46 Lin, "Fujian zhucai jiaju de chuangxin he yanbian," 163.
47 Lin Jianqing, "Fujian bowu yanjiuhui jilue," in Zhongguo Renmin Zhengzhi Xieshang Huiyi Fujian Sheng Weiyuanhui Wenshi Ziliao Bianjishi, ed., *Fujian wenshi ziliao*, vol. 25 (Beijing: Zhongguo Wenshi Chubanshe, 1991): 146–50.
48 Lin, "Fujian zhucai jiaju de chuangxin he yanbian," 164.
49 Lin, "Fujian zhucai jiaju de chuangxin he yanbian," 164.
50 Lin, "Fujian zhucai jiaju de chuangxin he yanbian," 167.
51 Lin Jianqing, "Zhucai jiaju sheji de yidian tihui," *Zhuangshi*, no. 10 (1960): 9.
52 On the dissemination of scientific knowledge see Sigrid Schmalzer, *The People's Peking Man* (Chicago: Chicago University Press, 2008); Schmalzer, *Red Revolution, Green Revolution*; and Miriam Gross, *Farewell to the God of Plague: Chairman Mao's Campaign to Deworm China* (Oakland: University of California Press, 2016).
53 For an example of such internal reports, see Zhongguo Nonglin Kexueyuan Anji Zu, ed., "Maozhu shiyan huibian" (August 1973). See also "Guang zhong zhuzi jieyue yong zhu," *Renmin ribao*, April 25, 1963, 2.
54 In this, China's Mao period actually shared a great deal in common with cultures of experimentation in Europe during the sixteenth and seventeenth century, when the house and everything in it was a possible source of scientific discovery. See Werret, *Thrifty Science*.

55 Wu Zhonglun, *Zenyang zhong maozhu* (Beijing: Zhongguo Linye Chubanshe, 1956).
56 Knowledge as repetitive practice and "making" vs. theoretical knowledge on paper is discussed in Kyoungjin Bae, "Joints of Utility, Crafts of Knowledge: The Material Culture of the Sino-British Furniture Trade during the Long Eighteenth Century," unpublished PhD thesis, Columbia University, 2016; and Yiyi Xu, "The Knowledge System of the Traditional Chinese Craftsman," *West 86th* 20, no. 2 (Fall–Winter 2013), 155–72. On the question of state knowledge acquisition and dissemination in twentieth-century China, see Eyferth, *Eating Rice from Bamboo Roots;* and Schmalzer, *Red Revolution, Green Revolution.*
57 Official advocacy for DIY, however, was always a double-edged sword. Although it was usually explained as a citizen's duty in order to free up all available resources for the grand socialist project, it was common knowledge that it was a sign of the government's shortcomings and failed promises. Uta Brandes, Sonja Stich, and Miriam Wender, *Design by Use: The Everyday Metamorphosis of Things* (Berlin: DeGruyter, 2013).
58 Valentina Boretti, "The 'Appropriate' Plaything: Searching for the New Chinese Toy, 1910s–1960s,'" in Megan Brandow-Faller, Megan, ed., *Childhood by Design: Toys and the Material Culture of Childhood, 1700–Present* (New York: Bloomsbury, 2018), 293–315.
59 Yang Qiyan and Liu Yousui, eds., *Zhuzhi dongwu wanju* (Beijing: Shaonian Ertong Chubanshe, 1957).
60 Yang and Liu, *Zhuzhi dongwu wanju*, 1.
61 Luwan Qu Gongren Wenyi Chuangzuo Ban, ed., *Maozhu* (Beijing: Renmin Meishu Chubanshe, 1971).
62 "Neirong tiyao," in Luwan Qu Gongren Wenyi Chuangzuo Ban, *Maozhu*, no page.
63 On the discourse of socialist commodities and the significance of productivist rather than consumerist discourses, see also Coderre, "A Necessary Evil."
64 Coderre, *Newborn Socialist Things.*

2 THE BRICK

COLE ROSKAM

ON APRIL 5, 1950, SIX MONTHS FOLLOWING THE ESTABLISHMENT of the People's Republic of China, the famed architectural historian Liang Sicheng (1901–1972), son of intellectual and reformer Liang Qichao (1873–1929), wrote a letter to general and party stalwart Zhu De (1886–1976) regarding the potential architectural expression of the newly established People's Republic of China. A new architecture was needed to capture both the revolutionary vigor and the cultural resilience of China's people, reasoned Liang, and it was important that such built form be "national, scientific, and collective" in its aesthetic, procedural, and technical basis, with any connotations of the nation necessarily linked to China's thousand-year-old traditions.[1] "In the past, architecture in China entertained people, and was semicolonial in its origins," Liang reminded Zhu. Looking forward, however, "China's new architecture will serve the people and will only adopt selected aspects of Western technology, rather than blindly adhering to foreign styles."[2]

In search of potential existing models for such an architectural statement, Liang identified the modest brick living quarters located in Zhongnanhai, the former imperial garden turned central headquarters for Chinese Communist Party leaders, as a potential paradigm for "New China." Liang appreciated the extent to which the compound's residential buildings seemed to suit "modern living standards and technological demands," though it was in the structures' use of gray, clay-fired brick that Liang saw the buildings' true value to the state. "Using brick rather than steel frame or stone construction reflects our modern economic strength," he argued, despite the material's negative associations with China's semicolonial past. The brick's facilitation of "the buildings' careful material and spatial composition, from small details like its tiles, porch, and flower garden to major elements like its overall proportions, wall treatment, and door and window configuration, captures the revolutionary spirit and historical foundation at work in new China's power."[3]

Although it is unknown how persuasive Liang's letter may have proven to party leadership, subsequent official campaigns to deliver to Chinese citizens "two-story houses, electric light, and telephones" (*loushang louxia*,

FIGURE 2.1. (from right to left) Mao Zedong, Zhou Enlai, Chen Yi, and Zhang Wentian chat outside Yinian Tang, a hall located within the Zhongnanhai compound, Beijing, October 4, 1956. Zhongnanhai Huace Bianji Weiyuanhui, *Zhongnanhai* (Beijing: Xinhua Chubanshe, 1981).

diandeng dianhua)—itself a translated iteration of an earlier Soviet slogan—underscore the government's embrace of architecture as an important delivery mechanism for party promises and, by extension, a key element in the country's physical and ideological reinvention through socialism.[4] At the same time, Liang's comments shift our focus from the practical and symbolic roles played by architecture in the PRC to the particular significance of the construction materials used in such architecture. Of these materials, and as highlighted in Liang's letter, the brick occupies an important if unexamined position.

Scholarship on socialist Chinese architectural production after 1949 has heretofore paid little attention to building matter, yet it needs to be understood as a vibrant and vital source of meaning that helped to imbue Mao-era architecture with a distinctly socialist charge. The steel I beam, for example, forged China's goals for heavy industrial output and the technical oversight of the Soviet Union into what was widely considered to be a modern and progressive object achieved through collective action. Bamboo, as Jennifer Altehenger has argued in the previous chapter, was a unique "hinge material" that possessed both a premodern and modern history that embodied the transformative power of a new, collective ethics rooted in both the constraints of China's limited material resources and the creative agency of craft.[5] By the mid-1960s, rammed earth had also become an important revolutionary material capable of inducing bottom-up social change through the process of its own production.[6]

The brick offered a similarly rich and adaptable source of meaning to the party, though it also possessed a certain physical and representational ambiguity that distinguished it from other Mao-era building materials. At the core of its uniqueness, paradoxically, was its very ordinariness. On one hand, the brick's specific and relatable size and weight, produced through an understandable and replicable manufacturing process (at least within China's major urban centers), directly linked it to laboring bodies while also infusing it with a certain, arguably proletarian quality. Anyone—men, women, or children—could pick up and stack a brick, which required a specific but not necessarily highly skilled expertise to produce and assemble into a range of things considered essential to socialist China, from furniture, sidewalks, chimneys, and furnaces to buildings and entire built environments.

At the same time, however, the brick's material modesty posed certain challenges to party messaging, particularly as it concerned the project of socialist Chinese modernization itself. Perpetually defined by its own physical and representational constraints, including masonry's load capacity, its material resistance to perfection, the presumed simplicity of its own straightforward production methods, and its own tangible modularity, among others, the brick found itself an unwitting source of tension and contradiction at work in the party's identity construction, particularly its reliance upon the act and objects of building as sources of political meaning.[7] As the party's messaging fluctuated over time in response to certain political or economic conditions, the objects that gave them material form also required change. The brick was not immune from these shifts, though its essential obduracy limited its ability to contribute to these swings and signified the building material as both an aspirational yet somewhat inconclusive emblem of progress in the PRC. Although brick was an industrially produced object, it could not match the technical heroism of steel, for example, nor could it translate the exquisite hand of the craftsperson into physical form like bamboo. Brick was also burdened by a certain understated urbanity derived from its own checkered past as a key building block in imperial-era China before its manufacturing process was industrialized in several of the country's treaty ports—Shanghai, Tianjin, and Guangzhou, among others—beginning in the late nineteenth century.

Sturdy, durable, and seemingly standard in its material properties and capacities, the brick was an essential if ambivalent actant in the production and promotion of the Chinese body politic under Mao.[8] A closer study of it reveals a familiar yet somewhat ambiguously modern object for some but not all of China's residents, and a material whose unassuming ubiquity paradoxically risked exposing the chronic unevenness of modernization itself. Despite its many limitations—in fact, because of them—the brick reveals the arduous, contradictory, and at times unsuccessful shaping, testing, and projecting of processes, images, and objects deemed constitutive to the production and reproduction of the socialist landscape and its citizens over time.

ARCHITECTURAL HISTORY AND THE BRICK

In many respects, a history of the brick is a history of China. Multiple references to brick construction techniques exist in imperial-era building treatises dating back to the Qin dynasty (221–206 BCE). During the Song dynasty (960–1279 CE), brick production underwent a process of standardization following the completion of imperial-era China's first building manual, *Treatise on Architectural Methods or State Building Standards* (Yingzao fashi; 1103 CE). The text identified thirteen types of bricks specified and approved for imperial construction projects, though different regions of the empire continued to deploy slightly different techniques based on factors such as the particular kind of clay used. Despite subsequent efforts to regulate brick manufacturing, these variabilities continued to shape brick's history during the Ming and Qing dynasties, as different materials, different levels of workmanship, different firing techniques, and different kilns all existed throughout imperial China, meaning that there was no such thing as one standard brick in China until the early twentieth century, if not later.[9]

Nineteenth-century automation and mass production innovations had an impact on brick manufacturing around the world, including China, and transformed the brick from a traditional into a modern construction material. This transformation did not come without a technological and ontological struggle, however. In Great Britain, brickmaking remained "the most imperfect of all the mechanical arts" despite significant progress achieved in mechanical fabrication methods; by the 1870s, it remained the only trade "in which the custom differs so much in different districts" due to the variance in clay quality.[10] Early studies of bricklaying by scholars of new business management models, like Frederick Winslow Taylor (1856–1915), proved influential in introducing new, more standardized construction techniques that increased workers' production rates and, in so doing, recast the brick as a contributing building component to capitalism, particularly within the context of a rapidly industrializing America. Despite these efforts, however, the brick seemed to maintain a fundamental, ontological recalcitrance in the face of rapid change. "Why is it, in a trade which has been continually practiced since before the Christian era, and with implements practically the same as they now are," queried Taylor in *Principles of Scientific Management* (1911), "that this simplification of the bricklayer's movements, this great gain, has not been made before?"[11]

In contrast to other modern building materials like concrete, steel, or glass, the brick retained a semiotic charge fueled by its own premodern origins—an implacability that made it an overlooked but undeniable agent in the new environments and experiences emerging through acts of modern architectural design. In both Europe and the United States, pioneers of architectural modernism saw the attempted reinvention of brick by and through capitalism as essential to their efforts to address the new economic reality's effects on their craft without abandoning the fundamental, tectonic basis of their discipline. Mies van der Rohe (1886–1969), for example, was perhaps best known for his sleek, transparent glass-and-steel towers, though he famously argued that architecture began by "carefully [putting] two bricks together."[12] Frank Lloyd Wright (1867–1959) purportedly began at least one public lecture by asking the audience whether they knew what a brick was. "It is a small, worthless, ordinary thing that costs 11 cents but has a wonderful quality. Give me a brick and it becomes worth its weight in gold."[13] The American architect Louis Kahn (1901–1974) urged students of architectural design to ask the brick what it wanted to be—an imagined dialogic encounter with inanimate matter that scholars have framed as both agreeable and frustrating, but ultimately an acceptance of the brick's obdurate endurance.[14]

Ambiguity regarding the brick's material and economic value also reverberated through its history in nineteenth- and twentieth-century China, though in distinctive ways. There, foreign racism toward Chinese residents and antiforeign sentiment on the part of Chinese residents influenced the relationship between foreign-imported red, indigenous blue or gray, and handcrafted mud-and-adobe brick. A brick's coloration and strength derived from several factors, including differences in firing temperature, the particular fuel used for firing, its chemical composition, and the material quality and chemical composition of particular soils and clays, among others.[15] Nevertheless, and in part based upon foreign impressions of the brick as a symbol of civilizational sophistication and cultural robustness, perceptions quickly formed as to the material and structural advantages of foreign versus local brick production in China, where foreign-manufactured red brick first arrived in treaty ports like Shanghai, beginning in the 1850s and 1860s, as ballast for merchants' ships. Localized red brick production emerged shortly thereafter through the establishment of foreign production facilities, machinery, and firing techniques in treaty ports such as Shanghai and Guangzhou; these bricks were also considered to be more durable than locally produced blue or gray varieties, though in reality there existed active interplay between foreign and Chinese bricks and practices in late Qing China that produced numerous physical and material variabilities, making it difficult if not impossible to determine one type's indisputable superiority over another. The clustering of industrialization in and around Qing China's international entrepôts, amid swaths of Qing territory seemingly unaffected by such technology, also fueled foreign opinions that high-quality brick and stone construction was somehow particular to Western civilization. Bricks were also commonly used in the construction of numerous school campuses funded by North American universities or missionary organizations in China, and they also influenced perceptions among foreign and Chinese observers of Euro-American architectural superiority relative to Asian building traditions despite masonry's centuries-long history in China, Japan, and elsewhere.[16]

By the 1930s, brick production had become an active but not necessarily pervasive industry in Republican-era China. In 1934, for example, Shanghai was home to approximately 118 factories devoted to bricks, earthenware, and glass, supporting 6,240 employees, as compared to 920 textile mills, 552 machinery-manufacturing plants, 434 clothing factories, 403 printing facilities, 329 metal industries, and 319 metal-production facilities.[17] Mass-produced brick was still an unknown quantity for much of the country even as it exuded a mundane, everyday quality in many of its urban areas. Despite its active participation in the production of these urbane environments and their distinctive atmospheres, to say nothing of the visible changes in fashion, media, and other forms of cultural production these spaces supported, brick seemed to lack the more utopian, progressive properties associated with materials like glass, steel, and reinforced concrete.[18] In such denial existed opportunities for reinvention, however. After 1949, with the country's automated brick-manufacturing facilities associated with the humiliations of the treaty port system, and much of its existing block and brick production composed of handcrafted, localized practices, CCP officials set about imbuing the brick with new applied and conceptual meaning as a progressive and distinctly socialist construction material.

BUILDING THE NEW NATION

As an existing, affordable building material and a quantifiable marker of human power, the brick was immediately valuable to the projection, production, and promotion of the new socialist Chinese state. One of the brick's most valuable qualities was the extent to which it could be characterized as both a technological action and a technological artifact.[19] The brick was itself a specific technology and the product of certain industrial practices, but it could also succinctly capture the proficiency of an individual worker's production in ways that steel, for example, arguably could not. More than any other modern building material, the brick epitomized what the Indian journalist, diplomat, and businessman Raja Hutheesing (1906–1991) observed during two early trips to the PRC, in 1951 and 1952, as China's "realistic approach to the immediate problems. China was content to seek remedies which lay within the scope of technical skill and equipment available to her."[20] As an established technology in China, the brick was theoretically easier and cheaper to produce than other building materials, thereby satisfying the country's immediate needs, though this also made it more difficult to redefine as somehow new and important to the country's socialist reinvention. Officials quickly recognized that capitalizing upon brick's rich semiotic potential would first require the material's infusion with new, identifiably socialist meaning. In doing so, the brick underwent a transformation not dissimilar to what had taken place in Europe and North America during the late nineteenth and early twentieth centuries, though with different ideological objectives in mind. Materially, the brick itself would not change; rather, it was the nature of the productive forces underlying its ontological profile— what, in fact, made the brick socialist—that would need to be rejuvenated with collective energy.

By 1951, state-run media had begun to identify and promote a handful of new, model construction practices and laborers such as woodworker Xie Wanfu and bricklayer Su Changyou (1925–1981) as emblematic of the reinvigorated forms of production beginning to emerge following liberation through collectivized thinking.[21] Su was a Shenyang-based bricklayer who purportedly could lay no more than a thousand bricks in one day until he studied more efficient, collective work procedures; redesigned his own working tools, including his trowel; and reorganized the flow of his building materials in relation to other workers accordingly. The redistribution of expertise in physical relation to the brick and the wall was key to these efforts, however. Rather than dividing a work unit into smaller groups composed of workers with one form of technical expertise, Su divided construction teams into groups consisting of a mixture of highly skilled and low-skilled workers, thereby maximizing the potential of each unit. The physical positioning of workers in relation to the wall was vital; a twelve-person team divided into three groups of four people could be arranged so that each group's two most highly skilled workers were responsible for laying the wall's most visible, outer surface. A third, mid-tier worker laid bricks inside the wall, ensuring a certain stability and consistency between interior and exterior surfaces. The fourth, lowest-skilled worker was given responsibility for the wall's central section, while unskilled laborers mixed and applied lime mortar to the structure. Each of these three subgroups worked on different parts of the same building project, theoretically ensuring an equal distribution of work completed in a rational and efficient yet collective manner.

Su's method was in fact not dramatically dissimilar from Taylorist bricklaying practices promoted in the United States and Europe, which were also based upon a hierarchical division between managers and laborers, based upon forms of expertise. Both methods also prioritized time over craft as the basis for evaluating success. "His new technique is now being applied on a nationwide scale, resulting in an overall increase in the speed of building," reported *China Reconstructs*—a shared if inconvenient goal of both capitalism and socialism, and one in part exposed by the brick's seemingly benign, apolitical ubiquity.[22] Where the state worked to distinguish Su's technique as uniquely socialist was in the new physical and procedural relationship it proposed relative to the brick itself. Despite the skill-based hierarchical organization of Su's team, it still lacked a managing supervisor responsible for overseeing construction; instead, all members of Su's work unit were expected to touch and engage with the brick regardless of their expertise. This produced an arguably more active, creative, and equitable connection with the brick itself—a link not unlike a performer's relationship to a prop, or the film projectionist's engagement with the projector.[23] Situating the worker and brick together on-site represented an intimate, collective endeavor between human and nonhuman participants, and a vital, liberating break

FIGURE 2.2. Bricklayers demonstrate the Su Changyu method. *China Reconstructs* 2, no. 2 (1953): 40.

from the excesses of China's past and the rigid class-based hierarchies of capitalism more generally.

"In the construction industry of old, pre-1949 society, the merchant and labor contractor controlled everything. Layers and layers of subcontracts and exploitation resulted in rough and sloppy work with inferior materials, giving rise to all kinds of dark, suspicious activity," explained a well-circulated instructional pamphlet detailing Su's methods. "After liberation, every place initiated its own organizational structures and plans for reform, giving rise to new systems of management and production to be studied."[24] Direct contact with the brick and the redesign of associated, mediatory tools, particularly trowels, was promoted as producing more efficient working methods and better structures. At demonstration events known as "exchange meetings" (*jingyan jiaoliu hui*), audiences could see these new systems in action, and other work units could share their experiences learning the new practices and objects responsible for the construction of a new China. One such event held in Beijing in 1954 included over a thousand people from thirty-one units gathered to watch two model work units demonstrate advanced bricklaying methods and their new, redesigned trowels.[25] As performative exercises in physical assemblage, these activities offered enactments of how individual workers, physically collectivized around the brick, would contribute to China's construction efforts, which state-run media outlets hailed as one of the country's most dynamic and largest industries.[26]

Redefined in part through the new socialist worker and building systems on display, the brick also came to embody them. Foreign visitors immediately perceived the intimate dynamic between object and workers as evidence of some new, distinctly socialist force at play, though for some it was not the brick's material enlivenment through its close engagement with an entire work team that resonated but rather the undesirable objectification of people that occurred through such close contact. In 1954, for example, the British labor organizer Sam Watson traveled to China and found the brick to be an apt metaphor for the Chinese people, whose rights he felt were being unduly limited by the "enslavement of the trade unions by the state." In Watson's eyes, the party considered "the worker and the laborer as just a piece of raw material—'the masses'—another brick, another paving stone, something to fit into the pattern."[27] The new political power on display in these patterns, of which the merging of brick and human was now a vital constitutive element, evinced brick's complicated semiotics within the new, ostensibly more productive systems at work.

The brick did not always require the revitalizing hand of the laborer to inform a particular building pattern, or practice, as socialist, however. Brick was also a relatively simple material to quantify at a time in which statistics became essential indices of economic advancement under Mao, and it helped produce relatable, numerical evidence that grounded the otherwise dizzying, state-supported accounts of the country's new socialist reality and its rapid materialization.[28] Hospitals, residential buildings, textile mills, cinemas, and hotels were not necessarily new to China, but their swift construction through purportedly new, standardized building practices, boundless reservoirs of human energy, and seemingly abundant, calculable amounts of materials helped imbue them with a potent ideological agency. Publicized details of a linen mill's construction outside Harbin between 1950 and 1952, for example, privileged numerical totals of the materials used in the mill's construction, including 26 million bricks, more than 3.5 million cubic feet of gravel, 37,000 tons of cement, 4,100 tons of steel, and 741,000 cubic feet of timber.[29] A ton of cement may have been difficult for readers to visualize; a brick was not. Statistics from the country's 1955 construction goals substantiate the brick's understated if undeniable importance to these efforts, with quantifiable numbers of bricks prominently featured in a range of major building programs, including one-, two-, three-, four-, and five-story residential buildings, elementary and middle schools, offices, hospitals, clinics, clubs, dining halls, bathrooms, laundries, and basement structures.[30] The brick itself proved a helpful measure, not simply of the state's new productive capacity or the collective labor being deployed but of the material dimensions and scale of renewal itself.[31] Its relatable physicality to the work being done, particularly to residents otherwise unable to see such construction, also provided an accessible and reassuring image of progress neatly accounted for, stacked, and mortared in tangible fulfillment of the party's commitment to the Chinese people.

For all of the quantifiable and qualifiable change and promise linked to China's socialist brick production, however, constructing socialism itself remained an uneven and incomplete endeavor. Although the brick's inherent technical ambivalence remained one of its key material advantages, the party struggled to overcome fundamental imbalances between city and countryside. For example, there existed major differences between industrialized brick production in China's urban environments and the kinds of bricks and brickmaking technology available to rural residents—disparities that could not be fully overcome by the party's efforts to emphasize and promote the equivalent speed of new brick construction, if not necessarily production, taking place in both urban and rural China. Despite early and enthusiastic claims of progress, China's own brickmaking capacity and technical know-how remained inadequate to supply the entire nation's vast terrain and complex construction needs, and by the mid-1950s, Soviet-originated brickmaking technology was an important source of technical building knowledge.

Published collections of translated building manuals from the period include numerous references to Soviet practices and expertise that also reveal the weaknesses in China's building technologies relative to its Soviet mentor and the daunting procedural difficulties at work in the party's efforts to shrink that gap. For example, one manual published in Chinese in 1958 is based upon Soviet engineering documents published between 1952 and 1955—a three-to-six-year lag that limited how quickly China could advance relative to its Soviet mentor or the socialist world more generally, despite all of the physical development already taking place. By the late 1950s, China had incorporated a range of Soviet-originated brick technologies into its own building industry, including processes such as fly ash brick production, which offered a means of recycling burned coal waste into a reusable building material; hollow brick and block construction, which provided a lighter, more economical product; and prefabricated panel techniques. Adapting Soviet expertise to suit China inspired material and procedural innovations designed with material economy in mind, but it also led to misfortune. In 1956, for example, the Ministry of Construction suspended experimentation with double-curvature brick vaulting construction techniques following several accidents during and after construction. Moreover, much of this development remained limited to major metropolitan areas; in rural China, industrialized brick production and construction methods remained particularly difficult and expensive to realize before the 1970s.[32]

In a February 1957 conversation with members of the second committee of the All-China Federation of Students, Mao himself admitted the CCP's difficulties in producing modernized physical environments capable of both sustaining and symbolizing China's socialist transformation. "You see, revolution is such a prolonged process; we have only engaged in construction for a few years; how can there be no difficulties? There are over six hundred million people in our entire country," explained Mao. "It is unlikely that we won't encounter any difficulties if our goal is to build in a country with a population of this size. Construction is even more difficult than revolution."[33] At another talk, with party cadres in Shanghai on March 20, 1957, Mao declared that "construction is also a sort of revolution. It is a technical and a cultural revolution: to unite all the members of society and people all over the country to struggle with the natural world."[34] Growing anxiety within the party concerning China's inability to match the productivity of either its advanced capitalist rivals or Soviet mentor were aggravated by the logistical and temporal limitations posed the process of construction itself, leading to an increasingly heavy practical and semiotic burden placed upon the nation's built environment.

NEW MATERIAL DISCIPLINE

In the build-up to the PRC's tenth anniversary, official desire for a singular, realized vision of socialist modernity infused the country's cultural production with new urgency. Architecture, like film, is a distinctly time-based form of cultural expression, and in an effort to address questions related to how to best represent the country's rapid industrial progress through physical matter, the party turned not only to the country's filmmakers but to its architects.[35] At a national housing conference organized in Shanghai in late 1958, architects from the country's most prominent design institutes delivered papers theorizing on the state of Chinese architecture. Much of this work, which was subsequently published in *Architectural Journal* during the first half of 1959, focused on the aesthetics and speed of China's socialist building production, and whether the country's architecture was adequately reflecting its development.

Having themselves been subjected to criticism for their own elitist tendencies in the Hundred Flowers and Anti-Rightist campaigns in 1957, architects took the country's building materials to task. "If all you have is brick and wood for materials, you are limited in terms of the architectural forms you can produce. If you have reinforced concrete and steel, you could build anything you want—a modern skyscraper or an ancient architectural object," wrote Yuan Jingshen, director of the Beijing Institute of Architectural Design. Faced with the prospects of not fulfilling the country's expectations for socialist progress, architects criticized the loose, seemingly limitless array of aesthetic and structural choices enabled by steel, concrete, or glass as reeking of capitalistic waste and excess. "We must not let these modern materials dictate the form of the architecture produced," admonished Yuan.[36] Liang Sicheng, who had first identified the brick as the most capable vessel for capturing the aspirations of the young socialist state, struggled to articulate a revised version of his argument based upon the party's intensified emphasis on the speed of material production. In an editorial originally published in *Guangming Daily* in February 1959 and republished in *Architectural Journal*, he noted that the "people speak of this era as 'The Age of Steel,' but in New China we are in 'The Age of the Steel Spirit'; steel is still scarce in China today, and its production level remains low, so our moment is reflective of steel's spirit, though in the future we'll have more, and other new materials. . . . But we must remember that we are the masters of our architectural materials, and not their slaves."[37] Disciplining the unruly modern materials of capitalism through a strict yet balanced aesthetic and organizational logic demonstrative of a distinctly Chinese socialism—a treatment similar to Su Changyou's earlier reinvention of the brick—was key.

Official, publicized frustrations expressed in relation to China's limited building capacity illuminate the fundamental crisis of meaning facing the party and its architectural production after ten years of rule, at a time in which the collective agency of the Chinese people was not, in fact, transforming the country's material landscape in accordance with the party's increasingly outsized ambitions. In the country's early days, the brick proved to be a useful connection between China's past and its modest, technologically oriented present. With the party's leadership more focused on China's current and future production, however, the brick, with its unassuming aesthetic and limited structural capacity, fell out of favor. Brick could theoretically house China's population in village communes, dormitories, and seven-to-eight-story apartment buildings; it could not span the interior dimensions required by a technologically sophisticated industrial plant or sustain the structural loads produced by a twenty-story skyscraper without steel and concrete reinforcement, however.

Ambitious undertakings, such as the Ten Great Buildings Campaign, launched and completed over the course of 1959, capture the party's desire for monuments emblematic of the country's progress under socialism despite the material challenges at work. The massive effort has also been understood as a search for an architectural language capable of imprinting key socialist Chinese artistic and economic values, including speed, efficiency, beauty, and economy, upon Beijing's skyline.[38] Yet the endeavor may also be considered a performative instillation of the party's desire to project its control over the public production and perception of rare, relatively luxurious, and disobedient building materials in China—granite, marble, glass, reinforced concrete, and steel in particular—through the architectural language of China's own past and the collective labor of the country's present. In fact, brick was used in the construction of all of Beijing's new edifices but was not accorded the same degree of publicity as steel or reinforced concrete, both of which figure much more prominently in the era's promotional literature.[39]

By the late 1950s, brick's own limited structural and material properties, coupled with its ubiquity in urban China, had led to its own semiotic regression at a time in which the party demanded more advanced industrial capacity, embodied in a material like steel, which was famously subjected to fervid mass mobilization, not merely through the Ten Great Buildings Campaign but in each of the era's countless backyard steel furnaces. These sites, which were famously intended to produce more steel for the country's industrialization, simultaneously demonstrated the power of the people's collective to physically transform an otherwise semiotically difficult, socialistically unproductive material into something new and (theoretically) useful. Brick's more mundane material and manufacturing properties rendered it impervious to such alchemy, though brick itself was used to build the country's steel furnaces. Makeshift brick kilns were also constructed throughout the country to provide building material for the people's communes; one Shanghai-based report, for example, enthused that "people took the initiative to tear down their own chicken sheds and fish tanks, and some even took the bricks used to prop up their beds and furniture, reinforce their walls, elevate their stoves, or pave their floors" to provide brick for construction. Seven million bricks—not counting those salvaged or scavenged from existing structures—were apparently produced during the Great Leap Forward.[40] Despite these ambitious scales of operation, however, the brick was unable to stir official attention in the same, communally spectacular way as

FIGURE 2.3. China, Sin Kiang, Sian [Xinjiang, Xi'an], August 1958. As an after-school-hours project, youngsters pave the sidewalks of their neighborhood under the supervision of their mothers. From Henri Cartier-Bresson © Fondation Henri Cartier-Bresson.

backyard steel furnaces. Easily deployed by all of China's citizens, including children, the brick's solid material knowability made it an important transitional technology toward some better future, but not the desired material endpoint itself.

Paradoxically, however, the brick still required a degree of expertise, and for much of the country it remained an aspirational material that exposed consequential gaps and incongruities in the production of China's new socialist landscape. In a December 1959 scrapbook detailing brick chimney production techniques and performance data assembled by a state-owned but locally administered architectural and engineering company based in Liaoning, one sees evidence of the burdens placed upon workers struggling to adhere to the party's vision despite lacking the expertise to build a local steel-smelting facility's chimney using reinforced concrete. In the end, the company relied upon brick, though it also presented problems: experts in advanced brick chimney construction were still rare in China, making the implementation of such technology simultaneously and frustratingly "complicated and simple" (*fanjian*).[41] Amid state-sanctioned images of material abundance, such reports of on-site struggles with brick contradicted the government's promotion of more advanced building practices, including

Soviet-influenced hollow brick and block production techniques, which officials optimistically hoped would spur development, particularly in rural areas, by alleviating the time and material required to produce handmade mud bricks while also necessitating less coal consumption than solid bricks.[42] By late 1961, however, inadequate machinery, limited infrastructure, lack of technical knowledge, and variable production standards complicated by unsustainable coal usage had inscribed the campaign's disastrous effects upon built environments throughout the country.[43]

BUILDING AND DISMANTLING THE CULTURAL REVOLUTION

As officials grappled with the consequences of their actions, the tenor of building production in China began to change—another ideological fluctuation with consequential implications on the brick's meaning in relation to the party's shifting policy goals. By the mid-1960s, the rise of yet another new building material in China paralleled Mao's own reassertion of control over the CCP and the country at large following the disastrous Great Leap Forward: rammed earth construction, in which moistened soil is pounded into place and left to dry to produce solid earthen walls that could be used for low-rise buildings. Beginning in late 1964, Mao urged officials and architects to launch a "mass design revolution movement" aimed at demonizing Soviet-derived models of automatized prefabrication in favor of on-site methods inspired by the proletarian "spirit" of rammed earth construction principles.[44] These practices purportedly originated from workers toiling in the famed oilfield and factories of Daqing, an oft-cited model city for socialist Chinese industrial production, and were intended to epitomize the integration of "city and country, workers and peasants, and mental and physical labor" advocated by Mao and his ideological adherents.[45] Celebrating rammed earth construction as a low-cost, vernacular practice requiring little to no technical skill effectively communicated the party's rejection of the Soviet model—and all of its technical knowledge—to the population at large.

It also continued the decline of brick's ideological worth, given that brick production did require some technical know-how and lacked rammed earth's immediate, visceral connection to the ground and the people who depended upon it. Many communes, government offices, and institutions around the country still depended upon their own brick-production facilities, which continued to deliver a degree of empowerment insofar as they enabled the efficient construction of relatively standardized living and working environments. Yet many of these facilities lacked the kind of technical capacity needed to sustain quality, long-term building production, leaving the brick caught between the same two ideological positions that would divide the party's leadership, namely, the grassroots revolutionary efforts of Mao and the "Gang of Four" as epitomized by rammed earth construction, and the aspirations for a technically sophisticated socialist economy emblematized by the progressive material proficiencies at work in steel and reinforced concrete.

Reconciling these inconsistencies with the party's own unfulfilled promises of social revolution prompted a search for more specific Chinese forms of socialism—work that also strengthened Mao's grip over the party and its political goals through a vilification of disobedient party members, erstwhile mentors like the Soviet Union, and Chinese history itself. Objects and practices were subsequently radicalized along with nearly every other facet of Chinese society in the name of furthering Mao's revolution. Like the victims of reeducation itself, the brick's role in Chinese society was completely upended by the Cultural Revolution. Although it was still a key component of China's material reality, it became increasingly problematic object to defend amid the violent purging of China's imperial past and any vestiges of bourgeois, capitalist values, and so-called class enemies. No longer simply a modest emblem of collective ingenuity and development, brickmaking was repurposed as a method of punishment for class enemies, exposing the incongruities at the core of China's socialism. As the astrophysicist Fang Lizhi (1936–2012) wrote in his memoir detailing his punishing and bewildering ordeal making bricks in Hefei during the Cultural Revolution, "they were asking us to use a two-thousand-year-old method of firing bricks to fire up China's modernization."[46]

At this unique moment of industrial and ideological transition, however, the brick again proved its resilience as an enduring index of labor and a basic, physical technology. Beginning in 1973 and extending through 1976, prefabricated, reinforced concrete and brick-infill building techniques were reintroduced to the country's architects through the pages of publications such as *Architectural Journal*. Framed as a redoubled commitment to hollow brick and prefabricated wall panel technology, the "Wall Reform" (Qiangti Gaige) movement evinced the fervid rhetoric of the Cultural Revolution even as the unassuming proficient material and technical nature of hollow bricks, concrete blocks, and prefabricated concrete wall panels themselves cloaked what was, in fact, a radical pivot away from the violence of class struggle and toward more technically sophisticated, standardized ways of making.

Distinctive, hollow brick production practices were promoted as conducive to lighter, more economically and materially efficient architecture, but they also inadvertently reflected nagging problems of material scarcity in Mao-era China and the search for alternative production models. In alignment with the political, economic, and cultural engagement with capitalist countries supported by Premier Zhou Enlai and other more moderate party leaders at the time, use of prefabricated manufacturing methods demanded more technological expertise than did construction with other building materials, making them both more expensive and politically controversial for a nation still immersed in a campaign organized around the emancipatory power of the proletariat.

Importantly, the promotion of more sophisticated methods of production around the country inevitably privileged certain segments of the workforce at the expense of others, and signaled the reemergence of technicians as vital contributors to socialist Chinese society. In 1975 a series of open forums were organized in which representatives from work units based in Shanghai, Zhejiang, Jiaozuo, Henan, Harbin, and Fujian each discussed their experiences with different kinds of building blocks, aerated concrete, large formwork for concrete casting, and cast-in-situ concrete in addition to "proletarian theory."[47] These forums hearkened back to the bricklaying demonstration events organized during the early days of the socialist Chinese nation. In so doing, however, they also fanned familiar tensions regarding individuated forms of technical proficiency and their implications for collective making, pushing architecture's productive and representational agency in new and unsettling directions.

China's prefabrication innovation was also taking place as it worked to maintain diplomatic ties with socialist allies while pursuing international exchanges with capitalist countries like the United States and Japan, specifically in relation to building technology.[48] In 1975, for example, a delegation of Chinese architects toured the United States to study American architecture, cities, and building practices, specifically precast concrete construction.[49] That same year, China agreed to build a brickmaking factory at Luang Prabang, Laos. In December 1976, a Chinese-designed clay brick factory was completed along the Demerara River in Guyana. The emergence of multiple technical and material flows, inputs, and outputs, involving both capitalist and communist nations, with China somehow and improbably at the center, suggests the rise of a distinctive, more liberalized politics at work through China's material culture, particularly in relation to architectural production. The brick, for all of its various limitations, helped to hasten this shift.

REASSESSING THE BRICK IN MAO-ERA CHINA

In rendering tangible the complex and shifting tangle of political, economic, and cultural forces that shaped Mao's revolutionary objectives, the brick reminds us that the socialist Chinese state's aspirations, particularly within the realm of technological development, often depended upon distinctly physical and material acts of manifestation. In this respect, the brick retains a potent ideological charge in post-Mao Chinese society despite the shimmery sheen of glass, plastic, and neon that now dominates the country's cities and, increasingly, its countryside. These material tensions emerged in the immediate wake left by Mao's death, and they continue to shape the country's complex relationship to objects and physical environments, particularly in relation to questions of expertise and labor.

A glance at the earliest architectural production of the early reform era, for example, including international hotel projects such as the Jianguo Hotel in Beijing, completed by Clement Chen and Associates in 1982, or the Great Wall Hotel in Beijing, designed by Becket International and completed in 1984, may suggest a displacement of the brick as a fundamental socialist Chinese building object in favor of high-rise steel, reinforced concrete, and mirrored glass curtain-wall construction. Indeed, China's initial embrace of these materials projected an urgent desire to modernize through an international architectural language evocative of the alternative forms of capital suddenly at the country's disposal. At these buildings' structural core, however, exists brick infill—evidence of the limited technical expertise prevalent throughout socialist China at the time, but more importantly, brick's undiminished multivalence at times of gradual if ultimately transformative change.[50]

In a country perpetually in search of a visual language capable of illustrating its own progress, buildings and their materials remain an important and vibrant matter.[51] In this regard, and despite the preponderance of reflective glass and glossy plastic surfaces throughout much of China's built environment today, brick remains an unassailable semiotic force in Chinese artistic and architectural production. The intimate relationship between workers and their bricks no longer figures as an essential component of party messaging—a gap that the work of artists like Yang Fudong, Ai Weiwei, and Wang Wei, among others, have capitalized upon. Embedded within a streetscape, or placed in the hands of a white-collar worker or a group of migrant workers, the brick now speaks to a different set of labor dynamics marked by the fleeting, transactional culture and associative themes of violence, disposability, loss, and exploitation that have emerged in relation to the seemingly perpetual construction and destruction of China's built environment, both under Mao and since 1978.[52]

Within the realm of contemporary Chinese architectural production, the design and construction of several recent cultural facilities, such as the Ningbo History Museum, designed by Wang Shu and Lu Wenyu's Amateur Architecture Studio and completed in 2008, and the Suzhou Imperial Kiln Ruins Park and Museum by Liu Jiakun (2016), acknowledges the brick's physical and conceptual durability while commemorating the distinctly material dimensions at work in China amid ongoing shifts in its economy and politics. Material scarcity may no longer pose the economic or political threat to the party that it once did, but the perceived virtues of constraint nevertheless enliven the façade of Wang's building, which features a rich and varied tapestry of brick and tilework salvaged from demolished buildings and overlaid upon portions of the building's concrete core. In Liu's repurposing of an imperial brick kiln for use as a museum and park, sections of the kiln were rebuilt in order to maintain the site's unique brickmaking process, while others were left in a state of ruin in an effort to prompt visitors to ruminate on the inevitable effects of time.

Both projects, and many other examples of contemporary Chinese architectural production, have deployed the brick and its ability to withstand technological or semiotic obsolescence to powerful effect. In so doing, such work illuminates brick's capacity to index the productive efforts of people over time gradually, and not necessarily spectacularly. Such humble, measured multivalence—an ability to engage bodies, concretize labor, project value, and effect a certain atmosphere—have made the brick an oft-overlooked but consequential material object in the literal and conceptual construction of a new China, both then and now.

NOTES

1. Liang Sicheng, letter to Zhu De, April 5, 1950, in *Liang Sicheng quanji*, vol. 5 (Beijing: Zhongguo Jianzhu Gongye Chubanshe, 2001), 82.
2. *Liang Sicheng quanji*, vol. 5, 82.
3. *Liang Sicheng quanji*, vol. 5, 82.
4. Eyferth, "Liberation from the Loom?," 152.
5. See chapter 1 of this volume.
6. See Liu, "Making a New World."
7. Gary Garvin, "Completing the Mies van der Rohe Brick Country House: An Odyssey," *Numéro Cinq* 7, no. 5 (May 2016). I'm grateful to Jonathan Bach for bringing Garvin's work to my attention and for his careful reading of an earlier draft of this paper.

8   This chapter builds upon existing scholarship regarding human and nonhuman agency in natural and social systems. See, for example, Bruno Latour, *We Have Never Been Modern* (New York: Harvester Wheatsheaf, 1993); Latour, *Reassembling the Social*; Amit Srvivastava, "Encountering Materials in Architectural Production: The Case of Kahn and Brick at IIM," PhD dissertation, University of Adelaide, 2009, 39; and David Edgerton, *The Shock of the Old: Technology and Global History since 1900* (Oxford: Oxford University Press, 2007). For a discussion of the brick's importance to socialist and postsocialist Vietnam, see Christina Schwenkel, "Post/Socialist Affect: Ruination and Reconstruction of the Nation in Urban Vietnam," *Cultural Anthropology* 28, no. 2 (2013): 252–77.

9   Alfred B. Searle, "Modern Methods of Brick-Making: Lecture IV," *Journal of the Royal Society of Arts* 58, no. 3015 (September 2, 1910): 903–17.

10 Richard N. Price, "The Other Face of Respectability: Violence in the Manchester Brickmaking Trade, 1859–1870," *Past & Present*, no. 66 (February 1975): 111. See also Nathaniel Lloyd, *A History of English Brickwork* (New York: Benjamin Blom, Inc., 1972; originally published in 1925), 6–38.

11 Frederick Winslow Taylor, *Principles of Scientific Management* (New York: Harper & Row, 1947; originally published in 1911), 82.

12 William J. R. Curtis, "Mies van der Rohe," *Architectural Review*, no. 1377 (November 23, 2011).

13 James W. P. Campbell, *Brick: A World History* (London: Thames and Hudson, 2003), 271.

14 See Réjean Legault, "Louis Kahn and the Life of Materials," in *Louis Kahn: The Power of Architecture*, edited by Mateo Kries, Jochen Eisenbrand, and Stanislaus von Moos (Weil am Rhein: Vitra Design Museum, 2012), 219–33.

15 Shu, "From the Blue to the Red," 316.

16 See Guy Morrison Walker, "Primitive Industrial Civilization of China," *The Chautauquan* 33 (April–September 1901): 130. See also Gregory Clancey, *Earthquake Nation: The Cultural Politics of Japanese Seismicity, 1868–1930* (Berkeley: University of California Press, 2006), 11–28. I am also grateful to Liu Yishi for his insight regarding this point.

17 "Labor Conditions in China," *Monthly Labor Review* 60, no. 1 (January 1945): 23.

18 See, for example, Weihong Bao, "Transparent Shanghai: Cinema, Architecture, and a Left-Wing Culture of Glass," in *Fiery Cinema: The Emergence of an Affective Medium in China, 1915–1945* (Minneapolis: University of Minnesota Press, 2015): 197–262.

19 Steven Lubar, "Representation and Power," *Technology and Culture* 36, no. 2 (April 1995): S54–S82.

20 Raja Hutheesing, *Window on China* (London: Derek Verschoyle, 1953), 89.

21 *Su Changyou xianjin qizhuanfa ji qita* (Beijing: Dongbei Gongye Chubanshe, 1952), 4–5; Wang Jun, *Mao Zedong yu Zhongguo gongyehua* (Fuzhou: Fuzhou Jiaoyu Chubanshe, 2001), 226, 233.

22 Chu Chi-ping, "The Plan Is Under Way," *China Reconstructs* 2, no. 2 (March–April 1953): 5; see also Monica Felton, "Rehousing the People," *China Reconstructs* 2, no. 1 (January–February 1953): 24–25.

23 See chapters 4 and 5 in this volume.

24 *Su Changyou xianjin qizhuanfa ji qita*, 4.
25 "Half a New City in Five Years," *China Reconstructs* 3, no. 5 (September–October 1954): 9.
26 "Half a New City in Five Years," 6–9.
27 Patrick Wright, *Passport to Peking: A Very British Mission to Mao's China* (Oxford: Oxford University Press, 2010), 295.
28 "Half a New City in Five Years," 6.
29 "Latest in Linen Mills," *China Reconstructs* 1, no. 6 (November–December 1952): 42–44.
30 *Jianzhu gongcheng gaisuan zhibiao*, vol. 2 (Beijing: Zhongua Renmin Gongheguo Guojia Jianshe Weiyuan Hui, 1955).
31 For a discussion of the significance of scale in relation to socialist Chinese architecture and painting, see Zhu Tao, "Building Big, with No Regret," *AA Files*, no. 63 (2011): 104–10; and Joan Kee, "Why Chinese Paintings Are So Large," *Third Text* 26 no. 6 (2012): 649–63.
32 Zhu Xiaoming and Zhu Donghai, "Jianguo chuqi Sulian jianzhu guifan de zhuanyi: Yi Tongji Daxue yuan diangong guan shuangqu zhuan gong jianzao weili," *Jianzhu yichan*, no. 1 (2017): 94–104; Xia Heng, Xia Zhenkang, Rao Xiaojun, and Zhao Rubing, "'San cai' yueshu xia de di ji jianzao: Zhongguo zaoqi gongye jianzhu yichan gongke zhuan jiangou yanjiu," *Jianzhu xuebao*, no. 9 (2020): 104–10. See also Eyferth, "Liberation from the Loom?," 152.
33 "Conversation with Second Committee of the All-China Federation of Students (excerpts), February 14, 1957," in John K. Leung, ed., *The Writings of Mao Zedong, Volume II: January 1956–December 1957* (Armonk, NY: M. E. Sharpe, 1992), 301.
34 "Talk at the Meeting of Party Cadres in Shanghai, 20 March 1957," in Roderick MacFarquhar, Timothy Cheek, and Eugene Wu, eds., *The Secret Speeches of Chairman Mao: From the Hundred Flowers to the Great Leap Forward* (Cambridge, MA: Council on East Asian Studies, Harvard University, 1989), 351–52.
35 For a discussion of the role of film in the Great Leap Forward, see Ying Qian, "When Taylorism Met Revolutionary Romanticism: Documentary Cinema in China's Great Leap Forward," *Critical Inquiry* 46 (Spring 2020): 578–604.
36 See, for example, Yuan Jingshen, "Guanyu chuangzuo xin de jianzhu fengge de ji ge wenti," *Jianzhu xuebao*, no. 1 (1959): 38–40.
37 Liang Sicheng, "Dang yinqi women zoushang zhengque de jianzhu xiaoxue fanxiang," *Jianzhu xuebao*, no. 2 (1959): 1–2.
38 *Jianzhu xuebao*, nos. 9–10 (1959); Zhu, "Building Big, with No Regret," 104–10; Paul Clark, "Beijing's Ten Great Buildings: Popular Responses over Three Eras (1959–2016)," *Asian Anthropology* 19, no. 3 (2020): 181–94.
39 See, for example, *Jianzhu xuebao*, nos. 9–10 (1959).
40 Dikötter, *Cultural Revolution*, 213.
41 "Foreword," *Zhuan yancong sheji ziliao* (unpublished building manual).
42 Jianzhu Gongcheng Bu, "Guanyu qing yanjiu tuiguang zhanniantu duokongzhuan he kongxinzhuan de tongzhi," May 19, 1961, in *Zhonggong zhongyao lishi wenxian ziliao huibian*, vol. 28, no. 281 (Los Angeles: Zhongwen Chubanwu Fuwu Zhongxin, 2020), 122–23.

43 Jianzhu Gongcheng Bu Dangzu, "Guanyu zai zhuanwagongye zhong tuiguang 'neiran shaozhuan fa' de baogao," December 19, 1961, in *Zhonggong zhongyao lishi wenxian ziliao huibian*, 124–26.
44 Zhonggong Zhongyang Wenxian Yanjiu Shi, ed., *Jianguo yilai Mao Zedong wengao*, vol. 11 (Beijing: Zhongyang Wenxian Chubanshe, 1996), 210; Liu, "Making a New World," 269–85.
45 Yan Zixiang, "Zhongguo Jianzhu Xuehui disi jie daibiao dahui ji xueshu huiyi zhongjie fayan," *Jianzhu xuebao*, no. Z1 (1966): 21. See also Yu, *Chang'an Avenue*, 158.
46 Fang Lizhi, *The Most Wanted Man in China: My Journey from Scientist to Enemy of the State* (New York: Henry Holt and Company, 2016), 153.
47 "Quanguo kongxin qikuai ji qiangti gaige jingyan jiaoliuhui zai Shanghai zhaokai," *Jianzhu xuebao*, no. 3 (1975): 25.
48 See Cole Roskam, *Designing Reform: Architecture in the People's Republic of China* (New Haven: Yale University Press, 2021), 56–75.
49 "Technology Impresses Chinese Architects," *MEMO* (October 27, 1975): 2.
50 Interview, Clement Chen III, January 14, 2014.
51 See Bennet, *Vibrant Matter*.
52 Philip Tinari, "If It Isn't Built, It Can't Be Torn Down: Notes on Wang Wei's Temporary Space," *Yishu* 2, no. 3 (2003): 72.

3 DESIGN AND HANDICRAFT

CHRISTINE I. HO

AN OIL STUDY BY AN ART ACADEMY TEACHER ATTESTS TO THE world of objects that surrounded a certain echelon of intellectuals in the early years of the People's Republic of China (figure 3.1). Yuan Yunfu's painting memorializes a table crammed with carelessly strewn excavated pottery spanning from the third millennium BCE to the fourteenth century, identifiable as Majiayao to Cizhou ware. The work entices the eye to linger upon textural contrasts of glossy glazes and matte painted decoration, muted range of earthy hues, and subtle variations in the swelling shapes and contours of the vessels.[1] What Yuan has depicted is not an imagined series of objects but rather a selection from the 2,792 artifacts that formed the study collection at the Central Academy of Craft and Design.[2] At the time of its completion, the work was described as a still life, but it might also be understood as part of a genre known as "decorative painting" (*zhuangshi hua*) that arose in the 1960s.[3] Decorative painting entailed more than the still life's associations with moralizing *vanitas* or display of capital accumulation; instead, the genre registered a singular pedagogical relationship to the material object. Works like Yuan's painting were understood as not merely recording physical things and their palpable materiality but also fleshing out the designer's pattern book from a veritable world of historically resonant objects; decorative paintings were studies of pattern, decoration, and form that connected the contemporary designer with an existing historical record of material culture. Such studies placed the student of design between two worlds of things: the material object itself and the lessons of design that it imparted, and the imagined objects of a disappearing material history that stood as shadow presences, a projected history of craft production and unknown craftspeople that haunted the imaginations of designers in midcentury China.

Central to design studies was the relationship between design and handicraft, between prominent intellectuals who extracted lessons from the crafted object and formerly anonymous artisans whose identities were promoted as representative agents of socialist national culture. The history of design

FIGURE 3.1. Yuan Yunfu, *The Spirit Vitality of Ancient Ceramics*, 1962. Gouache on canvas, 20 1/2 x 28 1/4 in. (52 x 72 cm). Estate of Yuan Yunfu.

studies in Mao-era China tracks a trajectory parallel to other nation-building movements of the twentieth century, in which elite intellectuals and the state, sometimes in collusion and other times in collision, joined together to recognize and promote handicraft as constitutive of national identity.[4] In postrevolutionary Mexico, Olinalá lacquerware was promoted as the material representation of indigenous *mexicanidad* identity, elevating the handicraft object as an ethnicized essence emerging through collaborations within transnational contexts. Cosmopolitan intellectuals recognized that the state's desire for nationhood could be a congenial vehicle for an already existing culturally nationalist nativism, only for these intellectuals to become marginalized as their projects became assimilated as cultural hegemony.[5] Similarly, the folk craft (*mingei*) movement in early twentieth-century Japan featured comparable conditions of intellectual rapport that coalesced from transnational alliances. These connections were nonetheless vigorously denied, even as elite rediscovery and reanimation of native and ethnic traditions contributed to prewar cultural nationalism—optimal conditions that would unite the identity of the nation with the ideals of handicraft.[6] Among intersecting histories of handicraft and the nation-state, the relationship between propagandistic address and the New Year's print (*nianhua*) has dominated discussions of folk culture in Maoist China.[7]

Self-proclaimed designers in early Mao-era China conceived of a socialist material culture embedded within folk-national histories of handicraft.[8] As a result, they did not bring the same polemical positions of techno-utopianism as their modernist counterparts, or the break between handicraft and design that has characterized the conventional thrust of design history, and thus they have remained unincorporated into a larger, global history of design.[9] Prioritizing artisanal production, chronicling craft as vernacular history, and promoting ethnic diversity and regional identities, they imagined that mass production could retain aspects of the handmade, employ indigenous materials, and incentivize small-scale regional manufacturing. Their ambitions cohered with, and later responded to, developments within the Soviet bloc and internationally: the equation between the folk arts—most visibly song and dance, but also handicrafts that foregrounded women's labor, such as embroidery, carpets, and toy-making—and mass culture would expand during the Cold War era, as the promotion of handicraft through international trade exhibitions and souvenir shops became a key feature of communist industry, while enacting principles of national contributions to socialist internationalism.[10] Rather than a material culture of propaganda, the conjunction of design studies and handicraft offers another narrative that incorporates China back into Cold War frameworks of circulating material exchange, one in which intellectuals exerted themselves in defining a national cultural identity that would be coterminous with economic and cultural partners, yet not divorced, as is often casually assumed, from the material culture that preceded New China.

To create a socialist design pedagogy and profession, design bureaucrats focused upon a new socialist object with a national identity that could be defined by modern ornament derived from historical handicraft. Ornament, as they understood it, was an untapped well that could offer an unarticulated yet immediately pleasurable entrée into national pride and cultural essence to students, producers, and citizens alike. In this sense, ornament was the most mass-oriented aesthetic experience and tool available to the designer. In the history of design, the separation of decoration from materialist conceptions of technical development, associated with Gottfried Semper and explicitly illustrated in Owen Jones' *The Grammar of Ornament*, has frequently been understood as the foundational origins of the design profession in response to increasing mechanization and industrialization.[11] The names of Semper, Jones, John Ruskin, and Adolf Loos would have been familiar to the figureheads of Chinese design as they encountered architects and theorists in Japanese translation and through their studies in Europe. Of interest here, however, is the architect Lars Spuybroek's reclamation of matter's relationship to ornament in his rereading of Ruskin's seminal writings on the subject.[12] Ornament, in Spuybroek's conception, is more than graphical elaboration. Rather, it is an abstract materialism that visualizes Ruskin's sense of surface as a geological skeleton that externalizes "all is inextricably woven into the world-earth."[13] Deliberately rejecting Loos's famous manifesto descrying ornament's erasure of material, Spuybroek returns ornament as expressive of material substrate. In understanding ornament as the Ruskinian *articulation* of material, Spuybroek thereby underscores surface elaboration as the possibility for relational and transdimensional sympathy for matter itself.[14] Such ambitions for resurfacing one's sympathetic relation to matter, especially by reclaiming ornament as a process accessing the meaning of material things, were also keystones for intellectuals in designing early Maoist material culture.

INSTITUTIONAL TRANSITIONS

Design as an intellectual and functional project to augment the interface between humans and objects was not a new concept to midcentury China, but it was under New China that designers saw the potential for reorganizing state-sponsored organs of design to accommodate an ambitious, wide-ranging national program for investigating craft production and integrating such populist, hand-derived design knowledge into industrial production of everyday goods to "dress, eat, reside, travel" (*yi shi zhu xing*). Central to this intellectual project was the establishment of the earliest state-sponsored institution devoted to design studies, the Central Academy of Craft and Design (Zhongyang Gongyi Meishu Xueyuan). From its opening in November 1956 until its incorporation into Tsinghua University as the Academy of Art and Design (Meishu Xueyuan) in 1999, the Central Academy remained a troubled institution throughout its four decades of independent existence.[15]

Although the Central Academy was an entirely new cultural organ created under Maoist cultural policy, the emergence of the national design school was due in part to existing design departments that had been established in the major art schools of Republican-era China. Its failure to thrive was also due to the modernist orientation of its faculty, who had worked as graphic and textile designers in the urbane, cosmopolitan hybridity of 1930s treaty-port cities and subsequently shifted these interests to the handicraft industry during their wartime sojourns in southwestern China. The design profession in socialist China built upon Republican-era design studies, having inherited institutional configurations of art education, intellectual and professional experiences developed in treaty ports, and a political commitment to rejuvenating the national economy. In its earliest stages, then, early-twentieth-century design was a field characterized by the integration of design pedagogy into fine arts schools; a heavily cosmopolitan awareness of Art Deco and modernist developments in Europe, the United States, and Japan; and the economic nationalism developing out of the National Goods Movement and centered around the handicraft industry.[16] During the Second Sino-Japanese War, however, design by necessity had been transformed by the imperative to create mass propaganda, including producing handbooks for illustrated announcements on village blackboards and decorating the arrangement of meeting halls, political conventions, and other public rallying spaces.[17]

Between 1949 and 1953, most design, functional art, and craft departments from the prewar years were reconstituted within preexisting schools. Perhaps most interesting, the foundation of the Sichuan Fine Arts Institute in Chongqing developed out of one of the nation's first schools for design and handicraft, the Sichuan Provincial Advanced Craft Vocational School, which had been established in 1939 by Li Youxing and his colleague, the lacquer craftsman Shen Fuwen.[18] In Shenyang, a functional art department was also inaugurated under the Lu Xun Academy of Art; when the academy was first formed in Yan'an, no design department existed, although cultural workers had designed halls, posters, and typography. Most prominent among these reconfigurations, however, were the art academies in Hangzhou and Beijing: the design (*tu'an*) department at the former National Hangzhou Art Academy became part of the East China campus of the Central Academy of Fine Arts, while the functional art department of the Beiping Art Academy was reorganized under the Central Academy of Fine Arts in Beijing, complemented by the Craft Research Studio spearheaded by Pang Xunqin.[19]

These piecemeal efforts did not satisfy intellectuals who had, at the first Literary and Art Workers' Association meeting in July 1949, proposed the profession of design as a new category of cultural work and deserving of an institutional home sponsored by the state.[20] The idea of a national academy specially instituted to promote design was the pet project of a group of intellectuals, the most vocal of whom was Pang Xunqin; he was supported by his friends and colleagues Chen Zhifo, Lei Guiyuan, Li Youxing, and Shen Fuwen, all of whom had previously trained in design in Japan or France and subsequently worked in graphic design studios and textile manufacturers in Shanghai, Nanjing, Suzhou, or Ningbo; they were also joined by their membership in the China Commercial and Industrial Artists' Association, founded in 1936.[21] Taking the École Nationale Supérieure des Arts Décoratifs and the Bauhaus as their national cultural and educational models, they would become the state bureaucrats of design in early socialist China, carrying out research projects on handicraft goods and educational programs aimed at artisans and craftspeople, and defining the parameters of the design profession.

Before the opening of the Central Academy of Craft and Design in 1956, the respective departments of design in Beijing and Hangzhou merged into one unit in Beijing in order to prepare, administratively and intellectually, for the enterprise of creating a national design school. With the exception of the future academy president Zhang Ding, the core faculty of the merged unit—most prominently Pang Xunqin, Lei Guiyuan, and Zhang Guangyu—were all figures oriented toward Europe and shaped by the cosmopolitan, urban, and commercial environments of Shanghai.[22] Moreover, in spite of their institutional affiliations, they stood slightly apart from the academic debates that were concurrently taking place within the fine arts, which had been roiled by discussions over the status of easel and oil painting, staged clashes between Soviet and culturally nativist models of artistic training, and the problems of integrating fine, popular, and propaganda arts.[23] Without engaging directly, the faculty of the future Central Academy of Craft and Design saw themselves as operating beyond the parameters of such contestations, compelled by inclination and training to seek an alternative mode, away from continually retreading the antitheses of high and low, elite and populist, foreign and national, and traditional and modern that dominated the fine arts world.

Such debates could perhaps also only be part of the privileged realm of the art academies, distinct from the immediate economic goals that the academy designers embraced. The designers of the Central Academy styled themselves as critical to reinvigorating handicraft, the supply and demand of which had been interrupted during the wartime, in order to modernize the designs to appeal to domestic and international consumers, to anticipate and understand market demand in order to better coordinate production and sales, to coordinate material supply and streamline processes to reduce waste, and, above all, to connect artisans with a material history of things that had been overlooked or neglected as cheaper, machine-made items came onto the market.[24] Their immediate, pressing purpose was clearly indicated by the administrative oversight of the academy: it was not headed by the Ministry of Culture as were the art academies, but rather supervised by the Handicraft Bureau under the auspices of the Ministry of Light Industry.²⁵ This arrangement created close, advantageous ties among the various enterprises managed by the Handicraft Bureau, allowing a flow of exchanges between artisans who would visit the Central Academy for short-term lecture series on the history of their respective crafts, as well as between students of design who would enter into craft institutes to participate in monthlong training sessions.²⁶

Still, the designers of the Central Academy did not see themselves as solely devoted to market demands. In its original, lofty ambitions, the Craft Research Studio at the Central Academy of Fine Arts was modeled after the interdisciplinary formations of Academia Sinica and the Central Academy of Social Sciences; this sense of intellectual alliance was shored up by invited lecturers such as the archaeologist Chen Mengjia.²⁷ Cleavages between economic purpose and elite intellectual heritage eventually bifurcated the Central Academy of Craft and Design's centrality to the production of goods, but not before design bureaucrats staked out the parameters of socialist design that would define a national style.

DESIGN PEDAGOGY

A set of foundational texts by Lei Guiyuan and Pang Xunqin, published immediately after the founding of the People's Republic but before the launch of the first Five-Year Plan, became highly influential in defining the intellectual heritage of the Central Academy. The earliest of their kind in New China, these textbooks were envisioned as part of a foundational pedagogy for students and artisans, balancing theoretical and historical concerns with pragmatic exercises for understanding design. Both handbooks registered transitional phases, employing the Republican-period term for design, *tu'an*, from the Japanese loanword *zuan*; the preferred term in contemporary usage is *sheji*.²⁸ Lei, Pang, and their other design colleagues recognized that the textbooks, which retained patterns of thought and ingrained concepts from Lei and Pang's professional training and work in the previous two decades in Hangzhou, Shanghai, Kunming, and Chengdu, could not fully address the new mass designer of socialist China. Subsequently, they went on to reconfigure these texts in a later collaboration, the widely distributed *The Organization of Design* (Tu'an de zuzhi) compiled for mass designers.²⁹

One of the most seminal textbooks for design published in the early People's Republic was the two-volume *The Theory and Method of New Design* (1950) by Lei Guiyuan, which elaborates on a shorter, similarly influential primer that Lei produced three years earlier, *New Studies in Design*.[30] Citing three French and German books in its bibliography—*Memento de la science ornementale, Pour comprendre l'art décoratif moderne en France*, and Leonhard Adam's 1940 widely read study of global prehistoric material cultures in *Primitive Art*—Lei's *The Theory and Method of New Design* presents a curriculum for designing what he refers to as *l'idée ornamental*.[31] Where Lei's first volume gives the principles of design in both French and Chinese as *l'intensité, la varieté*, and *la concordance* through varying exercises in form, the second volume elaborates upon the basic components of form in order to develop patterns out of observations of nature, moving from vegetal to animal sources of inspiration. His illustrations stage cross-cultural comparisons, aligning a Paul Vera graphic design next to images of Miao women, as well as the history of primitive decoration, heavily lifted from Adam's *Primitive Art*. In a world of ornament ordered in chronological order (Egyptian, Persian, Assyrian, Greek, Roman, Pompeiian, Carolingian, Renaissance, baroque, rococo, neoclassical, Arts and Crafts, Indian, and indigenous American), design culminates in China and the Soviet Union, which Lei characterizes as uniquely bringing together east and west, extracting from Xinjiang papercut patterns as much as neoclassical precedents. Assigned in design and functional art departments, *The Theory and Method of New Design* continues the Republican-era legacy of ornamental grammar as source material, framed by the principles of Beaux Arts functional design education but divorced from design as a technical exercise of maximizing industrial resources.

By contrast, Pang Xunqin's landmark *Problems in Design Research* presented a polemical approach, confronting the minor status of design and proposing what has sometimes been understood as a Bauhaus-like shift to uniting fine and functional art courses in primary-level art education.[32] Once Pang participated as part of the Central Academy work unit in the land reform campaign and underwent thought reform during the Three-Antis and Five-Antis campaigns, he returned to the Craft Research Studio to begin teaching, while completing a comprehensive text written at the behest of Shanghai's Dadong Publishing House, part of a larger commission that created a new series of art handbooks adapted for New China. Pang set out by describing design as a series of haptic encounters that form the surface of everyday material life, from the first moment of waking to the end of the workday.[33] All of these experiences with the material world—of clothing, architecture, everyday objects, and interiors—constitute the work of design as the interface between the material and spiritual realms, the haptic means by which an affective relationship with objects is produced, elicited, and performed.

Important to Pang is the idea that function elicits a host of more indefinable sensations; pleasure, comfort, and beauty combine to envelop a laborer's existence with the leisure and relaxation promised by new socialist life. He begins with the act of putting on clothes, observing the incised pattern on buttons that fasten clothing, as well as the various styles of clothing produced for men, women, the elderly, and children, and even myriad ethnicities; he then moves to chairs and stools that provide comfort to the body as well as repose and ease for the eyes. Design, Pang observes, is not limited to everyday goods but can be found in folk expressions, such as carved window patterns in village houses.

In the realm of architectural monuments, Pang suggests that design is found in public sites such as the Temple of Heaven, the White Dagoba in Beihai, the Forbidden City, the Great Hall of the People, and the Monument to the People's Heroes; the communal leisure represented by parks, theaters, and cultural palaces; and the commercial spaces of the urban street, including displays in shop windows. And an awareness of design is also to be found among people as they shop: what drives their choices when faced with an array of "umbrellas, wash basins, printed cloth blankets, sheets, and towels," or leads them to select a particular drinking glass or porcelain bowl? It is, as Pang writes, that "they choose what they like, a good model, a good pattern, a good color." After all, he concludes, when you ride a bus, weary from work, is it not the arrangement and colors of the bus's interior that lift your spirits, and allow you to forget your tiredness?

Although Pang's positive statement of design's potential seems commonplace today, his manifesto diverges in some significant ways from earlier, similar efforts by his colleagues to reconfigure it from a designer-oriented perspective to a wellspring of mass experience. Many other designers, such as Li Youxing and Lei Guiyuan, had previously sought to describe the profession as coordinating and centralizing the labor of craftspeople, or the duty of the designer as retaining a sense of aesthetic appreciation and historical continuity in handicrafts challenged by industrialization.[34] Others, such as the Yan'an cultural worker and exhibition designer Wu Lao, had treated design in a more piecemeal fashion, delving into its constituent specialties arising from propagandistic needs, from prescribing a repertory of art typography (*meishuzi*) for writing on village blackboards to instructing future designers in the presentation of meeting hall spaces.[35] Pang, instead, moves beyond the profession as a top-down exercise and seeks to conceive of design as mediating the basic registers of socialist life, the sensorial expression of mass culture that materializes from a primordial sea of collective knowledge and is embodied through everyday experience: "Why does design work continually advance in the lives of humankind? It is because that design is demanded in multiple aspects of life." As a result, Pang declares, design is more than simply iterating ornament and inscribing surface; it is situated within a Bauhaus-inflected conception as environmental, atmospheric, and devoted to improving the everyday.[36]

Pang's immediate project was to rehabilitate the status of design as a subject worthy of study. More than the other contested realms of cultural production, the profession was particularly politically suspect because it had originated in the cosmopolitanism, materialistic consumerism, capitalist culture, and landlord-oriented interests of Republican-era urban centers; the designers themselves were also plagued with equally dubious class backgrounds, having trained in and worked for imperialist enterprises such as the British-American Tobacco Company.[37] From a longer historical perspective, design's relationship to handicraft production was also rooted in regional craft workshops established to serve the imperial court, such as Jingdezhen, resulting in a legacy that still determined and directed the production of crafts that imitated court wares for landowning gentry and, of course, were particularly out of step with mass taste. Design's pedigree, from the bloodline of coordinated court production to Republican-era vernacular modernism, and specifically the aura of Shanghai, delimited Pang's argumentative scope as he sought to refute misconceptions about design: that it was a specious form of work that should remain uncelebrated and unacknowledged, that it was a feature of capitalist societies, that it lacked ideological significance.[38]

To define design as an object of mass culture, Pang argued that both shifts in demand and the longer history of material culture, in which artisans are conflated with the masses, evince a popular yet unenunciated responsiveness to the idea of design. Alluding to recent events in design's reception, including the lukewarm sales of printed cotton fabrics produced in 1950, the popular backlash against particular fabric patterns from eastern-seaboard producers in 1952, and the warm welcome given to Wenzhou-produced umbrellas at the Zhejiang Goods Convention, Pang identified these as expressions of mass sensitivity to design. But mass taste is not entirely trustworthy, as Pang noted, for, given their relative ideological consciousness and distance from feudal society, "not all the things that the people love are good."[39]

Pang's comments mirror a larger debate over the appearance of handicraft. As an essay by the critic Wang Xun published in 1950 prescribes, handicraft—defined as three realms of imperial crafts (*guanshi gongyi*), folk craft (*minjian gongyi*), and new everyday objects (*xin riyongpin*)—must be served by the large-scale production of new designs that would change consumer taste into mass taste, one that is healthy, auspicious, and beautiful.[40] To achieve the status that Pang desired, the designer, whom he referred to as a Stalinist "engineer of the human spirit," must simultaneously enable popular preference while also drawing out and inculcating higher ideals through everyday design. Design thus becomes a project of ideological education through sensorial experience.

The disjunction between the elite designer and the mass audience that underlies Pang's discussion rapidly became the focus of educating designers employed in work units managed by the Handicraft Bureau. The Craft Research Studio was designated as the intellectual linchpin that coordinated regional and municipal institutes of craft that had been established by 1953, including cloisonné and jade research institutes in Beijing and the Jingdezhen ceramic research institute, among others.[41] The designers who would be educated by the studio were handicraft practitioners themselves, selected from the artisans associated with each craft research institute. For these would-be designers, Lei Guiyuan pooled his resources with Xu Zhenpeng, Tian Shiguang, and Chang Shanren, overseen by Pang Xunqin, Zhang Ding, and Zhang Guangyu; together, they adjusted their notion of design pedagogy to suit their potential students. The unusual textbook that resulted diverged significantly from the textual orientation of their previous pedagogical exercises, even as it preserved the editors' primary commitments to historicizing design through vernacular material culture.[42]

The Organization of Design explains the internal logic of design thinking through the single example of designing patterns derived from tree peonies, chosen for their auspicious symbolism, healthy beauty, and potent historical associations as a native plant. To exemplify the evolution of vegetal ornament, *The Organization of Design* narrates the process of abstraction inherent in producing decoration, developing from an encounter with the natural environment into distillation, estrangement, and reordering, from realism to stylization (figure 3.2). With a bare minimum of commentary, the ninety pages of the textbook begin with a color photograph of peonies, noted as having been snapped in natural light without color correction, then expand into black-and-white photographs of buds and half-open blooms, then shift into contour line drawings, followed by historical examples of peonies found

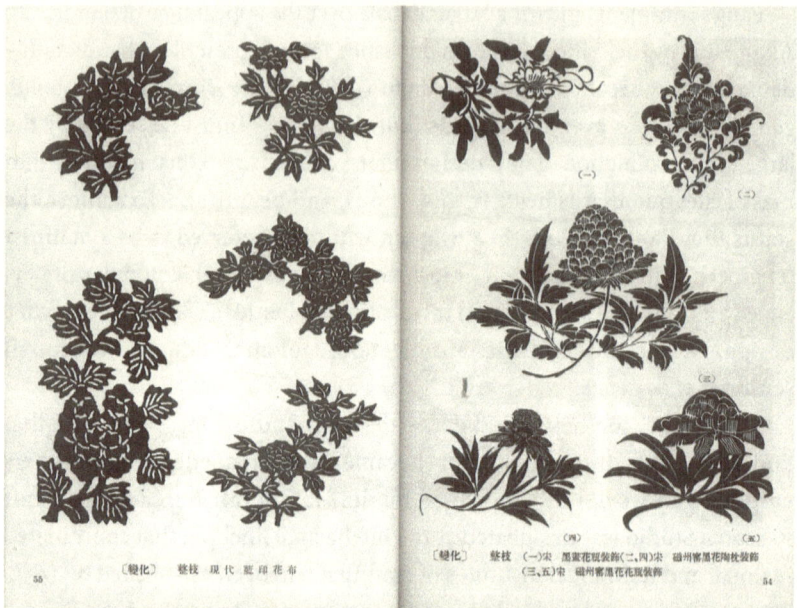

FIGURE 3.2. Craft Research Studio at the Central Academy of Fine Arts. From *The Organization of Design* (Tu'an de zuzhi). Beijing: Chaohua Meishu Chubanshe, 1955.

across media, an exhaustive collection that encompasses paintings, brocades, lacquer, *kesi* embroidery, mirrors, pottery and porcelain, papercuts, woodcuts, molded bricks, fresco painting, batik, jewelry, and architectural molding. The compendium ends with modern examples resulting from this process of extraction and historicization, the last object being a bookmark designed by Lu Jingda, a handicraft worker in Chaozhou. As such, the layout of the images suggests an domestic history of design—from plant life to folk and imperial craft, evolving into modern craft—absorbed as an intuitive, instinctual exercise of pictorial evolution while maintaining cultural and historical references. Distributed in an edition of 6,500 copies, *The Organization of Design* underpins the creation of iconic socialist objects, from Dongbei printed cottons (*dahuabu*) to the floral patterns found on everyday goods, from mirrors to pencil cases.[43]

HANDICRAFT: FUNCTIONAL ART OR COMMODITY?

The Organization of Design and other associated ornamental compendia on Dunhuang and Ming brocade patterns championed historicist and cosmopolitan orientations in order to define a socialist design identity, while also answering to an international market for folk crafts. The Central Academy of Craft and Design's preparatory organization, the Central Craft Art Research Institute, defined three objectives to "raise the standards" of handicraft as an export commodity: exploration of new materials and production methods in order to create model works that could raise the level of craft works, systematic collection and organization of ethnic and folk craft, and support of folk artists in raising the standards of production by researching and introducing foreign craft.[44] Design bureaucrats—Pang Xunqin, Lei Guiyuan, Wu Lao, and Yuan Mai—successively traveled with delegations to Eastern Europe on four important trips after 1954 to participate in trade fairs and to study international trends in designing handicraft, even as the People's Republic began to stage National Handicraft Exhibitions from 1953 onward.[45] The exchange of experts who arrived from Hungary, Bulgaria, Romania, Poland, and Czechoslovakia, among other countries, to inspect wares such as Wuxi clay figurines and Swatow ware for their viability in foreign markets, was employed to define China's own folk identity in the face of other national cultures, parallel to the dance exhibitions discussed in chapter 4 of this volume. Understood as the antithesis of Euro-American engagements of the previous decades, craft exchanges throughout the Second World highlighted the economic imperative for handicraft design to represent national identity.[46]

To answer to the market for light-industry commodities, handicraft institutes organized under the Ministry of Light Industry increased over the decade, each with hand-selected mass designers and artisans who were to be trained by the Central Academy through lectures on material culture history and exposure to historical objects, either as short-term visits to Beijing or by academy designers who traveled to regional institutes. Several other design departments had been simultaneously established under the municipal and provincial light-industry work units, such as the Craft Art Research Studio within the Shanghai Municipal Light Industry Research Institute. Rather than offering histories of material culture, these studios provided practical knowledge on materials, new techniques, imported machinery, and quantitative data on the larger market; they supplemented the "scientific" knowledge that Central Academy designers failed to impart.[47]

As a result, the authority claimed by the Central Academy designers was challenged by their dual mission, split between the historicist notion of handicraft design and the immediate problem of sales numbers. That the academy's research projects proceeded without directly accounting for mass taste through economic data did not go unnoticed. Addressing the simmering problems in an essay published during the 1956–57 Hundred Flowers Movement in the *Craft Art Newsletter*, the former printmaker and cultural cadre Ge Kejian discussed whether the handicraft industry would be better led by the Ministry of Culture or the Ministry of Light Industry: "When cultural bureau members go to handicraft production work units to guide creation, this is the result: you [designers] provide your opinion, they [the workers] follow their production contract to carry out matters."[48] Due to the success of Chinese handicraft exports, annual sales of which were cited as totaling three hundred million yuan in 1956, the Ministry of Light Industry's demands excluded the Central Academy's design knowledge. The result, as discussed throughout the newsletter, was that economic imperatives effectively trumped the designers' ability, and desire, to experiment with modern forms.

The inability to effect change in the handicraft industry spurred junior designers and senior administrators to sign a series of ten recommendations at the height of the Anti-Rightist campaign in early 1957, calling for the inspection of the academy's leadership and creation of a rectification committee to reconfigure the Central Craft Art Research Institute, to clarify the chain of command between the national and provincial ministries of culture, and to form a National Handicraft conference, among other stipulations.[49] The consequences of making these public demands were dire. At the first landmark meeting in Beijing of the National Handicraft Artists Representatives, on July 22–28, 1957, which gathered eighty thousand people involved in craft production, various cadres in attendance singled out Pang Xunqin as a target of criticism for having intervened in the handicraft sector of light industry.[50] In a speech, Qian Junrui, a cadre from the Ministry of Culture, singled Pang out for his role in the publication and distribution of craft-related publications as a conduit for "sowing poisonous seeds" across the nation, employing Mao Zedong's phrase for reactionary, counterrevolutionary thought and action.

The relationship between design and the designer was to be putatively nonhierarchical in concept, but it was hierarchical in practice: constantly held in tension were design derived from mass taste, and the designer as the intellectual pioneer responsible for historical inheritance from the laboring classes' material culture. At the same time that intellectuals sought to research and establish a notion of national design, state collectivization and centralization of the handicraft industry resulted in the erasure of the same histories that designers sought to maintain.[51] If the dream of socialist life was the wholesale redesign of everyday life, in metaphorical terms, to maximize the material conditions of the socialist utopia, the impact of Maoist cultural and economic policy was a continual ambivalence over the balance between folk culture and industrial advancement, a tug-of-war over vernacular nationalism and economic priority. The project of design as defined by Pang Xunqin, Lei Guiyuan, and their like-minded colleagues was unequivocally described by the light-industry officials as a blight upon the handicraft industry. Intellectual, time-consuming, experimental, and hence subject to failure, their idea of design work was also a project that was too cosmopolitan and European in its inclinations, far too interested in elitist visions of material culture without adequate grounding in market research and consumer taste.

DREAMING THE SOCIALIST OBJECT

In the wake of the criticism of Pang Xunqin, his colleague Zhang Guangyu sought to continue their joint vision of the possibilities for material culture, memorialized in one of the most unusual publications of the early People's Republic: *Decoration* (Zhuangshi). Succeeding *Craft Art Report* as a bimonthly magazine on the topic on September 5, 1958, *Decoration* was a short-lived journal in the early socialist mediascape, published in a run of a mere twelve issues until publication ceased abruptly in 1961. It was partially authorized by developments in Soviet material culture and design, especially *Dekorativnoe iskusstvo SSSR*, an exploration of Russian folk material culture that had begun publication eight months earlier.[52] From editorial choices in its presentation and format, *Decoration* was designed to stand out among standardized publication sizes. Its unusual proportions as a square format enabled expansive photographic spreads of design proposals using three types of technology: offset, intaglio, and relief printing.[53] While serving as an international promotional agent for Chinese handicraft, the trade magazine must also be understood as a pointed argument for design's alternate modernism, founded within the history of material culture.

With typography designed by Zhang Guangyu and graphics by Zhang Ding, the inaugural cover of *Decoration* combines a series of references bridging elite and popular, antiquarian and peasant, textual and lived traditions (figure 3.3). Brushed swathes of neon pink and mint green enclose the archaeologically derived yet vaguely Art Deco flaring forms of the title's characters with the cartoon-like naivete of the New Year's print-style dragon boat, its curve elongated in order to bear four triangular pennants. The dragon is itself rendered in a slightly crude yet charming amateur hand, reminiscent of the folk paintings that peasants were encouraged to produce

FIGURE 3.3. Zhang Guangyu and Zhang Ding, cover for the inaugural issue of *Decoration. Zhuangshi* 1, no. 1 (1958).

during the Great Leap Forward's amateur art campaign of outdoor propaganda murals. Each of the pennants is decorated with a symbol that appears as though derived from a rubbing from a Han-dynasty molded brick: a robe, cup, house, and wheel are arrayed from left to right, the graphic representation of dressing, eating, residing, and traveling, respectively; repeated throughout the magazine's interior, the four symbols are paired with chrysanthemums, lotuses, and peonies. This first cover of *Decoration*, now a landmark image often reproduced in surveys of modern design history, unites archaeological, folk amateurism, populist propaganda, and Art Deco elements to define the new visual identity of socialist Chinese design.

Encapsulating its producers' dream of socialist design, in which the physical experience of matter and materiality would give rise to ideal forms of affective experience, embracing what Genevieve Zubrzcki has termed the "national sensorium," the material culture featured in *Decoration* constituted a haptic and sensual supplement to the political pedagogy of the period.[54] Both the magazine and the objects that it featured, "inarticulate objects of desire," to borrow Chandra Mukerji's phrasing, were far from everyday lived experience, but they reveal something of intellectuals and their competing visions of modernity and modernism in early Mao-era China, in which a wholesale transformation of material life could be effected through designing culturally and nationally expressive surfaces to be enlivened through everyday touch.[55] Paradoxically, the histories of ornament developed by *Decoration*'s designers would become coopted as a rote language as light industry expanded into producing and exporting stereotypically Chinese objects, from jade carvings to carpets, for exhibition at international trade fairs.[56] *Decoration* and its predecessors present a far broader, more expansive set of sources for socialist material culture: their designers' wide-ranging exploration of the material culture of the past reveals why the Maoist material world was so frequently decorated with the auspicious symbols, archaeological imagery, and folk designs that socialist material culture was supposed to discard in favor of industrial modernity. In so doing, *Decoration* preserved the designer's dream of material culture and its possibilities in early Mao-era China.

NOTES

1 Wu Zhangshen, ed., *Yuan Yunfu hua ji* (Beijing: Beijing Shidai Huawen Shuju, 2015).
2 Yuanshi Bianxie Zu, *Qinghua Daxue Meishu Xueyuan (yuan Zhongyang Gongyi Meishu Xueyuan) jianshi* (Beijing: Qinghua Daxue Chubanshe, 2011), 26.
3 Zhang Ding, "Zhang Guangyu de zhuangshi yishu," in *Zhang Guangyu chatuji* (Beijing: Renmin Meishu Chubanshe, 1961), republished in the compendium of texts for design education *Gongyi meishu lunwenxuan* (Beijing: Zhongyang Gongyi Meishu Xueyuan Ziliao Shi, 1963).
4 Glenn Adamson, *The Invention of Craft* (London: Bloomsbury, 2013), 181–91.
5 Rick A. López, *Crafting Mexico: Intellectuals, Artisans, and the State after the Revolution* (Durham, NC: Duke University Press, 2010), 95–150.
6 Yuko Kikuchi, *Japanese Modernisation and Mingei Theory: Cultural Nationalism and Oriental Orientalism* (London: Routledge, 2004). See also Kim Brandt, *Kingdom of Beauty: Mingei and the Politics of Folk Art in Imperial Japan* (Durham, NC: Duke University Press, 2007).
7 Felicity Lufkin, *Folk Art and Modern Culture in Republican China* (Lanham, MD: Lexington Books, 2016), 159–73.

8   Ka-ming Wu, "Paper-Cuts in Modern China: The Search for Modernity, Cultural Tradition, and Women's Liberation," *Modern China* 41, no. 1 (2015): 90–127.
9   On the engineering of objects, metaphorical and technical, see Kiaer, *Imagine No Possessions*; Katharina Pfützner, *Designing for Socialist Need: Industrial Design Practice in the German Democratic Republic* (London: Routledge, 2018), 139–69; and David Crowley and Jane Pavitt, *Cold War Modern: Design 1945–1970* (London: V&A Publishing, 2008). On the gap in design history in China, see Leah Hsiao and Michael White, "The Bauhaus and China: Present, Past, and Future," *West 86th: A Journal of Decorative Arts, Design History, and Material Culture* 22, no. 2 (2015): 182; Wendy S. Wong, "Design History and Study in East Asia: Part 2: Greater China: People's Republic of China/Hong Kong/Taiwan," *Journal of Design History* 24, no. 4 (2011): 375–95.
10 David Crowley, "Stalinism and Modernist Craft in Poland," *Journal of Design History* 11, no. 1 (1998): 71–83; Penny Sparke, "The Straw Donkey: Tourist Kitsch or Proto-Design? Craft and Design in Italy, 1945–1960," *Journal of Design History* 11, no. 1 (1998): 59–69; Daniel Stone, "Cepelia and Folk Arts Industries in Poland, 1949–1956," *Polish Review* 54, no. 3 (2009): 287–310.
11 Stacey Sloboda, "*The Grammar of Ornament*: Cosmopolitanism and Reform in British Design," *Journal of Design History* 21, no. 3 (2008): 223–36.
12 Lars Spuybroek, *The Sympathy of Things: Ruskin and the Ecology of Design* (Rotterdam: V2 Publishing, NAi Publishing, 2011).
13 Spuybroek, *Sympathy of Things*, 85.
14 Spuybroek, *Sympathy of Things*, 102, 119.
15 The Academy of Art and Design has continued to celebrate its anniversary as the continuation of the Central Academy; see Qinghua Daxue, ed., *Qinghua Daxue Meishu Xueyuan jiansheng 50 zhounian jiaoshi lunwen ji* (Wuhan: Hubei Meishu Chubanshe, 2006).
16 The literature in English is brief; see Julia F. Andrews and Kuiyi Shen, *The Art of Modern China* (Berkeley: University of California Press, 2012), 89–91; Ren Wei, "The Writer's Art: Tao Yuanqing and the Formation of Modern Chinese Design (1900–1930)," PhD diss., Harvard University, 2015; and Christine I. Ho, "In Search of National Decoration: Archaeology and Ethnography in Wartime Chinese Design," *Archives of Asian Art* 69, no. 2 (2019): 121–54.
17 Chen Ruilin, *Zhongguo xiandai yishu sheji shi* (Changsha: Hunan Kexue Jishu Chubanshe, 2002).
18 Initially named the Chengdu Art Vocational School in 1950, it then merged with the Southwest People's Art Academy into the Southwest Art Vocational School.
19 Zhejiang Meishu Xueyuan, *Yishu yaolan: Zhejiang Meishu Xueyuan liushinian* (Hangzhou: Zhejiang Meishu Xueyuan Chubanshe, 1988).
20 Disici Wendaihui Choubeizhu Qicaozu, ed., *Liushinian wenyi dashiji, 1919–1979* (Beijing: Wenhuabu Wenxue Yishu Yanjiuyuan Lilun Zhengce Yanjiushi, 1979), 123–24.
21 Zhongguo Gongshangye Meishu Zuojia Xiehui, *Xiandai Zhongguo gongshangye meishu xuanji* (Shanghai: Zhongguo Gongshangye Meishujia Xiehui, 1937).
22 On their roles in graphic design, see Paul Bevan, *A Modern Miscellany: Shanghai Cartoon Artists, Shao Xunmei's Circle and the Travels of Jack Chen, 1926–1938* (Leiden: Brill, 2015), 53–92.

23 Julia Andrews, *Painters and Politics in the People's Republic of China, 1949–1979* (Berkeley: University of California Press, 1994), 137–61.
24 Zhang Daoyi, "Sheji, shengchan, xiaoshou—Tan sanzhe de guanxi," *Gongyi meishu tongxun*, no. 2 (1956): 6–9.
25 Deng Jie, "Jiaqiang dang dui gongyi meishu shiye de lingdao," *Gongyi meishu tongxun*, no. 2 (1956): 2–5.
26 Wang Fengyi, "Tigao riyong yongepin de meishu sheji he peiyang rencai," *Gongyi meishu tongxun*, no. 4 (1957): 35–7.
27 Tian Zibing, "Buyao hushi lilun gongzuo," *Gongyi meishu tongxun*, no. 1 (1956): 6–7.
28 Lu Shizhu, *Cong tu'an dao sheji: 20 shiji Zhongguo sheji yishu yanjiu* (Nanchang: Jiangxi Renmin Chubanshe, 2011).
29 The most popular design textbook in Republican-era China was Shinzō Komuro and Hisashi Matsuoka, *Ippan zuanho* (Tokyo: Maruzen, 1909), which the designer Chen Zhifo used as the basis for his *Tu'an gaishuo*.
30 Lei Guiyuan, *Xin tu'an de lilun he zuofa* (Shanghai: Wanye Shudian, 1950); Lei Guiyuan, *Xin tu'an xue*, Buding Daxue Yongshu (series) (Shanghai: Shangwu Yinshuguan, 1947). Many other similar *tu'an* compilations were also published at this time: a short list includes Shi Tao, *Tu'an xinbian* (Shanghai: Chunming Shudian, 1950); Tian Zibing, *Tu'an zi zuofa* (Shanghai: Wanye Shudian, 1951); Chen Zhifo, *Yingyong meishu tu'an bian* (Shanghai: Wanye Shudian, 1952); Chen Zhifo, *Zhongguo tu'an* (Shanghai: Wanye Shudian, 1952); and Wang Duan, *Zhongguo tu'an ji* (Shanghai: Beixin Shuju, 1953).
31 Henri Verne and René Chavance, *Pour comprendre l'art décoratif moderne en France* (Paris: Hachette, 1925); D. Duvillé, *Memento de la science ornementale dans laquelle sont présentés l'étude des lois de composition* (Paris: Roret, 1936); Leonhard Adam, *Primitive Art* (Harmondsworth, UK: Penguin, 1942).
32 Zeynep Çelik Alexander, *Kinaesthetic Knowing: Aesthetics, Epistemology, Modern Design* (Chicago: University of Chicago Press, 2017), 175–87.
33 Pang Xunqin, *Tu'an wenti de yanjiu* (Shanghai: Dadong Shuju, 1953), 1–4.
34 Li Youxing, "Sheji zhiye," *Gongyi*, no. 1 (1942): 2; Lei Guiyuan, "Gong zi yijie," *Gongyi*, no. 1 (1942): 3–5. See also the essays in Zhongguo Gongshangye Meishu Zuojia Xiehui, *Xiandai Zhongguo gongshangye meishu xuanji*.
35 Wu Lao, *Zenyang xie meishuzi* (Shijiazhuang: Chazhong Xinhua Shudian, 1947); Wu Lao, "Zhanlan gongzuo zhong de erge wenti" (1951), in Guo Qiuhui, *Wu Lao wenji*, Zhongguo xiandai yishu yu sheji xueshu sixiang congshu (Jinan: Shandong Meishu Chubanshe, 2011).
36 Most famously, Pang Xunqin seems to have visited some buildings associated with the Bauhaus when he was traveling in Germany in 1929. See Hang Jian and Jin Daiqiang, eds., *Zhongguo xiandai sheji yu Baohaosi* (Beijing: Renmin Meishu Chubanshe, 2014).
37 On a similar problem, see Laing, *Selling Happiness*, 223–34.
38 Pang, *Tu'an wenti de yanjiu*, 4–10, 18–21.
39 Pang, *Tu'an wenti de yanjiu*, 25.
40 Wang Xun, "Gongyi meishu de tigao he puji," *Renmin meishu*, no. 1 (1950): 69–70. Wang Xun writes of the design of everyday goods that "when peasants go to cities to

buy goods, they like red, green, and other happy colors; they like designs that represent a good life, because they have not enjoyed a good life for a long time and they desire things... As a result, conditions have arrived to expand the taste of the shallow, petty urbanites. Only when new objects produced from new methods appear will we return to the healthy flavor of worker's art."

41 Zhongyang Meishu Xueyuan Gongyi Meishu Yanjiushi, *Minjian diaosu gongyi* (Beijing: Chaohua Meishu Chubanshe, 1955); Zhongyang Meishu Xueyuan Gongyi Meishu Yanjiushi, *Minjian ranzhi cixiu gongyi* (Beijing: Chaohua Meishu Chubanshe, 1955).

42 Zhongyang Meishu Xueyuan Gongyi Meishu Yanjiushi, *Tu'an de zuzhi* [The organization of design] (Beijing: Chaohua Meishu Chubanshe, 1955).

43 *Tu'an xizuo xuanji* (Shengyang: Dongbei Meishu Zhuanke Xuexiao Gongyi Meishu Xi, 1956). Though difficult to give complete numbers, the print run of craft-related publications generally numbered around the low one thousands to around three thousand copies, in the case of *Folk Batik Floral Designs* (Beijing: Renmin Meishu Chubanshe, 1953), with an initial print run of 3,000; and *Suzhou Embroidery Designs* (Beijing: Chaohua Meishu Chubanshe, 1962), which had a run of 1,250. Fine-art-related publications (drawing, painting, sculpture, and so forth) usually were printed by the Beijing People's Art Publishing House in greater numbers, usually around 2,000–5,000 copies for art catalogs and around 20,000 copies for mass instructional manuals. As a guide to what was a relatively small field of professionals and students, *The Organization of Design* had a larger print run than the usual craft-related publication.

44 "Zhongyang Gongyi Meishu Xueyuan chengli Zhongyang Gongyi Meishu Kexue Yanjiusuo zai choubei zhong," *Gongyi meishu tongxun*, no. 1 (1956): 4–5.

45 Yuan Mai, *Baojialiya gongyi meishu pin xuanji* (Beijing: Renmin Meishu Chubanshe, 1958); *Luomaniya gongyi meishupin xuanji* (Beijing: Renmin Meishu Chubanshe, 1958).

46 Katherine Pence, "'A World in Miniature': The Leipzig Trade Fairs in the 1950s and East German Consumer Citizenship," in *Consuming Germany in the Cold War*, edited David F. Crew (Oxford: Berg, 2003), 21–50; Jennifer Altehenger, "Industrial and Chinese: Exhibiting Mao's China at the Leipzig Trade Fairs," *Journal of Contemporary History* 55, no. 4 (2020): 845–70.

47 Qinggongye Bu Gongyi Meishu Ju, *Gongyi meishu gongzuo jingyan jieshao* (Beijing: Qinggongye Chubanshe, 1958): 44–47.

48 Ge Kejian, "Queshi jiejue gongyi meishu shiye de lingdao wenti," *Gongyi meishu tongxun*, no. 4 (1957): 30–31; a response was published as Weng Yongnian, "Gongyi meishu yinggai mingque lingdao guanxi," *Gongyi meishu tongxun*, no. 6 (1957): 32–34.

49 "Guanyu gongyi meishu shiye de jidian juti jianyi," *Gongyi meishu tongxun*, no. 7 (1957): 1–4, signed by 36 figures, including Pang Xunqin.

50 Zhongyang Shougongye Guanliju, *Gongyi meishu de fangxiang wenti* (Beijing: Caizheng Jingji Chubanshe, 1958): 35–36.

51 Eyferth, *Eating Rice from Bamboo Roots*, 116–39.

52 Tao Tianli, "Sulian zhuangshi meishu jianjie," *Zhuangshi*, no. 1 (1958): 50; see also Susan E. Reid, "Destalinization and Taste, 1953–1963," *Journal of Design History* 10, no. 2 (1997): 177–201; and Tom Cubbins, "Dekorativnoe iskusstvo SSSR (1957–93)," in

Clive Edwards, ed., *The Bloomsbury Encyclopedia of Design*, vol. 1 (London: Bloomsbury Academic, 2016), 351.

53 Qiu Ling, "Huiyi wo yu *Zhuangshi* chuchuangshi de meibian gongzuo," *Zhuangshi*, no. 4 (1991): 48.

54 Genevieve Zubrzycki, *National Matters: Materiality, Culture, and Nationalism* (Stanford, CA: Stanford University Press, 2017), 5.

55 Chandra Mukerji, "Artisans and the Construction of the French State," in Zubrzycki, *National Matters*, 22.

56 Bianji Weiyuanhui, *Zhongguo gongyi meishu* (Beijing: Zhonghua Quanguo Shougongye Hezuo Zongshe, 1959).

4 DANCE PROPS AND THE RURAL IMAGINARY

EMILY WILCOX

IN 2009 I WAS INTERPRETING FOR AN INTERNATIONAL CHOREOGraphy research project at the Beijing Dance Academy, a top conservatory in China. On the first day of rehearsals, Shobana Jeyasingh, the guest British choreographer who would be creating a new piece for the academy's dancers, announced that before starting, she wanted to see how they moved in their own work. After the dancers had warmed up, she asked each of them to present a segment they had recently performed.

As nationally ranked professional soloists, these dancers all had repertoires at the ready and typically loved to perform and be watched. Thus, I was surprised when they appeared hesitant in response to Jeyasingh's request. They whispered to each other and looked anxiously around the room. "We aren't prepared," one dancer finally responded. Thinking she knew what was wrong, Jeyasingh reassured them that costumes and music were not necessary. "Just dance the choreography," she said. "I just want to see how you move." However, the dancers still insisted this was not possible. To perform, they explained, they needed their props.

It was a classic case of competing cultural definitions. In both European contemporary dance and south Indian classical dance, the major forms in which Jeyasingh worked, dance is understood as an art form performed by the human body alone. With the exception perhaps of the latter's ankle bells, both regard the material trappings of performance, such as costumes and stage sets, as essentially external to the dance itself. Even special footwear is not required for these dances, which are both typically performed barefoot.

By contrast, Chinese dance, the style in which this group specialized, often employs props (*daoju*)—objects manipulated by the dancers as part of their performance. Rather than seeing these as external elements added for the stage, dancers regard these props as integral to Chinese choreography. Thus, the work is conceived of as a composition performed not by the human body alone but by a cyborgian assemblage (in Donna Haraway's sense) of human and prop together.[1] Huang Dongmei, one of the academy's dancers Jeyasingh worked with, is known for her award-winning solo *Red Apricot*, in which she moves with a large red silk fan.[2] Wang Lei, another dancer in the group, performs his iconic solo *Calligraphic Rhythms* with an oversized writing brush.[3] Like other props, the silk fan and the writing brush each have distinct material characteristics that shape the meaning and composition of the dances. These include signifying features, such as references to particular places, times, ritual events, artistic works, kinds of labor, and social roles and relationships. They also include kinesthetic and tactile features, such as weight, balance, drag, texture, and malleability. This combination of the signifying and the kinesthetic or tactile makes the props an essential component of the work's form. The props impact both how the dancer moves and how these movements are perceived by audiences. Just as the ballet *Swan Lake* would be incomplete without pointe shoes, and a tango would be lacking if performed by one person, so too would these Chinese choreographies not be whole if missing their props.

The history of dance props in contemporary China dates to the early years of the Mao era—particularly the 1950s—when dance was institutionalized as an important component of China's emerging socialist culture.[4] One reason props played such a large role in early Maoist dance is that they served as "object mediators," material objects that allowed dancers to embody socialist ideals by learning about the world around them. When creating new choreography for the stage in China during the 1950s and early 1960s, professional dancers were often called upon to perform rural styles and characters, even though they themselves often came from urban backgrounds. Dance props provided a physical medium through which urban and rural performers interacted with one another and urban dancers learned to portray rural characters on stage. This created a way for choreographers to situate dancing bodies within specific social contexts in their artistic works. The use of props, together with costumes and movements, helped ensure that dancing bodies were understood in a Marxist sense as subjects with particular class, gender, and geographic identities, not as universal humans who exist outside material relations. Props helped situate dancers in the material and social environment as conceptualized by a socialist worldview.

The majority of props employed in early Mao-era choreography were borrowed from existing performance forms practiced in rural and folk contexts. Writings of the period emphasize the experience of learning to grasp and manipulate props as a crucial element of the field research through which urban dancers developed the corporeal and affective repertoires needed to perform a variety of unfamiliar roles, such as tea pickers, milkmaids, farmers, and itinerant village performers. Learning to dance with props often required engaging with rural communities by "going down to rural areas" (*xia xiang*) and collaborating with "folk artists" (*minjian yiren*). At times, rural performers also traveled to urban areas to participate in "trial performances" (*guanmo huiyan*), events designed to expose urban audiences to the wide variety of rural performance styles. In these varied interactions, props came to symbolize the practice of "learning from the folk" (*xiang minjian xuexi*), an important tenet of socialist cultural production since the Yan'an years that had deep artistic as well as political and ideological significance. Thus, beyond being a visual marker of rural communities, props served as mediating objects that by way of their distinct material characteristics allowed urban dancers to explore physical sensations linked to rural life. Dancers further sought to infuse these sensations into their own bodily feelings and choreographic movements. This use of props created flows of artists traveling between city and country. It also helped maintain the rural aesthetic orientation of Chinese socialist culture after the central government moved out of wartime rural base areas and back into cities. In this historical context, dance props worked to bridge the rural and urban, making rural life graspable for urban performers. It also created opportunities for rural artists to visit urban areas and participate in national conversations about dance creation.

The research for this essay stems from bodily experiences of studying Chinese dance, not only watching others use props but also doing so myself. Through the embodied regimen of dance training, I learned to perform with silk water sleeves, metal swords, silk and bamboo fans, chopsticks, and handkerchiefs, among other objects. This physical practice helped me gain a kinesthetic appreciation and understanding of the complex embodied knowledge required to perform with props. Although Chinese dance has changed since the 1950s, the basic approaches to incorporating props into Chinese choreography have remained largely consistent. Thus, object-based "practice-as-research" methodology is one lens through which to read the material culture of dance props in the Mao era,[5] and bodily knowledge of performing prop-based Chinese dance is an analytical tool for the examination of early Mao-era documents, including dance films and manuals, photographs, and essays. In this way, material objects serve as both the focus of inquiry and a medium of knowledge production.

DANCING WITH PROPS IN MAO'S CHINA

Like many other aspects of contemporary Chinese dance, its extensive use of props is a product of the Mao era. It was during this period, particularly prior to the start of the Cultural Revolution in 1966, that professional dancers and choreographers, with support and direction from the Maoist state, created the modern concert dance genre known today as Chinese dance.[6] The introduction of props as a core feature of this genre in the early Mao era was not a historical accident or an inevitable outcome driven by global dance developments. Rather, it was a calculated choice that emerged out of conceptions of what constitutes good dance in a socialist society and how best to go about learning, creating, teaching, and promoting such work.

Dancing with props in the Mao era was a performed manifestation of Chinese socialist approaches to choreography as both an artistic and social practice. It included ideas about the material and signifying parameters of dancers' bodies and notions about who or what the core agents and sources of Chinese socialist culture are. As dancers in Mao's China created and popularized new movement styles, these styles brought with them a new field of material culture. This field included the dance props, the human bodies that performed with them, and the practices of social interaction, circulation, and embodiment that went into the creation of prop-based choreographies.

A look at representations of dance in China's popular media during the early Mao years offers a sense of the pervasiveness and variety of dances with props during this period. Visual documentation of this phenomenon can be found in photographs published in *China Pictorial* (Renmin huabao), an important magazine, founded in 1950, that served as a consistent source of dance news in the Mao era.[7] These photographs show a wide range of dances involving props—in which dancers either grasp objects while dancing or wear items that extend or transform their bodily shape and create trajectories through space as they move.

In "silk dance" (*chou wu*), the performers hold long streamers of silk fabric in their hands and use them to draw patterns in the air around their bodies while they are dancing.[8] In "peacock dance" (*kongque wu*) and "lion dance" (*shizi wu*), performers dress as animals, wearing either a false peacock tail and wings or baggy lion suits with oversized eyes, large moving jaws, and shaggy hair and manes.[9] In "tea-picking lantern" (*caicha deng*) and "picking tea and catching butterflies" (*caicha pudie*), dancers carry baskets and twirl small, painted folding fans in their hands while they imitate the motions of tea-picking and chase paper butterflies mounted on long, thin rods.[10] In "fan dance" (*shan wu*), dancers hold arm-length semicircular folding fans that they expand, contract, and arc through the air.[11] Numerous varieties of "drum dance" (*gu wu*) incorporate drums of all shapes and sizes, from the large "hourglass drum" (*changgu*) worn slung over the shoulder, to the small "waist drum" (*yaogu*) fastened on the hip, to the hand-held "Taiping drum" (*taiping gu*), which resembles an enlarged ping-pong paddle.[12] "Sword dance" (*jian wu*) is another common sight. Typically, it uses narrow metal swords about four feet in length, with a knotted red tassel (*suizi*) that dangles from the handle and spins as the dancer moves.[13] Dances that employ parasols (*san*), often painted with flowers or other colorful patterns, are also common.[14] There are also a number of "flower lamp dances" (*huadeng wu*), in which orb-like lanterns designed to resemble flowers are either held in one's hand or attached to the dancer's costume.[15]

Another common type of choreography features dancers interacting with animals depicted using props, such as in "dragon dance" (*long wu*), in which a line of dancers carries a long snaking dragon above their heads attached to poles, or "running donkey" (*pao lü*), in which a hobby horse is suspended around the dancer's waist so that she appears to be riding a donkey (there is also a similar variation involving a fish).[16] Other dances incorporate objects from everyday life as props, such as milk pails, cups and bowls, clothing and hair extensions, vehicles such as carts and boats, plates of food or bouquets of flowers, wedding paraphernalia, embroidery, water-carrying vessels, hats, etc.[17] Throughout the 1950s and the early 1960s, the high point of Chinese dance in the Mao era, it was more common to see dancers performing with props than without them.[18]

Dance manuals published during the 1950s offer further insight into how the material culture of props was disseminated during the Mao era. Since manuals were typically published when more people wanted to learn a dance than there were teachers available, they offer a record of dances that achieved especially widespread duplication, with many bodies learning to perform them simultaneously across the country and even internationally.[19] Attention to props was a major focus in these manuals. *Red Silk Dance* (Hongchou wu), for example, published in 1953, contains a musical score, stage plots, and step-by-step instructions on how to perform the dance, with the majority of its fifty pages dedicated to explaining how to maneuver the long silk streamers. Illustrations accompanied by text also explain how to construct the streamer props, by first fastening the long pieces of silk fabric to sticklike handles, then bundling and securing the fabric together for the first part of the dance, when they resemble torches, before the silks are released to flow

FIGURE 4.1. Dancers performing a tea-picking dance using fans and baskets as props. *China Pictorial* (Renmin huabao), no. 4 (1954). Used with permission from China Foto Bank.

fully into the air. The instructions show would-be performers precisely how to handle the props, detailing specific hand grips and other movement techniques that allow the dancers to execute the airborne circles, spirals, figure eights, and zigzagging lines necessary to complete the choreography.[20]

Recognizing that props are material objects with limited life spans and their own interactions with the physical environment, dance manuals also instructed readers on how to properly care for the props to maintain their maximum effectiveness. In a special section titled "How to Use and Take Care of the Props," the authors of the *Red Silk Dance* manual reminded readers that during the beginning stages of learning the dance, it is best to practice with old silk. "This is because if one uses new silk during the practice period, by the time of the performance, the silk color will already be faded, and the new silk will have turned into old silk. This will negatively impact the effect of the performance," they explained.[21] When selecting old silk for practicing, the authors continued, it is essential not to use any that contains a seam in the middle, since this will make it difficult to distribute force equally through the fabric and thus aggravate learning. When preparing for a performance, it is also important not to bundle the "torches" too early, since this will cause the silk to become wrinkled. After the show, one should also

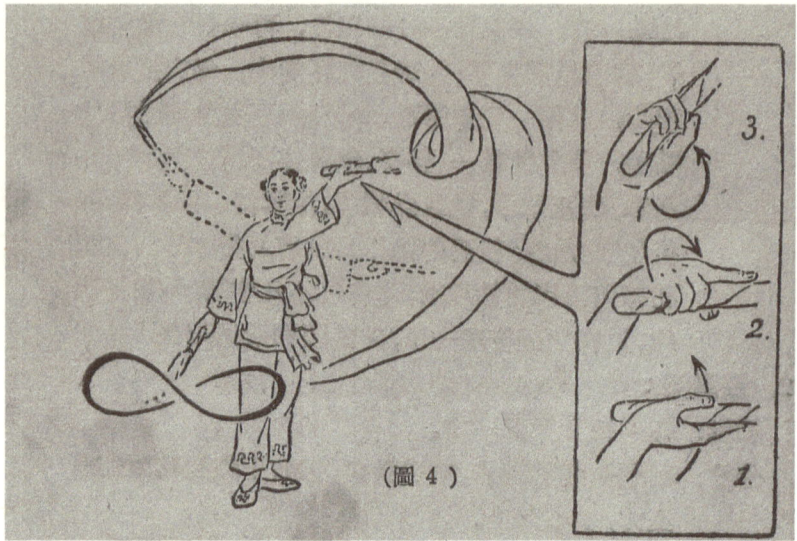

FIGURE 4.2. Detail from the dance manual *Red Silk Dance*. Wang Kewei, *Hongchou wu* (Shanghai: Shanghai Lukaiji Bookstore, 1953), 10. Courtesy of the University of Michigan Asia Library Chinese Dance Collection.

not toss the silks together but instead roll them up one by one and place them into a clean fabric bag for storage. In terms of appropriate spaces for rehearsal, the authors implored readers never to practice on concrete, since this will quickly damage the silk. They also reminded readers not to perform this piece outdoors, since "even the slightest bit of wind will easily cause the silks to be swept together, making them very difficult to control."[22] Finally, one should always rehearse on a well-swept floor to avoid having the silks whip up clouds of dust in the practice room.

Other instructional books from the period offer similarly detailed instructions on how to dance with props. One example is the 1954 manual *Selected Chinese Folk Dances*, which teaches dancers how to perform with silk fabric, lotus lamps, fans and handkerchiefs, butterfly wands, a donkey-shaped hobby horse, a whip, and a doll.[23] *Fan Dance*, published in 1958, instructs readers on how to manipulate large folding fans, as well as the hem of one's skirt, to perform this Korean-style folk dance.[24] The 1959 handbook *Sword Dance* similarly guides readers step-by-step through about forty different sword movement variations used in this dance.[25]

Dance films offer even further insight into how props were incorporated into choreography. There are at least nine such extant films produced in the PRC between 1950 and 1965, some of which are full-length narrative dramas and others are compilations of shorter works. Each of these films depicts extensive use of dance props.[26] Some uses are merely cosmetic, meaning that the props are not integrated into the movement and thus do not require special techniques to maneuver. The majority, however, are integrated and require the dancer to rehearse extensively to master the prop movement. In 1959's *Magic Lotus Lantern* (Bao liandeng), dancers perform with long silk streamers and swords, showing a high degree of body-object coordination that centers the movement of the prop as a focal point of the choreographic action. In these films, the props' material characteristics are clearly reflected in the dance forms. Scenes involving the silk streamers, for example, maximize the fabric's lightness and fluidity. The dancer casts them out in long, voluptuous lines that hang, float, and cascade through the air, surrounding her body in an ethereal nest of pastel swirls that evoke clouds, in this case fitting the character's role as a heavenly immortal. Scenes involving swords, by contrast, highlight the metal object's weight and ability to cut through the air without drag. Dancers spear the air in clean, crisp strokes and then allow the sword to wheel around on arcs and axes, creating momentum and speed that in turn amplifies the movements of the human operator.[27] This integrated use of props shows how physical features of the objects shape movement choices, producing contrasting choreographies that require the human body to move in different ways.

The 1960 film *Red Flowers Blossoming Everywhere* (Hong hua biandi kai), which features highlights from a workers' arts festival, shows how integrated prop–based choreography permeated beyond professionals to reach amateurs as well. One dance in the film, by a team from Anhui, stars a female lead deftly wielding a small silk folding fan and handkerchief, a pair of props commonly used in Han folk dances. Pulling and tossing them through the air with nimble arm swings and small wrist loops, she coordinates her own movements with those of a male partner, almost as if she is the conductor and he the orchestra. This creates the effect that each of his full-body actions amplifies the more delicate movements of her fan and handkerchief. Within her own movement, there is also a rhythmic contrast between the incessant drive of her bouncing footwork with the airy swooshes and flutters of the props. In contrast to the silk water sleeve and sword dances, which have a more serious tone, this dance is humorous and lively.

The thunderous finale of this film offers another example of integrated prop–based dancing and skillful coordination between groups of performers, here through the combination of dance and percussion. The scene is composed of horizontal lines of dancers brandishing differently shaped drums. Each line moves forward in success waves, each offering a fresh movement technique

FIGURE 4.3. Sword dance scene in *Magic Lotus Lantern* (Bao liandeng). Reproduced with permission from the private collection of Fang Bonian and the Pioneers of Chinese Dance digital archive.

combined with fast-paced drumming. Some dancers spin drums on straps around their necks and beat them mid-orbit. Others twirl their drumsticks in the air so quickly between beats that the sticks become invisible. Still others skillfully weave real-time rhythms produced by striking drums strapped to their necks or waists while they execute complicated choreography involving spins, steps, hip swivels, and jumps.[28] Here, like in many of the dance scenes found in Mao-era films, the movement of the props becomes as much of a focal point and object of appreciation as the movement of the dancers.

From an international perspective, the widespread and integrated use of props in Chinese choreography set the repertoires of Mao's China apart from trends in many other countries at the time. Documentation of competitions held at the World Festivals of Youth and Students (WFYS), the main international venue where China's dancers performed their work abroad during the early Mao era, suggests that props were very common in the works China sent to the festivals but were much less so among delegations from other participating countries.[29] The only other WFYS dance delegation that regularly performed with props was the North Korean one, and these two countries had a history of close interaction in the dance field.[30] In China's WFYS works, judging by those that won awards, props were nearly ubiquitous. Out of the total forty-one choreographies for which China won awards at WFYS

FIGURE 4.4. USSR National Folk Dance Ensemble performing the Chinese folk dance "red silk dance" in China in 1954. *China Pictorial* (Renmin huabao), no. 11 (1954). Used with permission from China Foto Bank.

festivals between 1949 and 1962, at least thirty-two employed props.[31] Several of these dances are recorded in the Mao-era dance films *Hundred Phoenixes Face the Sun* (Bai feng chao yang, 1959) and *Colored Butterflies Flutter About* (Caidie fenfei, 1963), and the integrated role of the props in the movement technique and choreography is quite evident in these recordings.[32] This association between props and the dancing of Maoist China is further expressed graphically in a poster printed for the cultural forum at the 1957 WFYS festival in Moscow. Of the five dancers of different national backgrounds depicted in the poster, only the Chinese dancer is using a prop, in this case a long, red streamer.[33] Another indication of this association is that when the Soviet State Folk Dance Ensemble visited China in 1954 and performed two Chinese pieces as part of its show, both used props.[34]

DANCE PROPS AND CHINA'S SOCIALIST CULTURE

What prompted this extensive use of props, and why did it become such an iconic element of dance performance in Mao-era China? Reading China's publications from the time provides insight into how these dances were created and the cultural imaginaries they were meant to provoke and exhibit. One source of such accounts is *Dance News* (Wudao tongxun), a professional bulletin published from 1951 to 1957 that served as China's first national news source dedicated to dance. In its articles, dancers often wrote about their motivations for creating performances that involved props and the methods they used to develop these works. Educators also discussed what they regarded as the pedagogical value of such choreography, while researchers explored the dances' historical and cultural backgrounds, and critics offered assessments based on aesthetic, ideological, and cultural values of the day.

A predominant theme in these writings is the role props played in mediating between social worlds. Specifically, props helped dancers cross the divide between urban and rural China, by bringing rural characters, rhythms, and images onto urban stages, albeit in revised forms designed for urban viewers. This effort to link urban and rural society and to make rural people and their expressions central to the culture of modern China was a long-standing commitment of Maoist thought and practice.[35] As studies of the CCP's turn to rural folk culture under Mao's leadership in late 1930s and early 1940s Yan'an show, this development was connected to the rising nationalism of the Second Sino-Japanese War, the nationwide debates over "national forms" (*minzu xingshi*) in the arts and literature, the rectification of artists and intellectuals, and the Yan'an *yangge* movement that transformed farmers' harvest celebrations and New Year's parades into political theater. All of these activities produced new expressive forms inspired by regional folk culture.

Recent studies of urban *yangge* in the early 1950s have shown that after the CCP moved its operations from its rural base areas back to the cities in 1949, it faced problems when simplified versions of folk culture, exemplified by *yangge* dance, failed to maintain the interest of urban residents.[36] During the land reform movement and early PRC, the CCP continued to view folk artists as important collaborators in its efforts to use the performing arts, such as revolutionary drama troupes, in rural China as a medium for promoting its political ideas and campaigns through the mid-1950s. However, bridging the gap between urban and rural culture remained an important challenge for the artists as well as audiences involved in these efforts. China's urban dramatists in the late 1940s and early 1950s spent a great deal of their time addressing the problem of how to understand, communicate with, and emotionally move rural audiences. At the same time, folk artists from rural areas often joined up with revolutionary drama troupes to provide expertise and technical knowledge, although the collaborations fostered between them and urban groups were typically fraught.[37] Given this historical background, it is not surprising that the divide between urban and rural culture was also a major point of concern for dancers. Props became one medium for addressing this perpetual dilemma.

By looking at the creative developments in dance, it is clear that rural culture continued to play an important role on urban stages in Maoist China through the 1950s and early 1960s. Rather than dying out shortly after the establishment of the PRC, as some scholars have speculated, historical sources show that dances derived from folk performance in the manner of the *yangge* movement continued to fill China's stages until the start of the Cultural Revolution in the mid-1960s.[38] Rather than abandoning folk dances, Mao-era dancers instead doubled down on their commitment to folk forms, which often involved props. The proliferation of props in the new choreographies of the early PRC period demonstrates urban dancers' ongoing engagement with rural forms, as well as their commitment to collaborating with folk artists and "learning from the folk," to cite one of the most common phrases in dance writings of the period. The extensive use of props in Chinese works of the 1950s and early 1960s shows urban dancers' continued interest in folk performance as a source of innovation in Chinese socialist cultural production. It also shows their ongoing efforts to perform rural identities by cultivating embodied investments in dance props as material vehicles of rural culture.

A typical account of how this process worked from the perspective of urban dancers in the early PRC can be found in an essay titled "How We Adapted and Rehearsed *Fan Dance*," one of a series of articles published in the inaugural July 1951 issue of *Dance News*.[39] Like most of the other articles in this issue, the essay explained the provenance of a dance that had received acclaim at the national folk dance "trial performance" held in Beijing a few months earlier, which lasted three days and featured ensembles from multiple regions across China. Many of its most successful pieces had been inspired by folk forms that used props. Apart from *Fan Dance*, for example, there had also been the premiere of *Red Silk Dance* discussed above, as well as those involving carts and boats and several different forms of drum dances.[40] As a writer for the state newspaper *Guangming Daily* attested, it had been a turning point in attitudes toward the study of local and folk dance, showing that "it really is as Chairman Mao said: studying the rich content of people's lives and critically learning from national art heritage, especially of the local and the folk, is the right direction."[41]

The trial performance was considered so important that the entire issue of *Dance News* was dedicated to it. The articles it contained operated as pedagogical tools for other dancers, providing models for correct choreographic practices that might offer inspiration for new works. "Learning from the folk" was a common theme in almost every article in the special issue, including "How We Adapted and Rehearsed *Fan Dance*." In such discussions, choreographers typically recounted how their ensemble members had traveled to the countryside and, often through experiences with props, gained a closer connection to rural life. In this process, the dancers also typically spent time learning from folk artists. As recounted in this article, the group came across their idea for *Fan Dance* while they were studying in China's northeast. Working with folk artists, the author reported, they had studied a particularly rich and complex local style of *yangge* dance, which was part of a comic folk theater genre called *bengbengxi* (also known as *erren zhuan*). In this process, they had come across an interesting popular northeastern folk dance called "catching butterflies" (*bu hudie*), also called "fan dance." The group first studied this dance and then worked together with a folk artist to adapt it for the concert stage.

According to the article, the part of their creative process that had been most transformative for the dancers was when they mastered fan movement. Initially, the author writes, the dancers had trouble inhabiting the roles of peasants, who were supposed to be the subjects of the dance, because the dancers themselves did not come from peasant backgrounds. The author wrote, "The performers knew intellectually that they were supposed to perform the new, joyful mood of today's peasants, but when they performed, they still more or less expressed their own thoughts and feelings (the thoughts and feelings of intellectuals)."[42] To resolve this problem, the group used visualization to establish a concrete setting for the dance in their minds: "We decided the time would be one midday around the Dragon Boat Festival and the place would be a hillside, in a path of wildflowers and grass next to a crop field. The story we would perform would be a group of healthy, humble, and lively village girls who sing and play in the untilled land. Birds would sing loudly, and beautiful butterflies would fly freely about. The girls would look for their favorite wildflowers and then use fans to chase and catch their even more beloved butterflies. After a few rounds of chasing, they would finally catch one."[43]

By way of this exercise, the author explained, the dancers eventually expressed a bit of the rural feeling the dance was aiming for. They reportedly used this story to discuss and determine the details of the entire fan dance choreography, including each section's emotional expressions, speed, steps, formations, and entire organization. Within this process, the fan had served as the medium that allowed them to gain a feeling for and embody the rural culture they were aiming to perform. The prop thus played a critical role as an object mediator when the dancers attempted to put themselves into the roles of rural subjects. Through the kinesthetic experience of manipulating this object—flapping and fluttering the fan in their hands while chasing the imaginary butterflies—the urban dancers gained a feeling of rural place and identity, which they used as a source of inspiration for their performance. For the dancers, grasping the props and learning to twirl and toss them in just the right way helped them to shed their bodily habits of urban intellectuals and cross into a mode of embodiment that was, at least in their idealized version of it, more consistent with rural life.

Judging from articles published in *Dance News* during the 1950s, the props that were most frequently adopted in Mao-era Chinese choreographies during this period came primarily from two sources: field surveys of rural folk performances and crossover techniques borrowed from Chinese opera. In both cases, learning to manipulate props was considered essential for dancers to embody characters and comportments appropriate to socialist performance. In one essay, for example, a choreographer from the South-Central Cultural Work Troupe explained how learning to perform the "walking lotus boat" (*zou lian chuan*) technique from folk performers and dancers training in Chinese opera helped company members portray the lives of fishers in New China.[44] Other choreographers reportedly drew inspiration from the deep reservoirs of rural culture that could be learned from studying and performing dragon and lion dances.[45] Still others, focused on the silk sleeves and combat weapons used by actors in Chinese opera, argued that physically mastering the techniques to wield these materials was necessary for dancers who intended to play characters in many new dramas, whether featuring classical or folk themes.[46] Meanwhile, field reports on folk dance forms practiced in various regions of the country contained long lists of object-centered genres, such as lantern, drum, fan, and parasol dances, and the like.[47] To perform rural dances, and by extension rural identities, meant dancing with props.

RURAL PROPS ON URBAN STAGES

Previous studies of folk aesthetics in the socialist culture of Mao's China have often emphasized substitutions, by which new objects and imagery associated with the iconography of socialism were inserted into and thus ended up becoming an integral part of rural folk forms. In the Yan'an *yangge* movement, for example, the *santou*, a dancer dressed in a special costume and carrying some type of open umbrella, who would traditionally lead a rural *yangge* procession, was replaced in the new CCP-sponsored version by two dancers dressed instead as workers and peasants and carrying a hammer and a sickle.[48] Similarly, in a new form of *nianhua*, or New Year's prints, introduced in the early years of the PRC, traditional symbols such as door gods were replaced by new socialist symbols such as PLA soldiers.[49] The prop-filled choreographies of the early Mao-era dance stage present a different direction of substitution from these earlier accounts. That is, they offer examples of how objects from rural folk culture were inserted into and ended up becoming an integral part of China's socialist culture. Although often embodied by dancers who came from urban backgrounds, the prop-based dances and their attendant techniques—whether mastered through direct field research and study with folk artists or secondhand from films or popular manuals—allowed these urban performers to bring elements of rural culture to life on urban stages domestically and internationally.

The introduction of props into Mao-era Chinese choreography came about as part of a larger mission espoused by early PRC choreographers to "inherit and develop" (*jicheng yu fazhan*) China's new national dance culture by building creatively on local performance practices from all over the country.[50] Because of this mission, dancers in Mao's China were expected to spend a great deal of their time and energy conducting field research, studying with folk performers, and publishing scholarly accounts that confirmed the links between their choreographic creations and existing practices, whether from rural village life, historical accounts, or the opera stage.[51]

Beyond the Maoist concern with folk culture, however, these dances with props also served another ideological function. That is, they ensured that dancers appearing on stage could never be viewed simply as "bodies," in the sense of a self-determined, universal, abstract human individual that could be theoretically divorced from a specific social context.[52] A foundational premise of Marxist views on human life, which Maoist thought also adopted, was the idea that all humans are situated in specific social, cultural, political, and economic circumstances and that all people are thus fundamentally shaped by their social and physical environments. Dancing with props is a way of manifesting this idea in an aesthetic and bodily sense. When the dancer moves with the prop in an integrated technique, the relationship between them is one of mutual entanglement. That is, the materiality and movement of one is mutually implicated in that of the other. From this perspective, the assemblage of the dancer and the prop in Chinese choreography of Mao's China actualizes in performance the concept of the socially situated and environmentally entangled human being that is at the core of a socialist worldview. In other words, dancing with objects not only allowed dancers to better understand and perform rural lives and experiences, it also placed them metaphorically into a social context, reinforcing the broader Maoist conviction that no human life can be understood detached from its concrete social reality.

NOTES

1. Donna Jeanne Haraway, *Simians, Cyborgs, and Women: The Reinvention of Nature* (New York: Routledge, 1991).
2. Video, www.youtube.com/watch?v=fgKBmiyqcJg.
3. Video, www.bilibili.com/video/av11512109.
4. In this chapter, I use the term "socialist" to describe a cultural phenomenon that began during the 1920s, enjoyed widespread influence from the late 1940s through the end of the 1970s, and continues to be part of the cultural landscape, albeit in varied and constantly changing forms, in China today.
5. "Practice as research" is a concept used in dance and performance studies. It refers to the idea that artistic activities, such as performance, can constitute a form of academic research.
6. Wilcox, *Revolutionary Bodies*.
7. Won Ho Chang, *Mass Media in China: The History and the Future* (Ames: Iowa State University Press, 1989), 33. *Renmin huabao* (henceforth *RMHB*) was one of the seven highest-circulation magazines in China in 1955. During the Maoist period, this periodical included reporting on both domestic dance creation and international dance groups that toured in China. See Emily Wilcox, "The Postcolonial Blind Spot: Chinese Dance in the Era of Third World-ism, 1949–1965," *positions: asia critique* 26, no. 4 (2018): 781–815; and Wilcox, *Revolutionary Bodies*. Here, I am only focusing on photographs of domestically produced Chinese choreography.
8. *RMHB* 1, no. 1 (July 1950); *RMHB* 3, no. 1 (January 1952); *RMHB* 5, no. 9 (September 1954); *RMHB* 8, no. 6 (June 1957); *RMHB* 12, no. 1 (1961); *RMHB* 13, no. 5 (1962); *RMHB* 14, no. 5 (1963).
9. *RMHB* 4, no. 6 (June 1953); *RMHB* 5, no. 3 (March 1954); *RMHB* 6, no. 7 (July 1955); *RMHB* 8, no. 6 (June 1957); *RMHB* 11, no. 18 (October 1960).
10. *RMHB* 4, no. 6 (June 1953); *RMHB* 5, no. 4 (April 1954); *RMHB* 10, no. 10a (October 1959).
11. *RMHB* 6, no. 10 (October 1955); *RMHB* 11, no. 4b (April 1960); *RMHB* 11, no. 6b (June 1960); *RMHB* 12, no. 9 (1961); *RMHB* 15, no. 11 (1964).
12. *RMHB* 3, no. 7 (July 1952); *RMHB* 5, no. 1 (January 1954); *RMHB* 6, no. 4 (April 1955); *RMHB* 7, no. 1 (January 1956); *RMHB* 8, no. 4 (April 1957); *RMHB* 10, no. 7a (July 1959); *RMHB* 10, no. 8b (August 1959).
13. *RMHB* 3, no. 7 (July 1952); *RMHB* 5, no. 1 (January 1954); *RMHB* 6, no. 4 (April 1955); *RMHB* 7, no. 1 (January 1956); *RMHB* 8, no. 4 (April 1957); *RMHB* 10, no. 7a (July 1959); *RMHB* 10, no. 8b (August 1959).

14 *RMHB* 6, no. 4 (April 1955); *RMHB* 10, no. 10a (October 1959); *RMHB* 11, no. 2b (February 1960); *RMHB* 11, no. 6b (June 1960).
15 *RMHB* 6, no. 4 (April 1955); *RMHB* 10, no. 10a (October 1959); *RMHB* 11, no. 2b (February 1960); *RMHB* 11, no. 6b (June 1960).
16 *RMHB* 4, no. 6 (June 1953); *RMHB* 6, no. 5 (May 1955); *RMHB* 8, no. 2 (February 1957); *RMHB* 11, no. 4b (April 1960).
17 *RMHB* 5, no. 7 (July 1954); *RMHB* 6, no. 5 (May 1955); *RMHB* 6, no. 11 (November 1955); *RMHB* 7, no. 12 (December 1956); *RMHB* 8, no. 6 (June 1957); *RMHB* 11, no. 6b (June 1960); *RMHB* 11, no. 16 (1960); *RMHB* 12, no. 7 (1961); *RMHB* 13, no. 1 (1962); *RMHB* 13, no. 10 (1962); *RMHB* 15, no. 4 (1964); *RMHB* 15, no. 8 (1964); *RMHB* 16,no. 2 (1965).
18 This description is based on a review of all photographs of dance published in *RMHB* from 1950 to 1965.
19 On the international circulation of these choreographies, see Wilcox, "When Folk Dance Was Radical."
20 Wang Kewei, *Hongchou wu* (Shanghai: Shanghai Lukaiji Bookstore, 1953), University of Michigan Chinese Dance Collection. For more on this dance, including a 1963 recording, see Wilcox, *Revolutionary Bodies*, 72–73, 85–86.
21 Wang, *Hongchou wu*, 49.
22 Wang, *Hongchou wu*, 50.
23 Chinese Dance Art Research Association, ed., *Zhongguo minjian wudao xuanji* (Beijing: Yishu Chubanshe, 1954), University of Michigan Chinese Dance Collection.
24 Chinese Dance Art Research Association, ed. *Shan wu* (Shanghai: Shanghai Wenyi Chubanshe, 1958), University of Michigan Chinese Dance Collection. During the Mao era, as today, Chinese dance includes both Han and ethnic minority dance. For more on this, see Wilcox, "Beyond Internal Orientalism; and Wilcox, *Revolutionary Bodies*.
25 Shanghai Experimental Opera Theater, ed., *Jian wu* (Shanghai: Shanghai Wenyi Chubanshe, 1959), University of Michigan Chinese Dance Collection.
26 *Bao liandeng* (Shanghai Tianma Film Studio, 1959); *Bai feng chao yang* (Beijing Film Studio, 1959); *Honghua biandi kai* (Beijing Film Studio, 1960); *Wu duo hongyun* (PLA August First Film Studio, 1960); *Xiao dao hui* (Shanghai: Shanghai Tianma Film Studio, 1961); *Caidie fenfei* (Beijing Film Studio, 1963); *Xuri dongsheng* (August First Film Studio, 1964); *Dongfeng wanli* (August First Film Studio, 1964); *Dongfang hong* (Beijing Film Studio et al., 1965).
27 Video, http://v.chinadance.cn/video/56747.html. Scenes begin at 36:35 and 53:40.
28 Video, www.bilibili.com/video/av10713997. Scenes begin at 36:44 and 72:00.
29 *Festival* newsletters from the 1951, 1953, 1955, 1957, 1959, and 1962 WFYS, stored in the World Festival of Youth and Students Collection, ARCH01667, International Institute of Social History, Amsterdam.
30 Emily Wilcox, "Crossing Over: Choe Seung-hui's Pan-Asianism in Revolutionary Time," *Journal of Society for Dance Documentation and History* 51 (December 2018): 65–97.
31 Song Tianyi, *Zhongwai biaoyan yishu jiaoliu shilüe, 1949–1992* (Beijing: Wenhua Yishu Chubanshe, 1994), 290–92.
32 Videos, www.youtube.com/watch?v=g19Jzcj_cPo and www.youtube.com/watch?v=rXQJ3ylq_9M.

33 A figure who appears to represent Latin America holds a tambourine, but he seems to be a musician, not a dancer. Poster, World Festival of Youth and Students Collection, ARCH01667, binder 9 (1957 Moscow), folder 1.
34 "Youmei de Sulian minjian wudao," *RMHB* 5, no. 11 (September 1954): 32–33.
35 Holm, "Folk Art as Propaganda"; Holm, *Art and Ideology*. See also Judd, "Prelude to the 'Yan'an Talks'"; Chang-tai Hung, *War and Popular Culture: Resistance in Modern China, 1937–1945* (Berkeley: University of California Press, 1994); and Wang, "Local Forms, Vernacular Dialects."
36 Hung, "The Dance of Revolution"; Hung, *Mao's New World*.
37 DeMare, *Mao's Cultural Army*.
38 Wilcox, "When Folk Dance Was Radical"; Wilcox, *Revolutionary Bodies*.
39 Yang Mingquan, "Women zenyang gaibian ji paiyan 'Shanzi wu,'" *Wudao tongxun*, July 7, 1951, 11–12. The *Fan Dance* discussed in this essay is different from the Korean-style version discussed in the handbook cited above.
40 Hu Sha, "Lun xiang minzu chuantong wudao yishu xuexi," *Wudao tongxun*, July 7, 1951, 5–7.
41 Fan Ming, "Kan wudao guanmo huiyan de jidian ganxiang," *Guangming ribao*, May 24, 1951. This article links such approaches to the goal of "realist art," although the term "socialist realism" is rarely used in these essays.
42 Yang, "Women zenyang gaibian," 11.
43 Yang, "Women zenyang gaibian," 11.
44 Wang Xi, "'Dayu chuan' pailian jingguo ji jingyan," *Wudao tongxun*, July 7, 1951, 27–29.
45 Tong Feng, "Cong yige you xingge de 'Long wu' tan qi," *Wudao tongxun* 6 (1956): 21–22; Wu Xiongyun, "Guanyu shizi wu," *Wudao tongxun* 11 (1956): 15–17.
46 Wang Ping, "Tan xiuwu de xunlian he qita," *Wudao tongxun* 6 (1956): 14–16; Wang Ping, "Dui wudao yanyuan xuexi gudian xiju wu zhong 'zhanqi wu' de wo jian," *Wudao tongxun* 10 (1956): 36–37.
47 "Quanguo minjian wudao buchong diaocha biao," *Wudao tongxun* (June 1955): 15; Liu Zhijun, "Shandong sheng minjian wudao fenbu qingkuang," *Wudao tongxun* 8–9 (1956): 32–33.
48 Holm, "Folk Art as Propaganda," 21–22.
49 Hung, *Mao's New World*.
50 Wilcox, "Dynamic Inheritance."
51 An example of this is *Zhongguo minzu minjian wu jicheng*, which documents folk dances, many of which involve props, based on long-term field surveys. The collection is huge and has a separate volume dedicated to each province and autonomous region. For more on this practice, see Emily Wilcox, "Dancers Doing Fieldwork: Socialist Aesthetics and Bodily Experience in the People's Republic of China," *Journal for the Anthropological Study of Human Movement* 17, no. 2 (Fall 2010, published 2012).
52 By contrast, this was a common image of the dancer promoted in American modern dance during this same era, also with ideological implications. See Rebekah Kowal, *How to Do Things with Dance: Performing Change in Postwar America* (Middletown, CT: Wesleyan University Press, 2010).

5 MOBILE PROJECTIONISTS AND THE THINGS THEY CARRIED

JIE LI

IN 1949, THERE WERE FEWER THAN SIX HUNDRED MOVIE THEATRES in mainland China. By the early 1980s, the film exhibition network in the People's Republic expanded to some 162,000 projection units, most of which were mobile movie teams showing films outdoors in rural and urban areas.[1] Such an expansive media infrastructure helped to unite and mobilize a vast and diverse populace behind the Communist Party's utopian visions. In this sense, the Chinese revolution was a media revolution. Central to the Maoist media network yet neglected in historiography, mobile projectionists physically carried the material infrastructure of cinema to a populace scattered across a vast territory not covered by any electrical grid, thereby "wiring" or "electrifying" the nation with audiovisual propaganda. Mobile projectionists became "physical and spirit mediums"—their bodies were extensions of the machines they wielded and were as much a revolutionary medium as the film prints they carried.

The typical mobile movie team in the Mao era consisted of three to four members, sharing tasks such as generating electricity, projecting, organizing logistics, and making extrafilmic propaganda. They transported the heavy machinery and personal baggage on wheelbarrows, cattle, carrying poles, or simply their shoulders. They traveled by foot, horse carriage, tractor, self-tinkered automobiles, or boats, breaking ice over frozen lakes, building bridges, and repairing roads along the way. They set up open-air cinemas on threshing fields and pastures, in forests and deserts, on construction projects and battlefields. Like military guerrillas, these "cinematic guerrillas" conducted "battles," or film screenings, on any terrain and in any climate.

The "physicality" of cinema at the grassroots in Mao's China encompassed both the corporeality of bodily senses, needs, and performances as well as the materiality of media apparatuses. Mobile movie teams and their material practices demonstrate how human bodies and acts supplemented and extended poor infrastructure in the Mao era, such that material shortage found compensation in bodily sacrifice and spiritual enrichment. Whereas cinema had originated in the West and expanded around the globe mainly as a capitalist commodity associated with urban modernity, in socialist China it took different routes through the countryside and served not only economic but also political goals: to mobilize the populace behind the party's utopian visions and to enchant them with communist ideology, teleology, and eschatology. The work of mobile projectionists helps us reconceptualize Maoist propaganda—not just as homogeneous and mechanical indoctrination from the central leadership but also as heterogeneous ritual performance and participation at the grassroots. In ways reminiscent of religious clergy and proselytizers, projectionists not only mediated messages from a central authority or divinity but also served local communities and their particular needs. As ventriloquist voices of the state, projectionists reinterpreted and adapted the films' stories and messages to mobilize audiences for current politics or local priorities.

MACHINES: THE CINEMATIC APPARATUS

The open-air film apparatus, or technological infrastructure, brought by mobile movie teams included generators and projectors, screens and film reels, loudspeakers and gramophones. Foundational film theories of the 1970s, also dubbed "apparatus theory," took as their premise the invisibility, imperceptibility and immateriality of film's infrastructure, with classical Hollywood cinema magically unwinding in hermetically sealed spaces.[2] Yet only a small fraction of Mao-era screenings took place in movie theatres built as such. In most cases, mobile movie teams and local people had to create and improvise cinema's infrastructure anew with almost every screening. Hence cinema's materiality was keenly seen, heard, touched, and even smelled and tasted by projectionists and audiences. The interaction between such materiality and human bodies and senses is what I mean by cinema's "physicality," which became foregrounded due to both technological wonders and technological failures.

Although there were sporadic efforts to bring cinema to the countryside in the Republican era,[3] most rural people in China encountered films for the first time only in the 1950s. While many villagers associated mobile movie teams with itinerant drama troupes, audiences also marveled at the modern wonder of film technology.[4] Screening sites swarmed with people as far as the eye could see, and projectionist reports and memoirs are replete with examples of how country bumpkins marveled at the electrical miracle of the technology, such as old peasants trying to light their pipes at the projectionist's light bulb, or audiences of a war film returning the next morning to look for leftover artillery.[5] As a former projectionist writes for the *Qinghai Film Gazetteer*, in the early 1950s many Tibetans rode their horses for tens of kilometers to listen to the team's gramophone, hoping to sing a local song with their microphone. These audiences could not help but wonder: "How can a hanging white cloth envelop thousands of troops? How can a high-mounted wooden box speak in so many voices? How can that 'lon lon' sounding power generator (Tibetans call it "mother" of electricity) draw lightning from the sky?"[6]

GENERATORS AND HUMAN POWER

The power generator was the bulkiest, heaviest, loudest, most volatile, and most important machine brought by the mobile movie team. Often weighing around two hundred kilograms each, power generators and projectors in 1950s China were nearly all foreign makes, either remnant American or Japanese machines or newer models imported from the Soviet Union or Eastern Europe.[7] Age, disrepair, primitive means of transportation, and exposure to a rough natural environment, as well as lack of technical manuals and trained technicians, meant frequent mechanical breakdowns. Since the generator was noisy and flammable, the movie team also brought a long cable (some thirty meters) to keep it both connected and at a good distance from the projector and loudspeakers. Watching the generator to troubleshoot and to forestall fire and electrocution and with children running amok, the generator operator could rarely pay attention to the movie.[8]

If technology was precarious and perilous, then projectionists' bodies played a compensatory role. Guidelines admonished them to shield their machines from shock, falls, rain, snow, sandstorms, heat, and cold during transport and screenings.[9] Refraining from drinking, smoking, and chatting, generator operators kept an eye on the transformer, listened carefully for noises, touched many buttons, and attended to burning smells.[10] Many also took precautionary measures, from regular cleaning of machine parts to sewing a cotton bag to keep the gasoline from freezing.[11] Some projectionists risked their lives to save machines from a collapsing building[12] or covered them with their own raincoats and blankets in a thunderstorm.[13]

Doing a physically demanding job that required mechanical or engineering skills, female projectionists received special media coverage as embodiments of new socialist ideals of gender equality.[14] All-female movie teams carried a

FIGURE 5.1. A 1966 poster portraying Hebei's "Three Sisters Movie Team." Author's personal collection.

similar symbolic currency as the iconic image of the female tractor driver printed on the 1960 edition of *renminbi*. For example, articles in film magazines from 1963 praised an all-female movie team from Heilongjiang for carrying 150-kilo generators on their shoulders through quagmires, all the while thinking of the Long March.[15] After overenthusiastic villagers "helped" them transport their equipment but shook up the fragile generator so that its water tank started leaking during the screening, the women had to postpone their supper and keep filling the water tank amid the icy wind and snow.[16] A 1966 poster portrayed the model "Three Sisters Movie Team" from Hebei as crossing a snowy mountain to bring film to villagers, towering above pine trees that symbolize their resolve and self-discipline (figure 5.1). Model projectionists used bodily self-sacrifice and inventive bricolage to resolve technical issues like the wind blowing away the screen, failing generators, and brittle, overused film reels.[17] As their bodies compensated for poor technology, their self-sacrifice emanated an electrifying spirit and pathos that reportedly moved the masses they served. As bodies became extensions of technology, they contributed to the generation of energy as much as the machines they carried.

Indeed, the movie team not only *carried* a power generator—they *were* a power generator. The joining of projectionist bodies to their machines of image projection and sound amplification generated the electricity, energy, passion, labor, and mass assembly needed for all forms of revolutionary projects and socialist construction. Throughout the Mao era but especially during the Great Leap Forward and the Cultural Revolution, local cadres summoned mobile movie teams to generate electricity for the lights and loudspeakers at conferences and rallies, even for all-nighter shifts for agricultural or construction projects.[18] The films themselves became a secondary, even dispensable, means toward the end of mass mobilization. Cinema thus became sheer electrification that both inspired and conscripted the masses to "make revolution" day and night.

Besides serving revolutionary mobilization, the human-powered generator could also mock, undermine, even subvert the films' propaganda intent. In the 1970s, movie teams at the commune level used lightweight pedal generators as well as 8.75 mm–format projectors and films to bring recordings of Jiang Qing's model works (*yangbanxi*) to the most remote corners of the land.[19] It was in this decade that cinema became regular monthly or bimonthly events at the village level. However, since the same few films were shown over and over again, both projectionists and their audiences became blasé about their ideological messages. Writer Ah Cheng describes a typical screening in the Yunnan mountains in the 1970s: "You needed several men to take turns powering the generator by pedaling. Sometimes the man pedaling tired and the electricity would fluctuate, causing the sound from the loudspeakers to become slurred, distorting the well-known arias. Meanwhile on the screen, an uplifting scene of the "heroic deeds" might have started boldly but would suddenly lapse into hesitation . . . Other times the man on the pedals changed the tempo on purpose, creatively improvising, and the old films would send the audience into fits of laughter."[20]

Since little comedy or eros was featured on the silver screen, the material and bodily practices of projectionists and audiences could often introduce extrinsic new meanings and sensations to films, sometimes changing the genre and tone of films from heroic martyrology into campy comedy, from propaganda into carnival.

THE SCREEN AS A FLAG, SAIL, AND LIGHTHOUSE

More than generators and projectors, the movie screen itself held the greatest visual prominence for audiences and became the key architectural element of mobile open-air cinema. As the state extended the film exhibition network into ever more grassroots levels, hanging up movie screens became akin to raising flags in territorial conquests. Calling themselves "vanguards on the cultural front" who "hack through brambles and thorns" in order to "spread the seed of socialist thought to the broadest masses of people,"[21] mobile projectionists opened up "virgin lands" that did not yet know cinema.[22] The fixing of the screen was itself an attraction and a spectacular display of the projectionists' acrobatic virtuosity, whether it was scaling up the pillars of a temple theatre or lassoing a rope like a cowboy. Audiences were also eager to help tamp down the earth to stabilize the bamboo poles, to tighten the rope that secured the screen, and to cast shadows with their hands when the light turned on.[23]

Lighting up a dark firmament in the open air, the screen had an enchanted quality, "enveloping thousands of troops," magnifying tiny insects, drawing the far near, conjuring up the past and divining the future.[24] Some compared the screen to a sail that takes audiences through an ocean of dreams, and if "Sailing the Sea Depends on the Great Helmsman," as a hosanna to Chairman Mao put it, then his translucent image on the screen provided both the illusion of live presence and summoned otherwise dispersed villagers into a congregation.[25] From the 1950s to the 1970s, projectionist reports on villagers' encounters with cinema often mention Mao's appearance in newsreels as the greatest attraction. Rural audiences would applaud, take off their caps, or shout "Long live Chairman Mao!" Some allegedly asked the "projectionist comrade" to "slow down, let Chairman Mao stay a bit longer!" Those who saw Mao onscreen would tell fellow villagers, "Chairman Mao came out to talk to me!"[26] Beyond the illusion of live presence, Mao's translucent image on film literally lit up dark villages without electricity. In this sense, the screen was also meant as a lighthouse that provided orientation and anchor in Mao's "revolutionary wind and waves."

Real wind blowing the screen, however, gives a twist to the metaphor of the sail, as the screen itself became subject to distortion, and film characters took on grotesque grimaces and warped figures.[27] Bending the surface of the screen or even breaking the rope holding the screen altogether, the wind created unpredictable comedy, farce, and a sense of the uncanny out of didactic film texts. In her novella *A Tale from the Cultural Revolution*, Wang Anyi describes how "sent-down youths" (*zhiqing*)—urban youths dispatched, from 1968 to 1976, to the countryside for rustication—assembled in the middle of the night at the sounding of a bugle for a screening of a revolutionary ballet: "The wind blew the screen like a sail on the sea, twisting the bodies of the characters on-screen so they all looked miserable.... The exaggerated gestures of the characters seemed absurd in this kind of night. The sound of music is engulfed by the wilderness, but the sound of the wind was omnipresent, filling the space between sky and earth."[28] The visual and auditory signals of cinema were not only distorted by the wind and other elements of nature but also swallowed up, overpowered, and rendered infinitesimal by the sky, the earth, and the air in between.

Indeed, even under optimal conditions, open-air screens, often two by three meters or the size of a "double blanket,"[29] were tiny in relationship to the large audience, who blocked one another's vision, so that those in the back often could see little more than a bunch of "heads and rears."[30] Sometimes rural audiences traveled a long way to a planned screening location, only to see a "white cloth film" when the projector or generator broke down, or if the movie team came so late that the film screening lasted into sunrise.[31] Even when films ran smoothly, audiences often watched a blank screen during the changing of the reels.[32] The materiality of the screen, in other words, could rarely be overlooked in open-air cinema.

FILM REELS AS PRECIOUS SCROLLS

Having discussed generators and screens, let us turn to the fragile and flammable materiality of film reels. Articles in *Film Projection* magazine liken projectors and films to "guns and bullets" that help to "occupy the thought front" in the vast Chinese countryside.[33] A 1963 slogan admonished projectionists to "love machines as your life, protect film prints as you would your eyes. Cutting out or damaging a film frame is equal to wasting a flatbread. Ruining a film is even more critical—you can account for the economic numbers but cannot account for the political impact of millions of audiences not educated by the film."[34] Since each reel had to be screened hundreds or even a thousand times, a ruined one could mean a ruined career for any projectionist. In work photos (figure 5.2), they often posed with their projector while checking a print frame by frame, since loosened projector parts or even sand blown in by the wind could cause reels to break, scratch, or even burn.[35] Prints could also get wet from the rain during a screening or fall into a river during transportation, requiring immediate and tedious attention to prevent the celluloid from being irredeemably spoiled.

Despite all the care given to film reels, they inevitably got snapped, scratched, and scrapped, so that an overused print often unwound as a palimpsest scroll of human foibles. Scratched films and other technical problems contributed to an experience of "disrepair and noise," as Brian Larkin characterizes Nigeria's media infrastructure.[36] Similarly, Chinese

FIGURE 5.2. Work photo of a projectionist in Heilongjiang in 1973. Courtesy of Cheng Yuntao.

viewers of open-air cinema in socialist China associated their filmic reception with "the noise of the real": fuzzy, scratched images and hissing or crackling sounds that made dialogue incomprehensible to even Mandarin-speaking audiences.[37] The snapping of film reels further provoked audiences to boo and hoot, while children jumped up to fight over the discarded "treasures" of celluloid fragments.[38]

The scratches on the celluloid could also be correlated with the film's popularity and familiarity to audiences, who memorized dialogue aloud or commented on the plot. Single copies of popular movies with a brief rental period were sometimes shared among multiple movie teams conducting screenings on the same night, requiring a "copy runner" to deliver the reels between two or more locations, also causing frequent interruptions. Waiting for the copy runner to arrive, the audiences were held in suspense about what would happen next.[39] Alternatively, projectionists filled the gap by summarizing the plot of the last reel, sometimes in prosimetric form with a bamboo clapper, so that a feature-length film took on the quality of traditional, serialized vernacular storytelling.

Thus, I would like to consider film reels "precious scrolls" in two senses. The first refers to their precious and fragile materiality, which demanded meticulous care from projectionists. The second valence analogizes films to "precious scrolls" as *baojuan*, premodern Buddhist and Daoist vernacular texts intended for performance.[40] Like premodern precious scrolls as religious propaganda, film reels came to life through the incantation of projectionists and received reverent attention from audiences. Whereas precious scrolls often began with an invitation to Buddha and bodhisattvas,[41] socialist cinema began with revolutionary icons and mediated encounters between a revered Chairman Mao and his loyal masses.

In the early years of the Cultural Revolution, newsreels about Mao's meetings with Red Guards and parades at Tiananmen Square were dubbed "red treasure films" (*hong bao pian*) in the same way that *Little Red Books* (popular excerpts from Chairman Mao's writings) were called "red treasure books" (*hong bao shu*).[42] Movie teams went on special tours with such films to make sure that they were screened in as many places as possible, so as to re-create revolutionary rallies with every screening. Villagers welcomed the movie team with ceremonious pomp and circumstance—often with a procession of gongs and drums, whereby the village chief himself would carry the print with red ribbons and a Mao portrait from its last projection site.[43] Whereas landlords, counterrevolutionaries, and other "black elements" were banned from these screenings, all "revolutionary masses" were invited to bring their "loyal, boundless proletariat revolutionary feelings." Since failure to attend such screenings might invite criticism or worse troubles, audience numbers rose to new heights.[44]

BAMBOO CLAPPERS AND LANTERN SLIDES

Mao-era film projectionists were not merely machine operators but instead used their voices, bamboo clappers, lantern slides, and other tools to enhance the liveliness of the cinematic event, even turning it into a kind of cinematic liturgy (figure 5.3). In a vast and diverse country, mobile projectionists were like missionaries who disseminated, translated, and explicated propaganda for their grassroots congregations. Their human mediation of cinema transformed and diversified an industrialized, standardized mass cultural product to suit local needs.

The wooden clapper (most often bamboo) is a percussive instrument routinely used by opera troupes and traditional storytellers to punctuate their narrative ballads with a crisp, rhythmic, staccato sound. Especially popular in North China, its associated performance genre, clapper talk (*kuaiban* or *kuaibanshu*, also known as *shulaibao*) developed from ballads

FIGURE 5.3. A 1966 propaganda poster of a rural projectionist with bamboo clappers and lantern slides. Courtesy of chineseposters.net.

sung by beggars to professional and amateur stage performances in the socialist era.[45] A former projectionist reenacted her prescreening clapper talk from the 1950s: "Audiences, settle down and be kind, a few rules to keep in mind. First rule, most crucial: order at the site is essential. No pushing, no fighting, no running and screaming. Tall chairs should be laid low, and clear out a central path. Why clear out a middle road? If you block the light, people can't see. Second rule . . . "[46] Given the improvised infrastructure of film exhibition spaces—without sloped seating or fire safety—projectionists used clapper talk and other oral performance genres to focus audience attention and discipline their collective behavior.

Clapper talk also addressed the comprehension challenges grassroots audiences faced at cultural, linguistic, and acoustic levels when introduced to the new medium of film. A 1953 report stated that after watching the film *Lenin in 1918*, many peasants could not tell which character was Lenin.[47] When watching Soviet World War II films in the early 1950s, rank-and-file army audiences applauded at the wrong places, such as when the enemy (German) troops appeared.[48] Even though imported films were dubbed in standard Chinese (Putonghua, or Mandarin), most rural folk only understood local dialects. Moreover, the acoustic quality of the loudspeakers and film prints in the 1950s was often so poor that even the projectionists had trouble discerning the spoken dialogue and thus relied on print publications to grasp the story.[49] Lastly, some cinematic language—such as flashbacks, intercutting, and dream sequences—also baffled audiences.[50] To aid their comprehension and to guide their reception, projectionists provided introductions of the film before, explanations during, and discussions after the screening, so as to ensure audience understanding of its plot, characters, and takeaway messages.[51] Absorption into the film's story world came to depend on the extrafilmic narrations of projectionists.

Such live performances are reminiscent of exhibition practices of silent cinema elsewhere,[52] with special resonance with Japanese film lecturers called *benshi*, who drew on traditional storytelling arts to add a live soundtrack to silent films, playing multiple roles as narrator, voice actor, and audience representative leading communal responses to cinema.[53] Whereas live narration and musical performances became largely extinct in other parts of the world, oral performances flourished alongside the growth of the film exhibition network in the People's Republic from the 1950s to the 1970s. Some projectionists were chosen for the job precisely because of their singing or storytelling skills, or their talents in composition or improvisation. Many projectionists also took lessons and trained with local storytellers and folk performers, such that they became the apprentices, heirs, and disseminators of "speaking and singing" traditions. While clapper talk and other performances were initially subsidiary to the films, their liveness, heterogeneity, and local nature often constituted a greater attraction than the more formulaic cinematic propaganda of the central government.

Apart from clapper talk, mobile projectionists systematically produced, projected, and narrated lantern slides, which came to be known as "rustic films" (*tu dianying*).[54] Hubei peasants came up with the following clapper ballad: "Rustic film is tip-top / clear on news and policies / giving technical guidance too / a great way to share experiences / at once propaganda and entertainment / inspiring commune members to work hard!"[55] Often part of an itinerant film projection team's repertoire, lantern slide projection was considered to have certain advantages over film in its technical ease, localized content, and slower speed, allowing room for performance by local subjects, artists, and projectionists. Cheap to purchase and easy to produce, lantern slides could be projected using gas lamps, not bulky generators, in areas without electricity. People watched the slideshow as they did cinema—as a concentrated collective in the darkness—but it could be presented slowly and could be subject to repetition on audience demand.[56]

In addition to mass-produced slides, many movie teams made their own after interviewing local heroes, learning local histories, writing a script, and painting a slideshow.[57] Photographic slides were also popular in reflecting "real local people, places, and events," and communes were urged to invest in photographic technology to enable peasants to see themselves on screen.[58] Some model teams, such as the Three Sisters Movie Team in Hubei, even animated their slideshows using a four-lens projector so people could see a red flag waving, a horse running, people walking, and birds landing on plum blossoms.[59] Just as their production depended on handicraft, the temporality of these slideshows depended on the hand that pulled the slides and on the commentary that accompanied the show—the "time of gesture and speech" that endows every magic lantern show with a performative quality not found in film projections.[60] The coordination and cooperation among members of the movie team resembled the virtuosity of a chamber music trio. Such handmade, live narrated slideshows, like the models they extolled, "put a local face" on the "Party-state's rural goals,"[61] so that even though film production was exclusively controlled by the central government, movie teams created local media content with the help of their audiences.

Lantern slides were also used for the introduction of agricultural techniques and popularization of scientific knowledge. After watching lantern slides of *Canal Prospective Blueprint* (Yunhe yuanjing guihua), laborers at an irrigation project agreed that "three years of bitter battle will give happiness to ten thousand generations."[62] A projectionist from Canton recalled how her team aided a local township government to fight against a pest by advertising a new insecticide. They tried but failed to capture the likeness of the rice planthopper (*Delphacidae*) with a drawing, so they asked the local cadre to catch a few such insects from the rice paddies and trapped them inside the lantern slides to be projected live onto the screen, while agricultural technicians explained the workings of the insecticide. The heat of the light bulbs agitated the insects, such that they became especially "animated." Thus the slide projector turned into a microscope and an "insect trap."[63]

Bamboo clappers and lantern slides were thus lightweight yet crucial material technologies and cultural techniques adopted by mobile projectionists for making localized propaganda. Similarly flexible media technologies projectionists carried and deployed for extrafilmic propaganda included microphones, gramophones, radio sets, cassette tape recorders and players, mimeographed pamphlets, and propaganda posters.[64] If mobile projectionists were clergy-like "spirit mediums," their film screenings resembled liturgical congregational worship in which the movie was only one component. A sample agenda published in *Film Projection* magazine in 1954 inaugurated the film screening by playing phonograph records of revolutionary songs. With the audience congregated, the projectionist would show lantern slides announcing the public tribunal of a "bad element" and give a speech mobilizing the masses to attend it. She would then sing a ballad about industrialization, followed by fifty slides depicting a new steel capital. Only then would she introduce the story and characters of the evening's film. During the changing of the reels, she would briefly summarize the previous reel. Finally, the next day, she would hold a discussion to solicit audience responses.[65]

Mobile film screenings thus became a tool for grassroots cadres to communicate and implement local policies, or "core work" (*zhongxin gongzuo*) in CCP bureaucratic jargon. Throughout the 1950s, movie teams collaborated with local cultural centers and theatre troupes to engage in "socialist distant horizon education" (*shehui zhuyi yuanjing jiaoyu*), promoting rural collectivization and showcasing Soviet collective farms, as well as ongoing industrial and infrastructural constructions.[66] From the Great Leap Forward to the Cultural Revolution, local cadres invited mobile projectionists to screen films at political meetings, because cinema attracted large, attentive crowds. Even when no political meeting was planned, it became customary for the party secretary to give a speech with the movie team's microphone.

Some village leaders got so carried away with the amplification of their voices that they would go on and on.[67]

Local cadres and mobile projectionists also invited audiences to use their microphones to give testimonials to their revolutionary faith. During the Great Leap Forward, for example, a Jiangsu movie team found an independent farmer (*dan'ganhu*) ready to join the commune and invited him to come on stage after the screening and publicly declare his change of heart, which supposedly convinced many other independent farmers to join the commune as well.[68] Another movie team staged a "martial arts contest" for young commune members, giving them microphones so that they could pledge to finish the harvest at unprecedented speed.[69] During the Socialist Education Campaign, films emphasizing class struggle, such as *The White-Haired Girl*, were rescreened, and audience members who identified with the prerevolutionary suffering on the screen came onstage to tell their own stories, therefore providing a "vivid and concrete lesson on class struggle" for "young people unfamiliar with past bitterness."[70] Cinema thus became a form of political shamanism that summoned memories of past grievances. It also transformed audience members into spirit mediums possessed by ghosts of the so-called feudal past, which was to be exorcised to ensure the purity of the revolutionary community.

THE WEIGHT OF BODIES

Projectionist reports and memoirs from the early 1950s highlighted their pioneering expeditions into inhospitable terrains in order to bring cinema to China's most peripheral populations. These narratives speak of crossing perilous rivers and braving enemy gunfire, suffering tropical diseases and surviving bandit attacks, but such risks and hardships were remembered as adventurous challenges rather than daily struggles.[71] As film screenings became more routine, *Film Projection* magazine also gave voice to some common gripes about the job, as captured by the following doggerel, published in 1957:

> Traveling fifteen kilometers a day to show films,
> Sleeping five hours a night in makeshift shelters,
> Hoping for a year of screenings without glitches,
> Despairing at four seasons without respite,
> A lowly third-rank official, a belly full of grievances,
> The horizontal scroll reads: Serve the People.[72]

According to a Guangxi film exhibition history, many projectionists had to delay their marriages, whereas those who were married didn't have much of a chance to go home, as summarized in another popular rhyme: "Don't let your daughter marry a projectionist man, otherwise she'd spend her days and nights all alone. On the rare occasion that he stops by home, he'd throw you a pile of stinky clothes" (you nü mo jia fangying lang, riri yeye shou kongfang, ouran yici huijia zhuan, diuxia yidui chou yishang).[73] In the 1960s, however, the everyday hardships of projectionists were again sublimated through a rhetoric of bodily sacrifice, and their representation in professional magazines also transformed from disgruntled state workers to labor models, so they became superheroes who "ate one meal a day yet traveled a hundred *li*" and who "climbed mountains at night instead of sleeping."[74]

Mobile projectionists used a wide range of modes of transportation—from automobiles, horse-drawn carriages, and boats to bicycles, hand-pushed carts, and shoulder poles—depending on the local terrain and available infrastructure. An all-female movie team from Shaanxi rode on a horse cart with their machinery and personal belongings, but they also had a bicycle for copy-running and for the team leader to go ahead and arrange the screening location, security, publicity, food, and accommodation for the team.[75] A Jiangsu movie team had a "movie boat" that served as their transportation and accommodation over three decades.[76] By the 1970s, many commune movie teams could expect the production brigade at their next screening site to send a few men to pick up the machinery.[77] Former sent-down youth projectionists in the "Great Northern Wilderness" got lifts on jeeps, trucks, or, more commonly, tractors and horse carts. One interviewee related vivid memories of the roads his team traveled, and how they got soaked in the rain and froze in the winter even when wrapped up in thick blankets. To counter the cold, they drank liquor, but if a projectionist got drunk, he might mess up the screening, and ruined film was rumored to be punishable by heavy fines or prison sentences.[78] In the summer, it sometimes got so hot that the horse galloped into the river with all the luggage and machinery. When the road was muddy and the horse was tired, they would sometimes be stranded in the grassland. The coachman would whip the horse, which would howl with pain but still refuse to budge, and the movie team would despair, thinking of the hundreds of people waiting for the movie.[79]

Teams usually slept in schools, temples, shrines, silos, toolsheds, theaters, and villagers' homes.[80] They brought their own bedrolls and mosquito nets but still had to endure the bitter cold of winters and bugbites in the summer. A poem from 1965 put it in romantic terms:

The sky is our mosquito net, the earth our bed
Not enough blankets? We'll find cover under the snow
So long as the herders can watch movies
A thousand bitter hardships are swept aside.[81]

The challenges of finding adequate accommodation go some way to explain the relative scarcity of female projectionists, despite their prominence in propaganda.[82] Besides overcoming grassroots prejudice against seeing women—especially unmarried women—doing "a man's job,"[83] pregnancy and motherhood also augmented the physical hardships of transporting bulky equipment, riding on bumpy roads, and swallowing spicy and unfamiliar foods.[84] Lacking childcare, a female projectionist at a Fujian coal mine left her older child alone at home and carried her younger child during screenings.[85] Most female projectionists would stop conducting itinerant screenings after childbirth. If they stayed within the film exhibition sector, they might sell tickets at movie theaters, train new projectionists, or maintain machines.

Mobile movie teams bought food from peddlers or town markets, or ate in villagers' homes. Except during crackdowns on "capitalist tails" (*ziben zhuyi weiba*) in the 1960s, peddlers followed projectionists, adding their steaming aromas and hawking cries to screenings, which sometimes undercut the films' high socialist messages. A Beijing sent-down youth recalls how the open-air screen was often encircled by the dim lamp of peddlers with baskets and pushing carts, mostly selling roasted sunflower seeds, five-spice roasted peanuts, dried tofu, and even lamb kebabs, liquor, and homemade cigars. While onscreen newsreels (sometimes several years old) showed laboring or fist-raising masses shouting anticapitalist slogans, offscreen "capitalist tails" continued to peddle their wares to eager consumers, sometimes even beneath banners stating "Learn from Dazhai," the model communist village from the 1960s to the 1970s.[86]

Many projectionist reports and memoirs mention the touching hospitality of rural folk, even comical anecdotes about how naive villagers mistook onscreen characters for live actors and cooked up enough food to feed a theatre troupe.[87] Similar stories recount how villager children mistook the automobile that came with the movie team for livestock and tried to feed it grass.[88] Such "funny" stories highlight the abject poverty of many rural audiences. A former projectionist recalled a meal from the mid-1950s at the home of the "village party secretary, the richest man in the village," who generously offered the movie team cured meat that his family had parsimoniously hoarded for two weeks since Chinese New Year, not knowing that it was already spoiled and rancid.⁸⁹ Another former projectionist recalled how she could never get used to eating steamed wheat buns because she was a rice eater from the south, and another member from an urban middle-class background had trouble swallowing the food villagers prepared—often maize porridge mixed with vinegar and chili peppers.⁹⁰

Although movie teams paid for their meals, some cadres also drew on the collective budget to pay for feasts as well as the movie fee, angering villagers who considered the practice corrupt or unfair.⁹¹ Local cadres in Yunnan reportedly killed a sheep and several chickens to feed the movie team, along with 20–30 of their minions, so villagers composed a doggerel:

> When the movie is here, the cadres laugh.
> They'd drink like there's no tomorrow.
> Chicken and ducks fly in fright.
> Pigs and dogs fear for their plight.⁹²

Inebriated cadres sometimes gave long-winded speeches before screenings, inviting the catcalls of their audiences.⁹³

In the eyes of grassroots audiences, mobile projectionists were a privileged class, as evidenced by what they wore and ate. A villager from Ningxia recalled an all-female commune movie team whose members all wore leather shoes and leather jackets: "You could tell at once that they received a salary."⁹⁴ A villager from Gansu recalled how projectionists wore sheepskin coats or blue khaki Mao suit–like uniforms with four pockets and buttons up to the collars, whereas audiences had patches all over their clothes. Along with local cadres, movie teams also ate noodles or pancakes made of fine white flour instead of the villagers' daily fare made of coarse grain.⁹⁵ At reunions of former sent-down youths in which my parents often took part, people would speak about the former mobile projectionist with retrospective envy as the one who ate better than everyone else. The projectionists' material lives, then, also refracted the broader material conditions at the grassroots.

CINEMA AS A SPIRIT MEDIUM

Whereas Western classical film audiences and contemporary Chinese urban audiences easily forget our bodies as we sink into our upholstered seats in air-conditioned auditoriums that transport us into films' story worlds, the Mao era's mobile film exhibition in open-air and improvised spaces foregrounded physicality in terms of both corporeality and materiality. When machines had to be carried without mechanized modes of transportation over mountains or across rivers, we pay more attention to their bulkiness and weight, as well as to the roads, geography, and weather. When films break down, when electrical voltage fluctuates, when the wind blows at the screen, we notice the brittleness and flammability of celluloid, the human powering of the generator, and the makeshift shabbiness or absence of infrastructure.

Yet material scarcity demanded bodily sacrifice and contributed to a spirit of the sacred. Carrying heavy and ungainly power generators, movie teams *became* power generators, since their bodies and spirits extended technological infrastructure and contributed to the generation of revolutionary energy as much as did the machines. Raising screens like flags, sails, and lighthouses, they enchanted audiences with luminous images in villages without electricity. Taking meticulous care of precious film reels, projectionists made celluloid "precious scrolls" serve liturgical, educational, and entertainment purposes with their retellings of pious revolutionary tales. Using lantern slides and bamboo clappers, projectionists localized, diversified, and enlivened propaganda for their grassroots audiences.

In Mao's China, cinema was a physical and spirit medium. Both the material and the corporeal dimensions of film exhibition were physical—a media assemblage of generators and projectors, screens and film reels, microphones and loudspeakers, lantern slides and bamboo clappers, as well as the voices and gestures, labor and performances of mobile projectionists and sometimes their grassroots audiences. Human bodies thus supplemented and extended socialist China's impoverished and improvised technological infrastructure, which often translated into a "hot and noisy" (*renao*) cinematic experience and aesthetic. Here "hot noise" refers at once to loudness, disruption, and disrepair, as well as to the "sociothermic affect"[96] of mass assemblies enabled by cinema, along with all of its extrafilmic sights, sounds, smells, taste, and touch. Such hot noise contributed to revolutionary sound and fury on the one hand, and disruptive and even subversive noise on the other.

By "spirit medium," I underscore the *human* mediation of cinema by mobile projectionists, who wove together a mass media network and mobilized the masses with modern technologies, local traditions, and their own body and spirit. As crusaders of communist ideology, they wired the nation with audiovisual propaganda that went on to electrify their audiences. In ways reminiscent of missionaries, priests, and shamans, they solicited and staged testimonies to revolutionary faith, be they bitter memories of a pre-revolutionary past, denunciations of local landlords or other class enemies, or vows to contribute to a communist future. Thus Maoist cinema was also a form of spiritual enrichment that sought to compensate for material impoverishment, even if it sometimes highlighted the disjunctions between utopian images and material realities.

NOTES

1. *Yunnan Sheng dianying faxing fangying gongzuo jinian tekan* (Kunming: Yunnan Film Company, 1984), 2.
2. For a critical overview of apparatus theory, see Richard Allen, "Psychoanalytic Film Theory," in *A Companion to Film Theory*, edited by Toby Miller and Robert Stam (Malden, MA: Blackwell Publishing 1999), 123–45.
3. For example, see Thorn Hongwei Chen, "Cinemas, Highways, and the Making of Provincial Space: Mobile Screenings in Jiangsu, China, 1933–1937," *Wide Screen* 7, no. 1 (2018).
4. Tom Gunning, "A Cinema of Attraction[s]: Early Film, Its Spectator and the Avant-Garde," in *The Cinema of Attractions Reloaded*, edited by Wanda Strauven (Amsterdam: Amsterdam University Press, 2006), 383.
5. *Yunnan Sheng dianying faxing fangying gongzuo jinian tekan*, 14, 121–22; Guangxi Film Distribution and Exhibition Company, *Guangxi dianying faxing fangying shi* [History of film distribution and exhibition in Guangxi] (Guilin: Guangxi Film Company, 1995), 26–27; Li Gexin, *Jiangshu Qingdao de gushi* (Jinan: Shandong Sheng Ditu Chubanshe, 2013), 90.
6. *Qinghai dianying zhi* [Qinghai film gazetteer] (Xining: Qinghai Sheng Wenhua Ting, 1989), 194–95.
7. Chen Mo, *Huaji fangying*, 22–25; Also see relevant articles in the magazine *Dianying fangying ziliao* [Film projection materials] (henceforth *DYFYZL*) 3.54, 4.30–41, 5.18–38, 6.30–36. (Note: for each entry, the former number is the issue number; the latter numbers are page numbers. These were published in 1953–54.)
8. This was the general consensus of former projectionists and audiences I interviewed in various provinces, and remained true as late as the mid-1980s.
9. *DYFYZL* 6.21–27.
10. Magazine *Dianying fangying* [Film projection] (henceforth *DYFY*) 1963.2.10–11. (Note: the first two numbers are year and month of publication, also the issue number, and the last numbers are page numbers).
11. Chen Mo, *Huaji fangying*, 23–24.
12. *DYFY* 1963.2.18–19.
13. *DYFY* 1963.4.8; "Xin chengli de Hubei nuzi fangyingdui" [Newly formed Hubei all-female projection team], *Dazhong dianying* [Mass cinema], no. 1 (1953): 18–19.
14. Tina Mai Chen, "Propagating the Propaganda Film."
15. "Yixin yiyi wei nongmin: fang Heilongjiang sheng Shuangcheng xian di'er nuzi fangyingdui" [Wholeheartedly serving the peasants: Interview with second all-female movie team of Shuangcheng County, Heilongjiang], *Dazhong dianying* [Mass cinema], no. 9 (1963): 24–25. Also see Sun Jianwei, *Heilongjiang dianying bainian* [A hundred years of cinema in Heilongjiang] (Harbin: Heilongjiang University Press, 2012), 123.

16 *DYFY* 1963.4.8.
17 *DYFY* 1957.2.22–23.
18 Hu Guizhen, "Yige nongcun dianyingdui lao fangyingyuan de huiyi" [An old rural film projectionist's memories], *Shenzhou xinwen wang*, April 1, 2012. http://sznews.zjol.com.cn/sznews/system/2012/04/01/014894278.shtml. Also see *Dianying fangying* Editorial Office, "Xin Zhongguo dianying fangyingwang de shinian" [Ten years of film projection network in New China], *DYFY* 1959.18.1–8.
19 Guangxi Film Distribution and Exhibition Company, *Guangxi dianying faxing fangying shi*, 189–205.
20 Ah Cheng, "The King of Children" in Ah, *The King of Trees*, 173.
21 Lu Chun, "Zuo yige mingfu qishi de wenhua zhanxian shang de jianbing" [Be a veritable vanguard on the cultural front], *DYFY* 1957.4.16–19.
22 "Ba dianying song dao nongcun li qu" [Send movies into the countryside], *Dazhong dianying* [Mass cinema], no. 5 (1952): 28.
23 Chen Mo, *Huaji fangying*, 13; Mu Xiaoli, *Yigeren de xingzou* [One person's journey] (Ningbo: Ningbo Chubanshe, 2011), 146–47.
24 *Qinghai dianying zhi*, 194–95.
25 Guo Wenlian, *Yili wangshi* [Memories of Ili] (Hefei: Anhui Wenyi Chubanshe, 2013), 117.
26 "Ba dianying song dao nongcun li qu" [Send movies into the countryside], *Dazhong dianying* [Mass cinema], no. 5 (1952): 28.
27 Fan Xiufeng, *Cun shang de shi* [Village matters] (Shijiazhuang: Huashan Wenyi Chubanshe, 2010), 264.
28 Wang Anyi, "Wenge yishi" [A tale from the Cultural Revolution], in *Zhongguo dangdai wenxue jingdian bidu* [Chinese contemporary literary classics], edited by Wu Yiqin (Nanchang: Baihua Zhou Wenyi, 2016), 136–37.
29 Yao Juntao, ed., *Yilingba tuan zhi* [108 Regiment gazetteer] (Xinjiang: Xinjiang Dianzi Gongye Chubanshe, 2005), 378.
30 Qi Yujiang, *Hongdu qingshen* [Deep sentiments for the Red Capital] (Xi'an: Shanxi Renmin Chubanshe, 2011), 117.
31 Zhuang Zhijuan, "Sanci teshu de kan dianying jingli" [Three special film-viewing experiences], *Shiji*, no. 2 (2012): 44–45.
32 Guangxi Film Distribution and Exhibition Company, *Guangxi dianying faxing fangying shi*, 51.
33 Xie Fengsong, "Zhengque xuanpian: Tan nongcun dianying xuanchuan gongzuo" [Correct film choices: On rural film propaganda work], *DYFY* 1960.10.17.
34 Peng Jun, "Tantan anquan fangying" [On safe projection], *DYFY* 1963.4.27.
35 "Aiji hupian diandi jingyan" [Tips for protecting machines and film reels], *DYFY* 1963.2.12–13.
36 Larkin, *Signal and Noise*, 219.
37 Friedrich Kittler, *Gramophone, Film, Typewriter* (Stanford, CA: Stanford University Press, 1999), 14.
38 Yu Liang, *Naxie nian naxie shi: Yige nongmin de jiyi* [Those years: A peasant's memories] (Beijing: Haichao Chubanshe, 2014), 219.
39 Ge Fei, "Xiangcun dianying" [Village cinema], in *Yigeren de dianying* [One person's cinema] (Beijing: Zhongxin Chubanshe, 2008), 2.

40 Wilt L. Idema, *"The Immortal Maiden Equal to Heaven" and Other Precious Scrolls from Western Gansu* (Cambria Press, 2015), 1–2; Idema, *The Resurrected Skeleton: From Zhuangzi to Lu Xun* (New York: Columbia University Press, 2014), 217.
41 Idema, *"Immortal Maiden,"* 1.
42 *Jilin dianying faxing fangying jishi* [Jilin film distribution and exhibition chronicles] (Changchun: Jilin Film Company, 1994), 149–50; Zhang Huihe and Chen Yuqi, *Hunan dianying shiye* [Hunan film enterprise] (Beijing: Wenhua Yishu Chubanshe, 1992), 660; Clark, "The Triumph of Cinema."
43 Interview with former projectionist Zheng Aguai in Zhejiang, July 2015.
44 Guangxi Film Distribution and Exhibition Company, *Guangxi dianying faxing fangying shi*, 174; Also see Liu Guangyu, *Xin Zhongguo chengli yilai nongcun dianying fangying yanjiu* [Study of rural film exhibition since the founding of New China] (Beijing: Wenhua Yishu Chubanshe, 2015), 164.
45 Lü Yihuan, ed. *Minjian shuochang* [Folk spoken-singing] (Shenyang: Shenyang Chubanshe, 2013), 171–4.
46 Chen Mo, *Huaji fangying*, 16.
47 "Zuohao yingpian de xuanchuan jieshi gongzuo—duzhe laixin zongshu" [Take care to publicize and explain films: A summary of letters from readers], *Renmin ribao*, January 16, 1953.
48 "Nongcun fangying xuanchuan gongzuo jingyan jieshao" [Introducing experiences of rural film propaganda work], *Dazhong dianying* [Mass cinema], no. 17 (1954): 33.
49 Interview with former projectionist Zheng Yaoyu, Shengzhou, Zhejiang, June 2019; Bei Yan, *Shan de nayibian* [The other side of the mountain] (Guangzhou: Jinan University Press, 2012), 102.
50 *Anhui sheng dianying zhi* [Anhui film gazetteer] (Hefei: Anhui Cultural Bureau, 2001), 251.
51 *Guangdongsheng dianying faxing fangying gongzuo shiliao* [Historical materials concerning Guangdong film distribution and exhibition], vol. 1 (Guangzhou: Guangzhou Cultural Bureau, 1991), 184; Chen Qie, "Bozhong kaihua jieguo—ji Yanbian yong chaoyu jieshuo yingpian de jingyan jiqi tuiguang" [Sowing seeds, blooming flowers, bearing fruit: How Yanbian projectionists used Korean to explain films], *Dianying yishu* [Film art], no. 1 (1964): 27–30; Xu Dongqing, ed., *Jiangyin yu Zhongguo dianying* [Jiangyin and Chinese cinema] (Beijing: Zhongguo Dianying Chubanshe, 2010), 194.
52 Abel and Altman, *Sounds of Early Cinema*.
53 Hideaki Fujiki, "Benshi as Stars: The Irony of the Popularity and Respectability of Voice Performers in Japanese Cinema," *Cinema Journal* 45, no. 2 (2006): 68–84.
54 "Zhongnan zhaokai nongcun dianying yu huandeng faxing fangying huiyi" [The Central-South (Region) convenes a meeting on rural film and lantern slide distribution and exhibition], *Dazhong dianying* [Mass cinema], no. 6 (1965): 23.
55 See Hu Zhiren, "Producing More Lantern Slides," *Popular Photography*, Issue 1, 1960, 13.
56 Hu, "Producing More Lantern Slides."
57 "Dianying zai nongcun" [Cinema in the countryside], *Dazhong dianying* [Mass cinema], no. 4 (1964): 22–23; "Jiantiao huandengji, laidao qunzhong zhong" [Carry a slide

projector on a shoulder pole and arrive amidst the masses], *Dazhong dianying* [Mass cinema], no. 2 & 3 (1965): 44.

58 Hu, "Producing More Lantern Slides."

59 "Nongye zhanxian shang de wenhua jianbing—ji Hebei sheng Laishui xian 'san jiemei' dianying fangyingdui" [Cultural vanguards on the agricultural front: On the "Three Sisters" movie team from Laishui County, Hebei], *Zhongguo funü* [Chinese women], no. 1–2 (1965).

60 Thomas Lamarre, "Magic Lantern, Dark Precursor of Animation," *Animation* 6, no. 2 (2011): 127–48.

61 Hershatter, *Gender of Memory*, 90.

62 Ma Shijun, "Lingnan huahong yipian" [Red flowers in Lingnan], *DYFY* 1960.9.22.

63 *Guangdongsheng dianying*, vol. 2, 68; vol. 1, 185.

64 *Guangdongsheng dianying*, vol. 2, 31–32.

65 "Jieshao Guangdong sheng di 68 dui (nuzi dui) de xuanchuan gongzuo jingyan" [Introducing the propaganda work experience of Guangdong provincial team 68 (all-female team)], *DYFYZL* 5.60–62 (1954).

66 "Guanyu kaizhan chunjie nongcun wenyi huodong xiang nongmin xuanchuan zongluxian de zhishi" [Directives on propagating the general line to peasants through the arts during spring festival], *DYFYZL* 2.2–3 (1954).

67 Interviews with former rural projectionists in Hubei and Zhejiang, August 2015.

68 "Women shi xuanchuandui, you shi shengchan tujidui" [We are a movie team as well as a shock production team], *DYFY* 1958.16.16–17.

69 "Wudao Renmin Gongshe Fangyingdui de yiye" [One night of Wudao People's Commune Movie Team], *DYFY* 1959.2.21.

70 "Fang le dianying yihou" [After screening a film], *Dazhong dianying* [Mass cinema], no. 5 (1964): 22; "Pinxiazhongnong kan dianying" [Poor and lower-middle peasants watch films], *Dazhong dianying* [Mass cinema], no. 2–3 (1965), 47.

71 *Fujiansheng dianying fangying dadui chengli wushi zhounian jinian ce* [Commemorative volume for the fiftieth anniversary for the founding of the Fujian film projection brigade] (Fuzhou, 2001), 29–56, 194–5; *Qinghai dianying zhi*, 196–98.

72 "Fangying duiyuan de duilian" [Projectionist couplet], *DYFY* 1957.8.13. For similar gripes, see *DYFY* 1957.1.12, 26–27; 1957.2.7–8; 1957.6.3.

73 Guangxi Film Distribution and Exhibition Company, *Guangxi dianying faxing fangying shi*, 108.

74 "Fangying zhanxian hongqi piao" [Red flags on the projection battlefront], *DYFY* 1960.12.8–10.

75 Chen Mo, *Huaji fangying*, 30–1, 85–86.

76 Xu, *Jiangyin yu Zhongguo dianying*, 194; *Guangdongsheng dianying*, vol. 1, 182–83.

77 Shi Sanfu, *Qiaoshui lazhu qu* (Shanghai: Shanghai Renmin Chubanshe, 2013), 91.

78 *Fujiansheng dianying*, 44–45.

79 Interview with Lu Guoguang, former sent-down youth projectionist, 2012.

80 *Fujiansheng dianying*, 44–45; *Guangdongsheng dianying*, vol. 1, 187; Chen Mo, *Huaji fangying*, 29, 86.

81 Poem published in *Dazhong dianying* [Mass cinema], no. 7 (1965): 23.

82 *Guangdongshen dianying*, vol. 1, 187; Chen Mo, *Huaji fangying*, 86; *Fujiansheng dianying*, 44–45.
83 *Guangdongsheng dianying*, vol. 1, 182–3; Chen Mo, *Huaji fangying*, 16; interview by Peng Hai with a former female projectionist in rural Ningxia, April 2017.
84 Chen Mo, *Huaji fangying*, 53, 96.
85 *Fujiansheng dianying*, 71–73.
86 Cui Jizhe, *Zuihou de lang*, 98.
87 Li Liaolin, *Chuntian zhu zai wo de cunzhuang*, 58; Yu Dongxing, *Ma la huoche de difang* [A place of horse-drawn locomotives], memoir published online at http://qiancenglang.com/NewsTitle.aspx?ID=1942.
88 Yu, *Ma la huoche de difang*.
89 Interview with former projectionist Zheng Yaoyu, Shengzhou, Zhejiang, June 2019.
90 Chen Mo, *Huaji fangying*, 16, 32, 95.
91 *DYFY* 1957.2.17, 1957.4.40.
92 *Yunnan jinnian*, 81.
93 Wang Xinpeng, *Women xin sanjie* [We three new classes] (Beijing: Zuojia Chubanshe, 2008), 149.
94 Interview by Peng Hai with a villager (female, b. 1962) in Ningxia, April 2017.
95 Interview by Peng Hai with a retired worker (b. 1961) who grew up in Gansu and moved to Ningxia for work, April 2017.
96 Adam Yuet Chau, "The Sensorial Production of the Social," *Ethnos* 73, no. 4 (2008): 485–504.

6 OUTSIDE OBJECTS AND MATERIAL PROPAGANDA

DENISE Y. HO

AT FOUR O'CLOCK IN THE AFTERNOON OF JANUARY 12, 1962, THE Shenzhen train pulled into Guangzhou Station. As a shipment of two-pound "small packets" (*xiaobao youjian*) from Hong Kong was being unloaded, dozens of people rushed forward in an attempt to steal the packages. Police at the train station fired at the crowd, some were detained and questioned, and eventually ten were arrested. This minor incident was observed by an agent for a small-packet middleman and reported in a Hong Kong intelligence file without further comment.[1] Yet this aborted theft of small packets was noted because of its political sensitivity: mainland China was suffering from the "three hard years" of famine that followed the Great Leap Forward, and people in Hong Kong responded by mailing food and medicine to their relatives at the rate of about one million packages a month. While the flood of small packets was surely a relief to its recipients, it created embarrassment for Chinese officials, who told Hong Kong visitors to Shenzhen that food packages were neither welcome nor necessary.[2] In the face of Chinese propaganda about material life in "New China," the small-packet industry served as a tangible contradiction. Against the diasporic newsletters that celebrated the motherland's material plenty, care packages provided a lifeline in an era of privation.

As material goods crossed China's borders in the Mao period, such outside objects became part of socialist China's material landscape. The border between South China and Hong Kong (and sometimes Macau) was a key site for the transport of two categories of objects: those carried by travelers in their baggage and those sent as so-called "small packets." Individuals going to China to visit family or to study were allowed to bring certain amounts of goods with them duty-free, and those who wished to send items more regularly could do so through the Hong Kong post, the Macau post, or a variety of intermediaries who specialized in the trade. Outside objects entered China throughout the Mao era and after, but small packets became an internationally known phenomenon in the "mailbag rush" of the famine years.

The circulation of outside objects, licit and illicit, was not unique to socialist China. Trade within the Eastern bloc yielded consumer goods, like imported things in the Soviet Union's TsUM department store.[3] Diplomats and other officials abroad returned with gifts; Soviet tourists in Europe hoarded their foreign currency allowance, attempting to smuggle the vodka and watches they had bought instead of food and drink.[4] Sometimes such items ended up in black markets, which existed all over the socialist world. In border areas, foreign goods were especially prevalent, as in the case of the divided community of Sonneberg in East Germany and Neustadt in West Germany.[5] In Mao's China, likewise, foreign things found a place in both the official and unofficial economies.

The phenomenon of relief packages was also not unprecedented. In the aftermath of World War I, American Jews sent remittances, clothing, and food to Europe; the Joint Distribution Committee fed an estimated two million people a day in the Soviet Union, relief that included the transmission of individually purchased ten-dollar packages.[6] After World War II, Americans could send ten-dollar Cooperation for American Remittances (CARE) packages to West Berlin beginning with the 1948 airlift.[7] At the level of the state, socialist countries organized the delivery of packages as part of the economy. Torgsin stores in the Soviet Union delivered their own mail-order packages and licensed the delivery of packages from abroad.[8] Such accommodation—which also accumulated foreign exchange—stretched from East Germany's Intershops to the Bank of China and the China Travel Service's offices in Hong Kong.[9]

Like imported, mailed, or smuggled goods elsewhere in the socialist world, China's outside objects provoked both desire and anxiety. Some items were scarce necessities, like crucial medicine and high-energy foods. Yet to receive them was to accept assistance from "overseas connections" (*haiwai guanxi*), and to acknowledge the shortages produced by the country's socialist system. While the phenomenon of small packets was not particular to China or to socialism, the South China border and its "mailbag rush" was unique: its two colonies and historic entrepôt connected a significant diaspora with communist China, the small packets were a grassroots phenomenon, and the severity of China's famine was unprecedented. Outside objects thus took on great political valence. Cross-border travelers and overseas Chinese senders brought and sent consumer goods—from food and medicine to clothing and magazines—in a way that challenged the state's representations of material prosperity.

THE BORDER

On June 9, 1898, China and the United Kingdom signed a treaty that extended the boundaries of Hong Kong beyond Hong Kong Island and Kowloon to a line that connected Deep Bay (Shenzhen Wan) in the west to Mirs Bay (Dapeng Wan) in the east, with the exact limits to be determined by later surveys.[10] In the early years of the border, China Customs was primarily concerned with opium and munitions, and even with the advent of the through train in 1911, itinerant traders were relatively few. Beginning in the 1920s and 1930s, merchants began taking the train, carrying everything from kerosene and nails to flour and sugar, now subject to taxation. During the Japanese occupation, China Customs was closed and the border was militarized.[11] Yet smugglers continued to ply their wares, crossing the Shenzhen River at night. A native of Shunde remembers fleeing from occupied Hong Kong to Shenzhen in 1942, and then taking ten of his family's thirteen dollars to make a living trading between Shenzhen on the China side and Sheung Shui on the Hong Kong side. "If people wanted alcohol, then you'd buy alcohol. You had to carry your own tins and fill them up. You'd pretend that you were a farmer and hang the tins off a carrying pole ... with that ten dollars, I made it all the way to peacetime."[12]

Official travel was reinstated after the defeat of Japan in the Pacific War, but with the Chinese communist liberation of Shenzhen in October 1949, through-train service was again discontinued, with travelers having to disembark at Lo Wu (Luohu) and walk across the border. Yet outside of the checkpoints, the border was still not a hard boundary. Throughout the Mao era, provisions were made for villagers from both Hong Kong and China to cross back and forth, whether it was for daily farmwork or for grave-sweeping at the Qingming Festival. In 1952 Hong Kong's commissioner of police described three main border stations, two permanent police posts, and seven observation towers: "The frontier is partially wired, otherwise open, and there is a jeep road along it."[13] A travel guide from the same year explained the divided community of Sha Tau Kok (Shatoujiao): "There is a boundary stone in the Eastern Peace Market: one side is British territory and one side is Chinese territory; it is very easy to get them confused!"[14]

Despite a persistent porousness, both British and Chinese authorities instituted a new regime of border control. On the Hong Kong side, in 1950, British authorities began requiring entry permits and instituted a quota system, allowing no more than fifty natives of Guangdong to enter each day with documents permitting their reentry to China.[15] Hong Kong also introduced a number of cards and passes: a certificate of identity; a frontier pass (*tongxingzheng*, after 1956 called a reentry Permit), which allowed residents to return without being subject to quota; and an entry permit, for Chinese not from Guangdong and Chinese from Taiwan.[16] In 1951, the China side imposed a system of entry and exit permits for Guangdong, and in 1956 began to issue "hometown introduction letters," which had to be stamped at the destination in order to exit later.[17] There were also periodic moments of loosening border controls on both sides, such as during Chinese New Year and school summer vacation and to encourage participation in exhibitions and fairs in Guangzhou.[18]

The regulation of movement across the border took place in the context of continued waves of migration from China into Hong Kong, sometimes via Macau. For example, when border controls were relaxed in 1956 for two Guangzhou exhibitions, Hong Kong recorded a population gain of over seventy thousand in six months. Originally the responsibility of the Hong Kong police, immigration work grew so much that the Home Office in London recommended a new Department of Immigration. Established in August of 1961, it came into being just before an influx of an estimated 142,000 in 1962.[19] The movement, dubbed "the great exodus," was highly politicized. As Laura Madokoro has shown, Hong Kong authorities highlighted their commitment to maintaining stability, Chinese propaganda portrayed the separation of families as an attack on tradition, and at the United Nations High Commission for Refugees in 1962, British and Hong Kong officials argued against using the word "refugee" in order to establish that famine migrants were "illegal."[20]

Border control also operated against the backdrop of the Cold War. When China entered the Korean War in 1950, the United States launched an embargo, which was followed by one from the United Nations in 1951; while the UN sanctions ended when the war did, the American prohibition lasted until 1972.[21] Hong Kong had long been a transshipment point for the China trade and a site of small-scale industry using Chinese materials. A microlevel example demonstrates how blurry the boundaries were: Leung Yuk Jan's family manufactured oyster sauce for export; they sometimes furtively bought Chinese oysters from Shajing, using others' names and manipulating forms from the Hong Kong Agriculture and Fisheries Department.[22]

But despite the embargo, the two economies remained intertwined. Apart from illicit channels for smuggling, Hong Kong became an increasingly important trading partner, exporting goods that could not be supplied from the socialist world, like certain pharmaceuticals and machinery. On the receiving end, in this period, at least 80 percent of Hong Kong's meat and half of its vegetables came from China.[23] Fruit from both North and South China came to Hong Kong by sea, rail, and truck, with a border crossing at Man Kam To (Wenjindu) designated for agriculture. The transportation of fruit, delivered to a market in Yau Ma Tei and dominated by migrants from Dongguan, followed a cycle both seasonal and quotidian. Li Kit Fai remembers waiting with the other coolies for the sight of a ship's flags and the cry "Ship berthed!" Bananas came directly from China by barge and were carried in 300–400-kilogram baskets, two workers using one shoulder pole.[24] Thus the Hong Kong and China border, a material boundary that was an ideologically charged "Bamboo Curtain," was blurred by migration and trade, official and unofficial.

TRAVELERS AND BAGGAGE

The 1950 imposition of border controls between Hong Kong and China limited travel and made family visits less frequent. China Customs noted that with the need for a frontier pass, the number of Hong Kong travelers decreased from over ten thousand visits a day to one thousand, a number that halved again in 1952 as a result of the Three-Antis and Five-Antis Campaigns.[25] A decade later, in the first year of the Hong Kong Department of Immigration's existence, legal border crossings for 1961–62 numbered 418,036 from China and 408,811 to China, the vast majority being Hong Kong people with reentry permits.[26] Individuals continued to cross the border for significant events, such as the funeral of a parent.[27]

A moment of loosening restrictions demonstrates the pent-up demand for travel. In 1956, both governments decided to take the occasion of Chinese New Year—and for the Chinese, two separate exhibitions, on agricultural products and on Czechoslovakia's socialist construction—to lift controls. As of February 10, the Hong Kong government did not require its residents to apply for a frontier pass. On the Chinese side, Guangzhou established a special committee to welcome Hong Kong and Macau "compatriots" (*tongbao*), making arrangements to facilitate their travel: visitors could obtain tickets to the exhibitions at various Hong Kong outlets; upon registering with local police, they could get temporary ration coupons for grain, oil, and sugar, and their exhibition tickets could even serve as discount coupons for hotels, food stores, and restaurants.[28]

In addition to newspapers and word-of-mouth, visitor guidebooks from the period reveal how one embarked on a journey to China. One guide, which may have been published before the 1956 Chinese New Year exception, explained to a prospective traveler where to apply for the frontier pass, and what information was needed. Hong Kong identity cards would be stamped upon crossing at Lo Wu (Luohu), and a note to the reader explained that this stamp was not important—perhaps travelers worried that the stamp would cancel the ID card.[29] Once the stamp was obtained, the traveler could walk across the border to Shenzhen, where he had to fill out a letter of introduction, which was to be stamped by local authorities at his destination. This letter was necessary for applying for a temporary residence permit and any ration coupons, and the requisite stamp was required upon exiting China at the end of the trip.[30] After this, one could change money, pass through luggage inspection, and enter Shenzhen Station, where a cup of tea cost one *jiao* (four cents) in 1958.

Though the guidebooks varied in their political positions, they all addressed a central concern for any traveler: what could be carried into China, and what could be brought out. For example, in the guidebook published in 1956 by Hong Kong's *Xinwanbao*, a pro-PRC daily newspaper, one finds a straightforward outline of customs regulations. The guide reprinted an official notice from Guangzhou, which stressed that visitors could only carry daily use items for their own individual consumption, that contraband was forbidden, and that all valuables—including gold and silver jewelry, watches, and fountain pens—had to be declared upon entry.[31] Daily use items were tax exempt, and there were special categories for overseas Chinese settling down, students, and visitors bringing items to overseas Chinese.[32] The guidebook went on to detail customs regulations and lists of explicitly forbidden items, whether one was coming from Hong Kong or returning to Hong Kong. Travelers coming from Hong Kong were forbidden from bringing in weapons and drugs, Chinese currency or cheques, radio equipment, live pigeons, undeveloped film, and any media that might "harm China's politics, economics, culture, or morals." The list for travelers going back to Hong Kong was similar, including also any jewelry that was not originally registered, cultural relics and rare books, media that would reveal state secrets, and rare animals.[33] Reflecting both politics and proximity, live pigeons were not allowed on the way back, either.

In comparison with *Xinwanbao*'s direct listing of customs regulations, a strongly anticommunist guidebook from the same year provided explanations alongside restrictions. The guide urged travelers not to bring in any newspapers, magazines, or documents, telling readers that the Communist Party controlled speech and thinking. In a list of ten items that travelers "had to remember," returnees were told not to wear flashy clothing, to take too much cash, or to bring out any publications from the mainland. In a section on how to visit relatives and friends, the guide's authors described the gifts most appreciated for their "spiritual and material" comfort. At the top of the list was sturdy used clothing; cotton and woolens were best. Suggested foodstuffs included salted fish packed in oil that could be reused for cooking, brined pork or beef (favoring the former for its higher fat content), dried seafood for flavoring, milk powder for children, beans of all kinds, and peanut candy. Recommended daily use items were rubber shoes, toothbrushes, nylon thread, and plastics. Aware of its critical stance, the guide's authors forbade readers from bringing the guidebook itself into China.[34]

The same guidebook also acknowledged the material needs of the travelers themselves, including a list of questions like, "How does one sell used clothing and daily use items?" "How does one safely sell watches and fountain pens?" and "How does one rescue jewelry and bring it back to Hong Kong?" Whether the motive was to offset travel fees or to provide additional assistance to relatives and friends, the guide recognized that visitors often sold what they brought. Such items could be given directly or sold to street vendors, but in the face of crackdowns, the recommended choice was an official institution for this purpose, the "Service Center for Transferring the Personal Effects of Hong Kong and Macau Compatriots." If one wanted to sell watches and fountain pens, the trick was to dispose of them while staying at a hotel, right when one was about to leave. As for jewelry, one recommended method was to prepare fakes for the purpose of registration, and then return wearing the originals.[35]

Despite the cautious tone of the anticommunist guidebook, archival materials from a few years later demonstrate that the Chinese state took a much more practical view toward overseas Chinese travelers and the sale of items in their luggage. A 1959 document from Bao'an County, which shared a border with Hong Kong, passed along to relevant organs, including local customs offices, established set prices for all manner of commercial goods brought over by overseas Chinese. Such items included simple electronics (flashlights, camera parts, binoculars), parts and materials (woolen yarn, rubber washers, needles, wire, razor blades, tire inner tubes), and small consumer goods (fountain pens, ballpoint pens, toothbrushes).[36] Together with the guidebooks, such local customs documents demonstrate that people found not only recipients but also buyers—licit and illicit—that provided opportunities for profit. Smuggling in this period supplemented and even complemented the state-run economy.[37]

The window of opening in 1956 led to a dramatic increase in people and goods crossing the border. In the second half of the year, visitors brought in an average of ten bags each, an upward trend that continued the following year. Indeed, in 1957, purchasing stations at the border recorded spending 4,820,000 yuan to buy visitors' items, twice as much as the year before.[38] Between these official transfers and items sold on the black market, mainland China was flooded with consumer goods from outside of China. *Internal Reference*, a newsletter for cadres, reported from Shanghai in November of 1956 that a significant number of foreign products were appearing on the market. These included daily use items, from toothbrushes and nylon socks to containers (soap dishes, washbasins, dishes, kettles) to clothing (more socks, belts, shirts, sweaters), originating from the United States, Great Britain, Japan, India, and Hong Kong (even including counterfeit American products!). Such items were sold in official stores, totaling an estimated 1,498,000 yuan in the first half of October 1956 alone.

According to *Internal Reference*, these goods originated from Guangzhou, often via overseas Chinese returning home or students coming to study. The appearance of foreign products even resulted from enterprising Shanghai department stores contracting with China Customs to purchase confiscated items, a practice that cultivated a brisk trade, with agents traveling between Shanghai and Guangzhou. Not inexpensive—one pair of imported nylons cost the equivalent of eight to ten pairs of domestic ones—these products were primarily purchased by "capitalists, high-level intellectuals, art workers, and a small number of young workers, cadres, and PLA soldiers." Despite such dramatic price differences, *Internal Reference* expressed concern that foreign products influenced the market for domestically produced items. A glut of imported toothbrushes at Shanghai's Number One Department Store, for example, caused the sales of domestic toothbrushes to fall by 20 percent.[39] From Moscow in 1947 to Shanghai in 1956, the allure of nylon stockings was hard to resist.

Though foreign products were desirable, they could take on heightened political import. An *Internal Reference* report from April of 1956 describes Hong Kong people visiting their native places and gifting used clothing to other villagers, saying, "No one in Hong Kong wants these things. I hear you in the mainland live very bitter lives, so I've brought them back to show you." This alarmist report linked the gifting of used clothing to other kinds of behavior, including showing photographs to play matchmaker, suggesting that even Youth League party secretaries were longing for "degenerate" lives in capitalist society.[40] Outside objects appeared in the context of great scarcity: in Bao'an County, cooking oil was rationed, goods like bicycles and radios were not even available for sale, and a family of six might have enough cloth for two sets of clothing a year.[41] In this way, outside objects served as material evidence of another economic system and way of life.

By the 1960s, outside objects were decidedly political. At one level, the Socialist Education Movement and its campaigns against corruption labeled imported goods and luxury things as the possessions of capitalists and landlords with restorationist desires. But more generally, the devastating famine that followed the Great Leap Forward made hunger so taboo that to speak of it invited accusations of "counterrevolution." Food packages sent from Hong Kong to the mainland were at once necessities and political contraband. One Hong Kong student in China stashed her care packages at her relatives', bringing the cheese back to share with her female classmates. A Shanghai middle schooler with Hong Kong relatives received "a whole suitcase full of tinned food, milk powder, rice, and cheese." As her classmate remembered, "She didn't dare touch the food. No one dared to touch it either. All of us said we would rather suffer along with the rest of the country."[42] Underlying these outside objects—for travelers, the recipients and consumers, and the Chinese state—were larger narratives of material prosperity and political legitimacy.

SMALL PACKETS AND "THE MAILBAG RUSH"

The practice of sending packages from Hong Kong to China predated the Great Leap Forward famine. For some, mailing goods to family and friends was a regular occurrence. Marine policeman Lee Kam-yung, for example, remembers sending two *jin* of sugar and two *jin* of oil to his mother and elder sister every month. "There were grain shops and oil shops that specialized in this kind of business; you gave them an address and you gave them money, and they would ship it for you. There were restrictions on sending cloth, really only enough to make one set of clothes."[43] Professional letter-writer Lee Lai, working out of one of the thirty-some stalls that clustered near the Yau Ma Tei post office, recalls writing names and addresses on neat packages filled with sugar, oil, beans, and clothing.[44] Letters from Bao'an County to Hong Kong in the Mao period record frequent mailings; in an October 1966 letter from Shajing Commune, a mother acknowledges the receipt of four yards of cloth, one spool of thread, two tins of tiger balm, one doll, and one towel, asking her daughter, "If you have money to spare, please buy me some calico."[45]

FIGURE 6.1. Hong Kong food store specializing in postal parcels. "Food Parcels to Red China" (1961), Hong Kong: British Pathé.

But in the same way that 1949 inaugurated a new border control regime, in that year parcel post service was suspended. In its place, the Hong Kong Post organized a system of two-pound small packets, not to exceed three feet in length, width, and depth combined, and only for goods—letters were not allowed beyond an invoice of the package's contents.[46] People in Hong Kong could send small packets directly via the Hong Kong Post, they could carry packages to Macau to take advantage of lower postage, or they could utilize a number of middlemen, who would handle packages on their behalf for a commission. Such intermediaries included hawker stalls, shops, and syndicates linked to the China Travel Service. For the Hong Kong Post, the small packets were a boon; since China's postal system included Hong Kong as part of China, the Hong Kong Post collected postage while China bore the cost of delivery.[47] However, China received customs duties on the small packets; in 1961, it was estimated that food packages entering at Lo Wu (Luohu) alone generated sixteen million Hong Kong dollars per month. At the level of the individual, customs duties were not insignificant: the mother in Shajing paid 3.46 yuan for her package, more than a child's school fees of 3 yuan per year in the same locality.[48]

Neither the sender nor the Hong Kong Post was ever fully confident of what Chinese customs regulations were. According to rules promulgated by the Ministry of Foreign Trade in October 1955, Chinese were allowed to receive packages from Hong Kong and Macau not to exceed 50 yuan in value, and not more than once a month.[49] A directive from 1959 explained that individuals could receive five yuan of goods per month for their own personal use, as well as used clothes, tax-free. Luxury goods like a watch or a pen were allowable if the recipient could demonstrate that this was the only one he owned.[50] However, in practice, regulations were unevenly applied; scarce items like certain medicines, for example, often passed through China Customs even when they exceeded the allowable amount.[51] Both senders and the postal service thus used returned packages as a way to measure restrictions and their enforcement.[52] Hong Kong newspapers, often relying on interviews with travelers from China, reported on quotas and changes over time.[53]

The reportage on small packets gained urgency as famine conditions spread after the Great Leap Forward. In 1959 an estimated 870,000 small packets were sent to China, and in 1960, 3,690,000. By July 1961, Hong Kong residents sent about one million small packets a month, a trend that held steady through the middle of 1962. Record-setting months went over two million small packets, though these spikes might also reflect months around Chinese New Year or when—in December 1962—the Hong Kong postmaster general lowered the postage rate by eighty cents.[54] During what local newspapers dubbed "the mailbag rush," the traffic in small packets was so high that it resulted in delays and missing packages; one response was for individual senders and middlemen to bring packages across the border to mail directly from the Shenzhen post office, where they could also evade restrictions on weight.[55] By 1963 the number of small packets began to fall off, numbering slightly over nine million for the year, and by 1965 the Hong Kong Post stopped compiling statistics, "as traffic [had] returned to normal."[56]

What was in the contents of the small packets? Some were packed by people themselves, while others were made up by the stores that handled the purchases. Some operations fulfilled orders with food stocked in China, with packages made up and dispatched directly from mainland warehouses. The Bank of China in Hong Kong even launched a program of food coupons, which could be mailed to China and exchanged in communal canteens.[57] China Customs estimated that 95 percent of packages contained food (grain, noodles and biscuits, dried meat and sauces, edible oil and sugar), while medicine, rubber shoes, and cloth made up the rest.[58] Estimates from the

FIGURE 6.2. Cashier in Hong Kong food store passing a wrapped parcel to a customer. "Food Parcels to Red China" (1961), Hong Kong: British Pathé.

Hong Kong Post suggest that by 1962, at the height of "the mailbag rush," small packets maxed out their two pounds with lard and other fats, sugar, and dried fish.[59] Archival material in China confirms the surge in packages. One report by the Shanghai office of the China Travel Service, which helped to transmit parcels, recorded that in 1962, packages were arriving at the rate of six thousand per day, estimating that 85 percent were foodstuffs (including grain, sugar, and tinned food) with the remaining 15 percent being medicine. Though the China Travel Service referred to the phenomenon as a "package struggle," it explained that those known as "overseas Chinese dependents," who had family abroad, clamored for still more goods. Allowing those with overseas ties to access more products, China Travel Service officials concluded, would be a good way to strengthen ties among overseas Chinese dependents, the state, the diaspora, and Hong Kong "compatriots." In addition, remittances and other transactions were channels for the state to get foreign currency.[60]

Local newspapers and international newsreels portrayed the images of "the mailbag rush." Hong Kong and Macau papers described "parcels piled up like mountains" at post offices, "dragon-like lines" at border crossings, a shop delivering 1,600 packages via eight rickshaws, and the incessant sound of stamping postmarks. They reported on prices so that senders could take advantage of price differentials, and listed practical details, such as limits and duties, even explaining that enterprising welders were on hand to seal kerosene tins for shipment. Newspapers in Macau even ran ads for small-packet middlemen, claiming guaranteed delivery and offering insurance.[61] Beyond Hong Kong and Macau, "the mailbag rush" made international headlines. In addition to print, the British Pathé service produced two short newsreels on the topic, one of which highlighted the fact that the food being sent originated in famine-stricken China. In addition to the irony that China was exporting food when its population was starving, the newsreel pointed out that the state profited twice: once when it received payment for food exports, and again when it collected customs duties when packets were mailed back.[62]

China's economic recovery was the primary reason for the end of "the mailbag rush." According to China Customs, by end of 1962, cloth rather than food made up the bulk of the packages, and in addition, customs officials began to enforce regulations more carefully, returning packages that exceeded the quota.[63] Yet another factor was politics. With the Socialist Education Campaign and its crackdowns on alleged corruption, the receipt of small packets—material proof of one's "overseas connections"—was not always welcome. According to a report in Hong Kong's *South China Morning Post*, people in China were asking their Hong Kong relatives not to send them too many packages, "to avoid being innocently involved in the campaign."[64] Yet packages continued to be sent after "the mailbag rush" ended; in April of 1966 a hawker in Sham Shui Po commented that he still posted about a dozen packets a day, stating that condensed milk, medicine, and clothing were still in strong demand, with certain areas lacking staples: peanut oil was needed in Hainan, and sugar in Shanghai and North China.[65]

But in the following months, as the Cultural Revolution developed, big-character posters sprung up at China Customs, condemning incoming packages. During subsequent years, the numbers of small packets continued to rise and fall. They increased with Cultural Revolution disruptions to the supply chain in 1967, but decreased with stricter customs enforcement and later policies of local revolutionary committees to forbid packages to landlords, rich peasants, counterrevolutionaries, bad elements, and rightists.[66] In these ways, the small-packet trade persisted as a barometer of China's economic and political conditions until October 15, 1970, when—coincident with the opening of the Canton Trade Fair—parcel post between Hong Kong and China was reopened. Then, following international standards, senders could mail bigger packages of up to twenty-two pounds.[67]

MATERIAL PROPAGANDA

When the China Travel Service's Shanghai office explained the rationale for accepting small packets, it invoked the policy of the United Front and China's work with the diaspora. The Chinese state sought to maintain good relations with overseas Chinese, and indeed food packages were arriving not only from Hong Kong and Macau but also from places like Malaya and Singapore. Though Chinese in Hong Kong and Macau were officially "compatriots," they were often seen as a subset of the diaspora. Overseas Chinese and their dependents were given special status in mainland China; as an example, members of the diaspora had their own set of customs regulations applied to their baggage.[68]

Bao'an County's newsletter for the diaspora, *Bao'an Village Dispatch* (Bao'an xiangxun), reveals how official propaganda rested on addressing material conditions, especially those related to everyday life. The newsletter is full of stories of people coming back to visit their relatives, with one explicitly about two brothers who, after visiting their old mother, vow never to be duped by Hong Kong rumors again. Taken together, the stories paint a happy portrait of Bao'an in 1958, just as it had established the first set of people's communes. The newsletter describes life in the communes, where daycare and elder care abound, impeccably clean canteens feature flowers and poetry, and visitors eat for free. It also details the lifestyles of dependents and returnees, who labor only if it suits them. Of central import was the preservation of remittances and property, for part of the newsletter's agenda was to encourage visitors not only to come home but also to make investments in their native villages.[69]

Throughout, *Bao'an Village Dispatch* paid great attention to commodities available in the collective. Commune members spend their pay in a flourishing village market to buy printed calico, clothing, shoes, and daily use items. In Shenzhen Commune, the children wear new clothes. A cadre at Nantou Commune asserts that children have two *liang* of pork every other day, and at its Xixiang Kindergarten students are having porridge with pork bones. In Niuhu New Village's canteen, members eat vegetables and get fish nine times a month, pork twice, tofu seven times, and beef four times; its cooperative store stocks salt fish, sauces, cigarettes, alcohol, milk, and school supplies. In Hubei Village, the canteen's convenience store offers Cantonese favorites like roast duck, cold cuts, pork, and dog meat.[70] Never does the text refer to the revolution, the party, or Mao; instead it describes children as the "motherland's successors" and extols the realization of ancient virtues like filial piety.[71]

But these overseas visitors were most likely taken to exemplars, to model kindergartens and canteens. In January of 1959, the official newspaper *Bao'an News* (Bao'an bao) reported that the Bao'an people's commune party committee was promoting the use of sweet potatoes, bran husks, rice-rinsing water, and tofu dregs as food substitutes.[72] A few months later, in April of 1959, Bao'an's First Party Secretary Li Fulin recorded occurrences of edema, prolapsed uteruses, and even starvation. In 1960, Buji Village had seventy-one cases of starvation-related illnesses, including forty-two of edema and ten of prolapsed uteruses.[73] The internal newsletter *Bao'an Report* (Bao'an tongxun), primarily focused on rice paddy production, revealed the problems of the local cadre in 1961: peasants were eager to engage in sweet potato sidelines, manure was in short supply and leading to conflicts, rice plants fared poorly after a recent typhoon, and no one wanted to be a cadre. Signs of discontent were manifest: commune members complained of working without food, many subsisted on meager diets of thin rice porridge, and some were running away.[74]

These reports, authored by Bao'an County's party committee, came just as "the mailbag rush" took off. In Nantou's Xinwei Brigade, commune members described theirs to be a "miserable village . . . Now there are only two roads to take: one is to move to other places, the other is to escape." In Longgang's Longdong Brigade, the peasants reportedly said, "We would rather be a dog elsewhere than a man in Chigang Village," and many tried to escape. In Henggang Commune's Xintang Brigade, an old peasant surnamed Liao leveled an accusation: "You cadres play tricks to underestimate the output and increase the task later on; the commune members eat little, and Wutong Mountain will be trodden bare."[75] Indeed, old Liao's prophesy came true the following year: Hong Kong recorded over 142,000 illegal immigrants, many of whom climbed over Wutong Mountain, known in Hong Kong as "China Mountain."[76]

These three levels of reportage, from overseas Chinese propaganda to official newspapers to internal reports, demonstrate the contradiction between the external portrayal of material plenty and the reality of scarcity and privation. Visitors were aware of this contradiction long before, as the Hong Kong guidebooks make clear. In the 1956 anticommunist guide, each suggested gift for relatives and friends came with an annotation to explain why it was needed. There were shortages of cotton, wool, and oil, and "in cities, children younger than seven or eight have no idea what peanuts even are." Addressing its readers directly, the guidebook noted, "You are like a person who 'brings coal in the snow.'" The final pages of the guide, entitled "How to View Today's Mainland China," urged visitors to make direct material comparisons: Was employment better or worse than before? How did the lives of cadres compare with ordinary city residents? In the countryside, was the food and clothing of peasants better or worse than before?[77]

A second kind of contradiction existed between the Chinese state's propaganda to the outside world and the narrative it presented to a domestic audience. Internal propaganda painted a dismal portrait of Hong Kong society. Using a graphic of bigger fish eating smaller fish, *Bao'an News* had a special column on Hong Kong news, with a steady pattern of topics: unemployment and water shortages, family separations and suicide. To a greater readership, the *People's Daily* used Hong Kong to provide object lessons in political and material correctness; in one article from 1956, a spy from Hong Kong attempted to bribe a young girl with a fountain pen, and in another report from 1964, a young woman in the divided border village of Sha Tau Kok (Shatoujiao) refused an arranged marriage with a Hong Kong man in favor of a suitor on the mainland side.[78] By the Cultural Revolution, outside objects were vilified, either for originating from a capitalist economy or for representing bourgeois desire. In 1967, at Man Kam To (Wenjindu), the agricultural border crossing where livestock were driven across a bridge into Hong Kong, the people's militia denounced a gift of honeysuckle tea and watermelons Hong Kong laborers left in the freight yard, holding a public criticism of the "sugar-coated bullets." In 1968, a member of a production team's revolutionary committee was criticized for allowing his grandmother to keep a plastic spittoon from Hong Kong; he was reprimanded in public that this was "an enemy situation, class struggle in daily life."[79] From luxury goods like the fountain pen to daily use items like a plastic container, outside objects contradicted the virtue of socialist austerity. In Cultural Revolution struggle sessions, personal possessions could become markers of class.

But the two-pound food package persisted as a potent form of material propaganda. It was possible for the *People's Daily* to denounce the temptation of luxury or attack the falsity of bourgeois desires, but food shortages challenged the very legitimacy of the regime. In April of 1961, a Hong Kong delegation to Shenzhen was entertained with Chinese opera and propaganda films, and told during the festivities that "the practice of posting food parcels to China was unwelcome ... [and] that this aid was not necessary." To the contrary: during its famine, China sent rice as food aid across the border, citing "the motherland's concern" for compatriots in the face of typhoons and floods. However, even Hong Kong's left-wing journalists and trade union leaders were receiving letters from relatives in China asking for food and

FIGURE 6.3. Mailing small packets at the Kowloon Post Office. "Food Parcels to Red China" (1961), Hong Kong: British Pathé.

relating their suffering from malnutrition and its attendant diseases.[80] In a 1963 summary report, Zhao Ziyang estimated that in some Guangdong work units, as many as 70 to 80 percent of cadres received food packages, condemning a "Hong Kong wind" in which people's "bodies [were] in the motherland but [their] hearts [were] in Hong Kong."[81]

The issue of food relief became an international concern. British officials, American officials, and the International Red Cross all wished to organize more intensive forms of famine relief. In January of 1961, Chiang Kai-shek started to campaign for an international effort, a ratcheting-up of a small-scale program Taiwan had launched in 1959 to drop food packages over South China.[82] Earlier Nationalist Chinese airdrops had included—in addition to propaganda leaflets—grain and cloth; thread and needles; towels, socks, and vests; and combs and soap.[83] But British authorities stressed the need to maintain the status quo, warning the American consulate that if a larger and US-sponsored program were to be launched, China might close off the small-packet system altogether, and the Hong Kong population—for whom the food parcels "represent[ed] a tangible means of helping their relations on the Mainland"—would blame both the Americans and the Hong Kong government.[84] The small packets were seen as the politically correct compromise, and as traffic increased, the Hong Kong Post set up special sections to handle the flood of food packages and assigned extra personnel.[85]

At the height of China's famine, small packets were indeed a compromise on both sides of the border. At the border, the flow of baggage carried into Hong Kong and packages mailed from Hong Kong became one and the same, as an estimated one in three border-crossers went straight to the Shenzhen or Zhangmutou (Dongguan) post offices to mail food into the interior. In the same way that some calculated the fat content of pork versus beef, others choose what to mail based on what items incurred the lowest customs duties. Low-tax items like rice crusts and breadcrumbs proved so popular that the price of rice crusts in Hong Kong soared. China Customs estimated that for 1960, the average traveler from Hong Kong to China carried over 150 pounds of food, rising to 175 pounds in 1961 and totaling 30,000 tons of food that year.[86] These solo burdens are illustrated by newsreels of the Kowloon-Canton Railway at Chinese New Year: people boarded the train in Hong Kong balancing numerous bundles on shoulder poles, often with the aid of porters.[87]

Outside objects, as baggage and as packages, were at once personal and collective. On an individual level, the material goods they contained were everyday, grassroots, and small-scale. But in the aggregate, material things from the outside had an impact, appearing in Chinese markets and shops in the 1950s and providing a lifeline to relatives and friends in the early 1960s. Outside objects remind us that the material culture of the Mao era includes not only the homespun items of domestic production and the commodities of China's light industry but also a larger landscape of pre-1949 objects, imported goods, and things carried and mailed. In the form of "small packets," they spoke back to socialist China's persistent narrative of prosperity, providing material propaganda that could be more powerful than words.

NOTES

1 Hong Kong Public Records Office (henceforth HKPRO), HKMS 158-1-214, January 1962. (HKMS stands for Hong Kong Manuscript Series.)
2 HKPRO, HKMS 158-1-214, April 1961. Statistics on the Hong Kong side do not match those published on the China side. For example, only 560,000 food packages are recorded for 1961. *Jiulong haiguan zhi* [Gazetteer of Kowloon Customs] (Guangzhou: Guangdong Renmin Chubanshe, 1993), 214.
3 Julie Hessler, *A Social History of Soviet Trade: Trade Policy, Retail Practices, and Consumption, 1917–1953* (Princeton, NJ: Princeton University Press, 2004), 319–20.
4 Elena Osokina, *Our Daily Bread* (Armonk, NY: M. E. Sharpe, 2001), 95; Anna Krylova and Elena Osokina, "People and Things under Socialism," *Soviet and Post-Soviet Review* 42 (2016): 147–51.
5 Edith Sheffer, *Burned Bridge: How East and West Germans Made the Iron Curtain* (Oxford: Oxford University Press, 2011), 52.

6   Bernard Kahn and Joseph A. Rosen, *Report on the Activities of the Joint Distribution Committee* (Chicago: United Jewish Campaign and Joint Distribution Committee, 1927), 13; Oscar Handlin, *A Continuing Task: The American Jewish Joint Distribution Committee: 1914–1964* (New York: Random House, 1964), 44–45.
7   Carolyn Hughes Crowley, "Aid in Small Boxes," Smithsonian.com, April 30, 2001.
8   Osokina, *Our Daily Bread*, 122.
9   Jonathan R. Zatlin, *The Currency of Socialism: Money and Political Culture in East Germany* (Cambridge: Cambridge University Press, 2007).
10 Treaty Series No. 16 (1898), "Convention Between the United Kingdom and China Respecting an Extension of Hong Kong" (London: Her Majesty's Stationery Office, December 1898), 1.
11 *Jiulong haiguan zhi*, 178–79.
12 Hong Kong University Oral History Archives, Oral History no. 38, 2002.
13 D. W. MacIntosh, *Policing Hong Kong* (Hong Kong: n.p., 1952).
14 *Xianggang Jiulong Xinjie lüxing shouce* (Hong Kong: Huaqiao Ribao Chubanshe, 1952), 97.
15 Hong Kong Annual Departmental Reports, Commissioner of Police, 1954–1955, 50; Hong Kong Annual Departmental Reports, Director of Immigration, 1961–62/1962–63, 9; 1964/65, 3.
16 Director of Immigration, 1961–62/1962–63, 24.
17 *Jiulong haiguan zhi*, 180; *Huanxiang xuzhi* [Instructions for returning to the village] (Hong Kong: Xinwanbao, 1956), 21.
18 Commissioner of Police, 1955–1956, 87–88.
19 Director of Immigration, 1964–65, 8.
20 Laura Madokoro, "Borders Transformed: Sovereign Concerns, Population Movements, and the Making of Territorial Frontiers in Hong Kong, 1949–1967," *Journal of Refugee Studies* 25, no. 3 (2012): 419–20.
21 Catherine R. Schenk, "Hong Kong's Economic Relations with China, 1949–55: Blockade, Embargo, and Financial Controls," in *Hong Kong and Modern China: Interaction and Reintegration*, edited by Pui-tak Lee (Hong Kong: Hong Kong University Press, 2005), 199–218.
22 Leung Yuk Jan, retired oyster sauce shop owner, May 24, 2010, Hong Kong Voices Oral History Archives, www.hkmemory.hk.
23 Schenk, "Hong Kong's Economic Relations," 212–14.
24 Li Kit Fai, chairman of the Fruit and Vegetable Trade Workers Union, April 3, 2011, Hong Kong Voices Oral History Archives, www.hkmemory.hk.
25 *Jiulong haiguan zhi*, 180.
26 Director of Immigration, 1961–62, 32.
27 Interview in New Haven, CT, January 22, 2019.
28 *Huanxiang xuzhi*, 2–3.
29 *Huanxiang fangang xuzhi* [Instructions for returning to the village and coming back to Hong Kong] (Macau: Ao'men Xi'nan Chubanshe, 1956), 5–7.
30 *Huixiang zhinan* [Guide for returning to the village] (Hong Kong: Da Kung Pao, 1958), 4, 11; *Huanxiang*, 20–21.
31 *Huanxiang xuzhi*, 4.

32 *Huanxiang xuzhi*, 8–9, 42–43.
33 *Huanxiang xuzhi*, 11–12.
34 *Huanxiang fangang xuzhi*, 1–3, 26–27.
35 *Huanxiang fangang xuzhi*, 29–32.
36 Shanghai Municipal Archive (henceforth SMA), B170-3-344-10, 3–12.
37 Philip Thai, *China's War on Smuggling: Law, Economic Life, and the Making of the Modern State, 1842–1965* (New York: Columbia University Press, 2018).
38 *Jiulong haiguan zhi*, 185–86.
39 *Internal Reference*, November 2, 1956, 75–76.
40 *Internal Reference*, April 18, 1956, 396–97.
41 Nan Zhaoxu, *Shenzhen jiyi: 1949–2009* [Shenzhen memory: 1949–2009] (Shenzhen: Shenzhen Baoye Chubanshe, 2009), 60, 70.
42 Zhou Xun, *Forgotten Voices of Mao's Great Famine, 1948–1962: An Oral History* (New Haven, CT: Yale University Press, 2013), 208–9.
43 Lee Kam-yung, marine policeman, Hong Kong Heritage Project, Interview No. 1420.
44 Lee Lai, owner of a writing stall, May 25, 2011, Hong Kong Voices Oral History Archives, www.hkmemory.hk.
45 HKPRO, HKRS 934-8-112.
46 *Hong Kong Post Office Guide*, September 1961.
47 HKPRO, HKRS 70-2-217, HKMS 158-1-176, HKMS 158-1-214. Parcel post was reinstated in 1970.
48 HKPRO, HKMS 158-1-214.
49 *Jiulong haiguan zhi*, 213.
50 SMA B170-2-769-12.
51 *Jiulong haiguan zhi*, 213.
52 HKPRO, HKMS 158-1-76.
53 HKPRO, HKRS 70-2-217.
54 HKPRO, HKMS 158-1-176, HKMS 158-1-214, HKRS 70-2-217. The average cost of shipping a small packet in 1961 was two Hong Kong dollars.
55 HKPRO, HKMS 158-1-214. Also *Jiulong haiguan zhi*, 214.
56 HKPRO, HKRS 70-2-217.
57 HKPRO, HKRS 158-1-214.
58 *Jiulong haiguan zhi*, 214.
59 HKPRO, HKRS 70-2-217.
60 SMA B6-2-425, 1.
61 Union News Agency, "Sending Food Parcels to Relieve Food Shortage on China Mainland," *Union Research Service* 22, no. 12 (February 10, 1961): 177–94.
62 British Pathé, "Food Parcels Sent to Red China," 1961; British Pathé, "Hong Kong: Food Parcels to China," 1961.
63 *Jiulong haiguan zhi*, 214.
64 "More Food Packets Sent to China," *South China Morning Post*, December 10, 1963.
65 K. F. Lam, "Parcel Post Trade Drops," *Hong Kong Standard*, April 4, 1966.
66 *Jiulong haiguan zhi*, 214–15.
67 "Parcel Post to China Will Resume Today," *South China Morning Post*, October 15, 1970; *Post Office Guide*, January 1972, 132.

68 *Jiulong haiguan zhi*, 185–89.
69 *Bao'an xiangxun* 1, no. 1 (1958): 4–5.
70 *Bao'an xiangxun* 1, no. 1 (1958): 1–3, 5–8.
71 *Bao'an xiangxun* 1, no. 1 (1958): 6–7.
72 *Bao'an bao*, January 3, 1959; Nan Zhaoxu, 33.
73 Nan Zhaoxu, 49–50.
74 *Bao'an tongxun*, 1961.
75 *Bao'an tongxun* 59 (1961): 64, 71.
76 Director of Immigration, 1965–66, 8.
77 *Huanxiang fangang xuzhi*, 26–28, 36–44.
78 *People's Daily*, April 24, 1956; February 19, 1964.
79 Nan Zhaoxu, 240, 259, 19.
80 HKPRO, HKMS 158-1-214.
81 *Zhongnan tongxun*, Vol. 21, July 11, 1963.
82 HKPRO, HKMS 158-1-214.
83 "Fujian sheng Jinjiang zhuanshu gong'anchu guanyu jinnian yilai diren 'xinzhan' huodong qingkuang he jinhou yijian de baogao," *Internal Reference*, June 29, 1957. See also British Pathé, "Formosa Food Air Drop on Chinese Mainland," 1961.
84 HKPRO, HKMS 158-1-214.
85 *Gongshan ribao*, January 8, 1961.
86 *Jiulong haiguan zhi*, 181.
87 Reuters, "New Year Gifts from Hong Kong," 1963.

7 THE PROBLEMATICS OF PLENTY

LAURENCE CODERRE

PHOTOGRAPHS OF SHOPPERS PERUSING MERCHANDISE WERE A staple of China's premier, internationally circulating pictorial magazines throughout the Mao era. Many of these images seem intended to show the world the power of New China's "civilizing" magnanimity. *Nationality Pictorial* (Minzu huabao), first issued in 1955, for example, consistently published images juxtaposing great numbers of consumer commodities, purportedly produced in technologically advanced factories, with ethnic minorities sartorially marked as "backward" and "other."[1] In instances in which shoppers are unmarked, too—presumed to be both urban and Han—abundance forms the focus. Among other things, such photographs promulgated the notion that the party-state's beneficence could and should be measured in the newfound material abundance it brought to far-flung places and coastal cities alike. Such pictures were not meant to highlight the act of consumption ostensibly in the offing or even the commercial realm in which they are set. Rather, they were intended to draw attention to the conditions of production—touted under the banner of CCP-led "socialist construction"—that made such plenty possible in the first place. In this sense, they are perfect examples of a "productivist" move wherein "production" becomes an alibi, if not an outright justification, for all manner of otherwise problematic consumer behaviors.[2] In these images, retail is putatively transformed into an ode to labor, not an exercise in whetting desire.

Mao-era photo essays and spreads were particularly effective at enacting this inverted set of associations through the further juxtaposition of production and shopping in quasi-narrative form. Consider "Prices Are Stable, The Market Flourishes" (Wujia wending shichang fanrong), a six-page spread in *China Pictorial* (Renmin huabao at the time), published in late 1970.[3] The term "market" (*shichang*) is somewhat misleading, here: it is the market of "supermarket," a place where commodities are bought and sold, not the market of "market economy." Indeed, if "prices are stable," as the title contends, it is because they have been fixed by the centralized economic plan; their stability is a foregone conclusion. The point of the photo spread, then,

FIGURE 7.1. Enamelware. "Prices Are Stable, The Market Flourishes," *China Pictorial* (Renmin huabao), no. 11 (1970): 36.

is to document the "flourishing" availability of consumer commodities brought about by the plan and, by extension, the CCP's stewardship of the citizenry's material welfare. That said, only five of the piece's twelve photos explicitly depict consumer marketplaces. (Two more do so somewhat ambiguously.)[4] We see shoppers—all, but for a small child, dressed in shades of blue, gray, and white—purchasing colorfully packaged canned goods, eggs, fruit, enamelware (figure 7.1), and bolt cloth. In each scene, customers are diligently attended by store personnel, aiding them to wade through the staggering number of goods that surround them. Tin-can pyramids reach for the ceiling; enamel basins overtake a wall; mountains of fresh eggs threaten to spill off a counter. But these images of retail abundance do not stand alone: they are interrupted by a group of five pictures—four of which, unlike the aforementioned five, are in black-and-white—unquestionably set in production locales. There are mounds of commune vegetables (cabbages, eggplants, cucumbers, melons) (figure 7.2) and farm-raised shrimp. We are also treated to industrial settings: a large-scale bakery, a plastics factory, a textile plant.

FIGURE 7.2. Harvest. "Prices Are Stable, The Market Flourishes," *China Pictorial* (Renmin huabao), no. 11 (1970): 33.

Taken all together, the implication of these images is clear: the store shelves are stocked as never before because production is finally in the tireless hands of the proletariat. As the short blurb accompanying the photo spread puts it, stable prices and a flourishing market "demonstrate the unparalleled superiority of the socialist system."[5] This is what progress looks like.

But progress is not risk-free. Quite the contrary—it is fraught with new perils. In this particular case, demonstrations of abundance in the productivist mode, as evidence of historical progress, must continuously be distinguished from spectacles of consumerist excess and/or commodity fetishism. Attempts of this sort to subsume consumption under production, rendering it politically acceptable in the process, teeter on the edge of disaster out of necessity, since they are predicated on precisely that which they would deny: the powerful desirability of consumer commodities. This is the crux of the "problematics of plenty"—the implicit challenges posed to the Chinese socialist project by and through invocations of material abundance—at play in the Mao era writ large.

ASCETICISM

Much of our collective understanding of the Mao period is structured by a notion of lack. Indeed, since the publication of economist János Kornai's analysis of the "classical" communist system in 1992, if not before, the political economy of Soviet-style socialism has been axiomatically defined in terms of material shortage, rather than plenty.[6] Important scholars of socialism and postsocialism, spearheaded by anthropologist Katherine Verdery, have gone on to argue that the failure of Communist Bloc regimes to consistently meet their citizens' desires for consumer goods accounts in no small part for these regimes' ultimate demise.[7] More recent research has highlighted the importance of overstocking and hoarding in the late Soviet period—anthropologist Serguei Oushakine contends that it was characterized by a "storage economy" as much as it was by a "shortage economy"—as well as the persistent articulation of pleasure, luxury, and happiness to consumption under the auspices of Leninist party-states.[8] Still, empty shelves and endless queues remain the most enduring hallmarks of socialist consumer culture, both in and beyond academia.

A general lack of consumer goods was never itself a goal of the socialist system enacted in the PRC or, for that matter, in the Soviet Union and its satellites, however. As the historian of the Stalinist period Sheila Fitzpatrick puts it, "While the Soviet regime may be said to have discouraged consumerism by keeping goods scarce, it was not ideologically on the side of asceticism. On the contrary, future socialism was always conceived in terms of plenty: according to the regime's Socialist Realist perception of the world, the meagre supply of goods in the present was only a harbinger of the abundance to come."[9]

In other words, while the system for allocating goods may well have been designed in the interests of fulfilling the needs and desires of a chosen elite (the *nomenklatura* in the USSR and the Eastern Bloc and those with access to "special supply" (*tegong*) outlets in the PRC), any resulting lack for the general populace was understood as something to be overcome rather than praised. Consider that while communism was imagined as commodity-free—unlike socialism, which had to negotiate the commodity's continued existence[10]—it was most assuredly *not* imagined to be free of the creature comforts currently available to the elite. Rather, communism would involve such general prosperity and abundance that restricted, present-day luxuries would become commonplace, to the benefit of all. Communism was regularly conjured in China as elsewhere as, in the words of Slavicist Helena Goscilo, a "Cornucopia-Utopia" and an age of plenty.[11]

And yet, it is the specter of material lack that lingers, arguably even more keenly felt in China than the former Soviet Union and Eastern Bloc. So much of the reform agenda since the late 1970s has been understood as a break from the past, especially in relation to consumerism. It is not for nothing that a key edited volume at the turn of the millennium characterized the increasing range of permissible consumer behaviors in the 1990s as a "consumer revolution" very much on the order of the political and social revolution of 1949.[12] To be sure, the changes in Chinese urban standards of living have been staggering over the past forty years; it is not my intention to minimize the significance of such changes. Nor indeed do I want to downplay the very real hardships of many, if not most, people created by a climate of (forced) egalitarian austerity and, yes, the poverty of the Mao era. My immediate point here, however, is that today's discourse of material abundance and variety is implicitly rooted in a notion of past deprivation and individual sacrifice for the sake of the collective. Over and above the realities of historical scarcity, in other words, there is a presentist benefit to remembering the past starkly.

That (imagined and historical) starkness has sometimes been characterized in terms of a specifically "Maoist asceticism," a nebulous moral doctrine of self-abnegation. In *Appetites*, for example, anthropologist Judith Farquhar frames her discussion of food and sex in the 1990s as part of a broader "shift from Maoist asceticism to capitalist boom," enacted throughout the decade.[13] Farquhar's object of study is the endpoint of this transition, but what exactly is the "Maoist asceticism" whence it begins? What is it that is ostensibly being left behind? Although Farquhar leaves her definition of the concept and its particularly Weberian overtones unexplored, it is clear from her general approach that its essence involves a moralistic denial of individual desires in the realm of material things and creature comforts:

> Within the culture of Maoism, which became well established in the 1950s and reached its greatest degree of ideological ambition in the late 1960s and 1970s, it was much more proper to speak of past suffering (in the old society), future utopia (when communism is achieved), and, in the present, work, production, and service. For at least two decades, the collective priorities of building Chinese socialism ruled all the surfaces of life. Although the everyday lives of quite material bodies persisted, of course, and wishes and discomforts could be spoken of casually and privately, the existence and indulgence of non-collective appetites were almost an embarrassment.[14]

The defining characteristic of "Maoist asceticism" becomes a form of quasi-sublimation, wherein personal desires are directed into the kinds of labor required for the emancipation of the masses to come, that is, communism.

This general understanding of the function of the ascetic in Chinese socialist construction predates Farquhar's intervention, of course. One of its most fulsome explorations and theorizations appears in the work of historian Maurice Meisner, who made it very clear that the doctrine of sacrifice found at the heart of the Chinese revolution was never intended to be an end in itself.[15] It was, rather, merely a pathway to expediting future success. Indeed, it is precisely the instrumental nature of this individual self-denial that led to the (retrospective, academic) invocation of the ascetic in the first place. And on this point, it is worth noting just how incongruous the notion of asceticism really is in this context. Mao-era slogans regularly extolled the benefits of frugality and thrift (*qinjian jieyue*) and decried wasteful extravagance (*puzhang langfei*), but one would be hard pressed to find many discursive references to "the ascetic" and/or "asceticism" (*kuxing* and *kuxingzhuyi*) per se. In other words, to deploy the concept of asceticism—"Maoist" or otherwise—in reference to this time and place is something of an anachronism, one that implicitly links Mao-era mores to religious practices eschewing worldly goods and pleasures.

For Meisner, at least, this linkage is purposeful and specific. It harkens back to Weber's analysis of Calvinism, the Protestant ethic, and bourgeois morality under industrial capitalism.[16] It must be said that the structural analogy between Calvinist modes of worldly restraint and abnegation and Mao-era exhortations in favor of (temporary) thrift does work uncommonly well: just as Weber's Protestants are called upon to sacrifice present comfort in the name of achieving a future paradise, that is, Christian heaven, after death, the Chinese masses must subtend their contemporary individual desires in the name of achieving a future classless society, that is, a communist utopia. As I read Meisner, however, we might also extend the similarities between the two moralizing systems beyond such temporal parallels to the nature of the labor prescribed in the present and the formation of idealized Chinese socialist subjectivities. To wit,

> the ascetic values which the model "red and expert" [*you hong you zhuan*] exemplifies are essentially the early bourgeois values which both Marx and Weber identified with the initial phases of modern capitalist economic development. If Chinese Communist ideologists choose to describe these values as "socialist" or "Communist," this does not make them so, nor does it in any way mitigate their fundamentally repressive character; in original Marxian terms, these values can be described as a reflection of conditions of

"alienated labor." That the "red and expert" prototype combines early bourgeois ascetic values with "post-bourgeois" Marxist goals is one of the curious paradoxes of modern Chinese history and one of the paradoxes of the history of Marxist theory in the modern world.[17]

This paradox may be explained, if not resolved, by acknowledging the extent to which the PRC's economy—especially in its emphasis on heavy industry—inherited its structures and metrics for "catching up to the West" from early industrial capitalism and, later, Fordism via the USSR.[18] In other words, we might find an explanation for the peculiarities of "Maoist asceticism" in the political economic foundations of the Chinese Revolution's modernization discourse. In doing so, we would get away from nebulous invocations of religiosity and begin to move toward a more considered discussion of labor, its forms, and the ideological and moral implications of those forms.

Needless to say, this is a call for research well beyond the scope of this chapter, which focuses on the complexities *effaced by* the notion of asceticism as applied to the Mao era, namely, that there is a considerable difference between choosing to deny oneself pleasure in the present for the purposes of an imagined, utopian future—an issue of morality—and being unable to access such pleasures at all—a function of present scarcity. The former requires self-abnegation on the part of the individual, would-be consumer; the latter does not. The former can therefore be characterized in terms of personal virtue, while the latter is evidence of a systemic problem. The resulting reality for the individual may be the same in each case, that is, material lack and desire unfulfilled, but the implications for the regime, ostensibly in charge of consumer product distribution, could not be more different.[19] Framing responsibility for material lack as a matter of affirmative, personal choice lets the system—and those in charge of it—off the hook. In the context of a teleological understanding of historical development, moreover, personal sacrifice not only gestures toward a future utopia; it also becomes evidence of sociohistorical progress, away from poverty and toward plenty. It is this narrative and its attendant associations that we see reproduced in the official cultural sphere.

SACRIFICE AS DUAL PROGRESS

On July 1, 1974, two brand-new Beijing Film Studio productions premiered in major Chinese urban centers. One was a full-length military feature entitled

The Scout (Zhenchabing). The other was a film adaptation of the eponymous Hunanese flower-drum opera *(huaguxi) Delivering Goods on the Road* (hereafter, *Delivering*) (Songhuo lushang), a work concerned with dangers on a very different kind of battlefield. Specifically, it focuses on the role of salespeople—in this case, saleswomen—in the ideological education of their clientele as to the forms of consumption permissible under socialism. *Delivering* was not the first cultural product to tackle such issues, nor would it be the last. It joined the cinematic ranks of *What's Eating You?* (Manyi bu manyi) (1963) and *Red Basket* (Hongse beilou) (1965), among others.[20] More importantly, *Delivering* built on the recent success of *Xiangyang Store* (Xiangyang shangdian), a nationally promoted northern regional opera *(pingju)*,[21] and preceded a collection of short stories, *Storm at the Counter* (Guitai fengbo), ostensibly written by workers at Shanghai Number One Department Store, by just a few weeks.[22] These works were then promptly pressed into the service of a mass mobilization campaign, extolling the virtues of political economic study and decrying the capitalist-restorationist threat posed by the commodity-form and commodity exchange in 1975. An essay considering *Delivering* from this vantage point, for example, appeared in the Chinese Communist Party's theoretical organ *Red Flag* (Hongqi) in the spring of 1975.[23] My own interest in *Delivering* here is less in its political economic implications vis-à-vis the commodity per se, however, than it is in its engagement with the ideological dangers posed by the prospect of material bounty.

Delivering itself is quite straightforward, depicting the interactions of three characters: an experienced saleswoman at the local commune's cooperative store *(gongxiaoshe)*, Fang Xiuchun, on her mobile route; a recent addition to the store's workforce and Fang's new partner, Young Lan; and a commune member/customer of poor peasant background, Mother He. Thanks to the commune's many bumper harvests, Mother He finds herself flush with cash in advance of her son's wedding, and she promptly goes on a shopping spree. In addition to throwing the newlyweds a large banquet of pork, chicken, and lamb, she also plans on setting her son and his bride up in style. Her shopping list therefore includes four pairs of nylon socks, four Dacron shirts (two for men and two for women), one georgette scarf, two embroidered pillowcases, two bedsheets, two quilt covers, one red brocade bed curtain, one women's watch (from Shanghai), and fade-resistant, durable wool yarn (also from Shanghai) in red and brown (2.5 *jin* of each).[24]

Putting the impressiveness of Mother He's purchasing power aside for the moment—Young Lan estimates the total in the five- to six-hundred *kuai* range—that the list specifies *Dacron* shirts and *Shanghai*-branded products marks Mother He as a savvy consumer as well as a prolific one.[25] New to her responsibilities of ideological policing, Young Lan sells Mother He what she wants, the only limitation being the size of Young Lan's carrying pole; she is referred to the cooperative store for some of the more expensive items on her list, like the watch, for example. When Fang Xiuchun hears of her colleague's big sale, she chides her for not talking Mother He out of her intended purchases, whereupon the two retail workers chase Mother He down, show her the error of her ways, and happily process her returned goods, once she sees the light. Taken in its entirety, *Delivering* is a tale of crisis doubly averted: on the one hand, Young Lan's mistaken belief that her role as saleswoman is to satisfy her customers' desires, whatever they may be, is corrected; on the other hand, Mother He will never hold her lavish banquet or give her fashionable bridal gifts, saving both herself and those around her from bourgeois taint.

The combination of these twin "successes" comfortably situates *Delivering* within the discourse of self-abnegation and sacrifice. It is crucial that she actually give something up. Indeed, the film's entire premise is that Mother He *could* acquire all of her desired goods, if not for the political vigilance of the heroic saleswoman Fang Xiuchun. Mother He is *able* to buy everything on her extraordinary list—she has both the money, that is, the purchase power, to do so and, crucially, access to plentiful goods. Mother He's money would be useless to her in her pursuit of four Dacron shirts, say, if her commune's cooperative store did not actually have Dacron shirts in stock. In fact, much of the global popular imaginary of socialist consumption concerns precisely the kind of frustrated desire that *Delivering* pointedly avoids. There is never any suggestion that the goods Young Lan does not have on her person as a mobile saleswoman will likewise be unavailable at the physical store; there is no room for empty shelves here. On the contrary, every desired product is assumed to be easily at hand, thanks to one of the commune's official retail channels. No need to wait around or marshal one's network of personal connections and black-market hookups. We the audience know this because, among other things, Young Lan makes the original sale; some of Mother He's desires are, albeit for a very short time, satisfied. It is only after the fact that her desires are deemed problematic, at which point they are not so much frustrated as excised and dissolved en bloc thanks to Fang Xiuchun's powerful ideological teachings.

Both Mother He's monetary wealth and the cooperative store's implicitly varied and abundant consumer commodities are rooted in the commune's recent agricultural surplus, made possible by a series of bumper harvests (*da fengshou*). As a poor peasant, Mother He is necessarily dependent for the bulk of her income on the commune of which she is a member.[26] That income corresponds to her share of the money accrued by that commune in the sale of whatever remains of its crops after meeting its responsibilities to its members and the party-state. This remainder is sold to the cities in commodified form in exchange for cash and/or factory consumer goods made available for individual purchase by commune members. Accordingly, most everything in this system depends on the size of the commune's harvest, and the cash burning a hole in Mother He's pocket must be understood as emblematic of a (purportedly) more general phenomenon of rising standards of living in the countryside. If Mother He has the wherewithal to throw a big wedding bash, then others must be riding high on the proverbial hog, too. Her success means everyone else's success, which ultimately signals socialism's superiority over capitalism.

This last systemic association is facilitated by a number of factors, not least of which is the repeatedly drawn contrast between Mother He's (and by extension, the rest of the commune's) present prosperity and the suffering experienced by poor peasants in "the old society." In fact, the underlying blame for Mother He's ideologically problematic consumption practices is laid at the feet of the former landlord class. In the past, throwing a wedding necessarily meant financial hardship. As Fang Xiuchun tells Mother He when trying to get her to change her ways, "In the old society, the poor were forced to borrow in order to treat their guests. The debt collectors were at the door before the wedding ceremony was over." Mother He agrees that there is no comparison with today. "Now that we poor and lower-middle peasants are in charge of our own affairs, when our kids get married, we can do things in style and set our sights higher." This kind of ambition does not do the peasantry proud, however. "Mother, how can throwing a wedding in the wasteful and extravagant style of landlords and capitalists be setting the sights of the poor and lower-middle peasants higher?"[27] The implication is clear: just because Mother He finally has the wherewithal to act like the profligate spenders of old does not mean she should. New times call for new rituals of consumption alongside everything else. Where there was once wasteful extravagance, there must now be thrift and frugality; the true poor and lower-middle peasants prove their revolutionary bona fides through restraint and self-abnegation. If plenty signifies developmental progress of a measurable, material sort, the willingness to sacrifice the kinds of pleasures historically born of plenty becomes the mark of a person's political progress.

And yet, at the same time, Mother He's (momentary) ideological lapse is framed as an entirely predictable effect of the commune's underlying material abundance. Indeed, she is not alone in her errant ways. While Young Lan makes the original sale to Mother He, Fang Xiuchun has gone offstage to serve another customer. Veteran saleswoman that she is, Fang makes a point of engaging in some propaganda work in addition to fulfilling her customer's ideologically appropriate desires. As part of that process, as she informs Young Lan upon her return, she learns that some commune members are engaging in problematic forms of conspicuous consumption in the name of wedding planning. It is at this point that Young Lan realizes that she has made a mistake in acquiescing to Mother He's demands, and the saleswomen go after their customer to try to set things right. That they ultimately succeed in doing so should not distract us from the fact that the problem Mother He gives voice to and embodies is imagined as widespread and arguably systemic. Where there is abundance, there is a risk of returning to old forms of capitalist excess. In other words, there is a risk of capitalist restoration.[28] Abundance itself may be seen as a good thing—a sign of developmental progress—but it is not without its dangers, ones that can only be mitigated through propaganda work, including, on the metacinematic level, the promotion of cultural products like *Delivering* itself.

THE CART BEFORE THE HORSE

In an ironic twist, however, the very works meant to model consumer vigilance and other "correct" behaviors in the face of developmental progress qua prosperity necessarily foreground that which they would inveigh against. In seeking to distinguish between ideologically acceptable and unacceptable forms of consumption on screen, for example, *Delivering* raises the prospect that "transgressive" forms of conspicuous consumption will actually appeal to the audience. Insofar as this is a version of the age-old problem of "negative examples" (*fanmian jiaocai*), it is perhaps not surprising. The more consequential point is a related one: not only does *Delivering* conjure danger, as often happens, it also conjures the possibility or necessity of a sacrifice *from the audience*. It cannot do otherwise, for the film itself turns on the representation of material abundance and the very same pleasures that Mother He is browbeaten into giving up. More precisely, we might say that, just as a moral doctrine of self-sacrifice requires the possibility of giving something up in order to have meaning, the representation of revolutionary thrift and discipline likewise requires the representation of plenty *in the present* over and above the promise of a comfortable, utopian future. Following this thread to its logical end, then, it is not that the ideological dangers posed by material plenty require mitigation via the official cultural sphere. Rather, the cultural products deployed in the name of such mitigation constitute displays of abundance of the very sort they themselves purportedly combat.[29] Indeed, when there is a pervasive shortage of "real" consumer commodities in the present, representations of abundance may be the *only* forms of plenty available to sacrifice.

This points to a significant wrinkle in what is often taken to be a linear temporality of postponement. To be deemed intentional, delayed gratification requires the possibility of instant gratification. To the extent that so-called "Maoist asceticism" makes a virtue of poverty and lack, transforming systemic failure into personal morality in the process, it does so by invoking the specter of abundance today. Indeed, it is predicated on it. So much so, I would argue, that it produces and reproduces that (future) abundance—or its simulacrum—in the present precisely in order to deny it. It is not unlike the famous marshmallow test of behavioral psychology, in which young children are promised an additional sweet upon an adult's return, if and only if they refrain from eating the marshmallow they currently have.[30] The test is meant to determine the depths of the subject's self-control when left to her own devices; the longer the child waits to eat the sweet she has, the greater her purported ability to keep her drive for instant gratification in check. That the second marshmallow never materializes is irrelevant to the proper functioning of the experiment, but the first marshmallow is essential. No marshmallow, no test. Likewise, when sacrifice is understood as progress—progress being the eternal goal—one must provide in order to disown. Causality is reversed. All appearances to the contrary, it is not abundance that necessitates the production of a doctrine of self-abnegation. Self-abnegation necessitates the production of abundance now, precisely in order to deny oneself its would-be pleasures.

This inversion of apparent cause and effect is not restricted to narrative works like Delivering. Instead, Delivering and other cultural products of its kind speak to a more generalized and generalizable representational logic.[31] The paradox of abnegation is at the very heart of the problem attending plenty in the waning years of the Mao era writ large, insofar as it is rooted in the interplay of productivism and desire. In this sense, we must reckon with a problematics of plenty not only emblematized in imaginative narrative but also extending far beyond the limits of the strictly fictional. The photos at this chapter's opening are a case in point: they implicitly purport to document "reality," even as they participate in the production of plenty—in this case, as a visual trope—on which any doctrine of individual sacrifice must be predicated. Admittedly, the relationship between the photograph and "reality" is particularly fraught in the Mao period. As China media scholar Jie Li demonstrates, the evidentiary truth claim implicitly undergirding journalistic photography was deployed at times like the Great Leap Forward in ways that both materially exacerbated harmful party policies and highlighted the constructed nature of the "real."[32] The upshot is not that photographs of bumper harvests were "faked" or distorted "reality" but rather that they remade "reality"—albeit not necessarily in their own literal image—as they circulated. In this sense, while we can by no means approach such photos as transparent representations of historical conditions, they are not wholly removed from them either. At a minimum, they contributed to the making of a world in which visual access to and consumption of abundance was relatively common, even when—especially when—commodities were not. This access was facilitated by photographs as well as urban window displays, forms that themselves bear striking similarities to so-called "new New Year's prints" (xin nianhua).[33]

Popular in rural areas of the north in the late imperial period, *nianhua* were originally produced in accordance with the lunar new year, as their name implies, but they quickly came to encompass all manner of colorful prints devoted to the theme of bounty and prosperity.[34] Originally meant to circulate as auspicious visual markers, the *nianhua* genre was recast in the 1950s not as feudal or superstitious but as a distinctly "Chinese" form, of and for the masses. The well-documented generic tension between *nianhua* and calendar posters (*yuefenpai*) in the first decade of the PRC is a testament to the ideological stakes of invoking plenty under a socialist banner.[35] The latter was the province of bourgeois artists, who used beautiful women to sell cigarettes and pesticide, while the former could be used to promote the coming of material abundance as party-led progress. That these new *nianhua* trafficked in tropes of plenty—especially agricultural plenty—turned them into prime modes of visual consumption as well. Indeed, it seems likely that *nianhua* and *nianhua*-esque images structured the ways in which photographs of bumper harvests, during the Great Leap Forward and beyond, were ultimately seen and understood. That is to say, it is likely that *nianhua* informed the way photographs of abundance, fueled by the medium's implicit truth claim, helped remake "reality."

More generally, the deployment of such visual tropes alongside (and at times over and above) the expansion of commodity production resonates with the quasi-magical thinking that defined Soviet socialist realism as a representational mode greatly influential in the PRC. Soviet scholar Evgeny

Dobrenko's notion of socialist realism as a representational technology that *produces* socialism, rather than reflecting it, seems an apt way to think about displays of abundance as generative simulacra, for example.[36] On the other hand, there is something to be said about the particular mechanism I have examined here in relation to material plenty. If, as Fitzpatrick famously argues, socialist realism's "tendency to view the present through the prism of an imagined future" means that "a dry, half-dug ditch signified a future canal full of loaded barges,"[37] what are we to make of the choice, effectively, to conjure the bustling canal of the future outright? Despite their many similarities, the two approaches require very different things from the viewer: one requires imaginative production as a condition of partaking in the future, while the other requires only imaginative consumption. The latter brings with it a particular set of risks and rewards, for progress measured in demonstrable plenty sparks desire as surely as it demands sacrifice.

NOTES

1. This role is part and parcel of what Ralph Litzinger has called the "developmental double bind" facing minority groups in the PRC. Litzinger, *Other Chinas*, 225.
2. See Coderre, *Newborn Socialist Things*, chapter 3.
3. "Wujia wending shichang fanrong" [Prices are stable, the market flourishes], *Renmin huabao* [China pictorial], no. 11 (1970).
4. The first comprises two rows of shiny bicycles and motorcycles. Two small groups of people—one in the foreground and one in the background—examine the products carefully; a display of some sort appears on the far wall. This is, in all likelihood, a department store showroom, a conclusion supported by the large windows facing the street. It is not wholly inconceivable, however, that this is actually a depiction of quality control, rather than commerce, an ambiguity reinforced by this image's position, immediately before the five pictures of production, within the larger photo spread. The second ambiguous photograph, on the other hand, immediately follows the production pictures and focuses on an impressive array of Beijing ducks, hanging from hooks in the familiar way. Only one man—the chef, apparently—is shown in the frame.
5. "Wujia wending shichang fanrong," 35.
6. Kornai, *Socialist System*.
7. Verdery, *What Was Socialism*.
8. Oushakine, "Against the Cult of Things." See also Bren and Neuburger, *Communism Unwrapped*; and Crowley and Emily Reid, *Pleasures in Socialism*.
9. Sheila Fitzpatrick, "The Good Old Days," *London Review of Books* 25, no. 19 (2003): 19.
10. See Coderre, "A Necessary Evil."
11. Goscilo, "Luxuriating in Lack," 78.
12. Davis, *Consumer Revolution in Urban China*.
13. Farquhar, *Appetites*, 3.
14. Farquhar, *Appetites*, 3.

15 Meisner, "Utopian Goals."
16 Weber, *Protestant Ethic*.
17 Meisner, "Utopian Goals," 108.
18 On the latter, see Werner, "Global Fordism."
19 Ci Jiwei makes an analogous point: "It is only at the level of understanding that an ascetic life differs from an impoverished one. Asceticism makes poverty meaningful; communist asceticism, which treats itself as a means of bringing about utopia, makes poverty both meaningful and temporary—and hence all the more bearable." Ci, *Dialectic of the Chinese Revolution*, 157–58.
20 One could conceivably add *Sentinels under the Neon Lights* (Nihongdeng xia de shaobing) (1964) to this list as well.
21 Guo Qihong and Sha Hu, *Xiangyang shangdian* [Xiangyang store] (Beijing: Zhongguo Changpian Chubanshe, 1974).
22 Shanghaishi Di Yi Baihuo Shangdian Chuangzuozu, *Guitai fengbo* [Storm at the counter] (Shanghai: Shanghai Renmin Chubanshe, 1974).
23 Hu Rong, "Shangpin jiaohuan zhong liang zhong sixiang de douzheng—cong Hunan huaguxi *Songhuo lushang* tanqi" [The struggle between two kinds of thought on commodity exchange: A perspective from the Hunan flower-drum opera *Delivering Goods on the Road*], *Hongqi* [Red flag], no. 4 (1975).
24 Liu Guoxiang, *Songhuo lushang* (Hunan huaguxi) [*Delivering Goods on the Road* (a Hunan flower-drum opera)] (Beijing: Renmin Wenxue Chubanshe, 1974), 3–4.
25 Only the latter is deemed troubling in its echoes of landlord conspicuous consumption practices and wasteful rituals. See Gerth, *Unending Capitalism*, chapter 1.
26 At times of relative ideological thaw, peasants could also supplement their incomes with crops and livestock tended on private plots.
27 Liu, *Songhuo lushang*, 9.
28 As I have written elsewhere, this view is consistent with an understanding of the commodity-form, espoused at the end of the Cultural Revolution, wherein its dualistic nature as a combination of both exchange-value and use-value constituted a revisionist threat to Chinese socialism. See Coderre, "A Necessary Evil."
29 In this, we see an extension of the notion that Maoism produces its own enemies.
30 Walter Mischel, *The Marshmallow Test: Mastering Self-Control* (New York: Little, Brown & Co., 2014).
31 See, for example, Pang, "Colour and Utopia."
32 See Li, *Utopian Ruins*, chapter 3.
33 See Coderre, *Newborn Socialist Things*, chapter 3.
34 For an overview of popular print culture in the late Qing era, see Laing, *Selling Happiness*, 43–59.
35 On this tension and *nianhua* in the 1950s, see, among others, Hung, *Mao's New World*; Yao and Wang, "Miandui 'yuefenpai,'"; James Flath, *The Cult of Happiness: Nianhua, Art, and History in Rural North China* (Vancouver: University of British Columbia Press, 2004); Flath, "'It's a Wonderful Life,'"; and Laing, *Selling Happiness*, 223–34.
36 Dobrenko, *Political Economy of Socialist Realism*.
37 Fitzpatrick, "Becoming Cultured," 217.

8 NATIONALIZING FOOD PROVISION IN BEIJING

MADELEINE YUE DONG

ON JANUARY 15, 1956, AFTER SEVERAL WEEKS OF MOBILIZATION parades filled with drum beating, gong striking, and firecracker lighting throughout the city of Beijing, two hundred thousand people braved the bitter cold and gathered at Tiananmen Square to celebrate the completion of the Socialist Transformation (Shehuizhuyi Gaizao). The top leaders of the state—Mao Zedong, Liu Shaoqi, and Zhou Enlai—surveyed the crowds from the Gate of Heavenly Peace. Following the capital city's example, almost all the cities in China completed the Transformation by the end of the month, and January 1956 essentially marked the end of private ownership of businesses in all Chinese cities. Along with the confiscation of enterprises owned by foreigners and by the Nationalist state and its officials (from the late 1940s to the early 1950s) and the redistribution of land (1950–53), the abolition of private ownership in the cities was the third component of the nationalization of the whole economy.

The Transformation converted almost all of Beijing's industrial, handicraft, and commercial establishments to state or public-private joint ownership, impacting about one hundred thousand businesses and two hundred thousand employees.[1] Since consumption dominated Beijing's economy, a large percentage of the businesses nationalized were in the food provision sector. The new system first created through the Transformation lasted for two decades, until the end of the 1970s. It affected both the residents' everyday consumption of items like vegetables and soy sauce and the specialty establishments, such as Liubiju, known for its pickled vegetables, and Donglaishun, famous for its lamb hot pot. Socialism changed what Beijing residents ate and how they accessed their foods, and the Transformation started it all.

How did the socialist system develop? What goals did the new system intend to achieve? How did a socialist system impact the availability of different kinds of food for the city's residents? And what did the new developments mean to the city's cultural identity?

FOOD HABITS OF PRE-1949 BEIJING

Twentieth-century Beijing's food habits came primarily from those of the Qing dynasty, highlighted by palace feasts, northern Han cuisine, and halal food. Many of these became associated with seasonal and holiday celebrations. Food in Beijing was in general divided into two broad groups: staples such as grains and root vegetables that constituted the bulk of daily consumption, and nonstaples such as meats, aquatic products, and leafy vegetables that supplemented and added flavor to meals. Nonstaples also included fruits, baked goods, and snacks. The dominance of staples marked the basic pattern of food consumption in Beijing until the last two decades of the twentieth century.[2] Staple grains were further divided into the refined (rice and wheat flour) and the coarse (sorghum, beans, corn, millet, etc.). In the early twentieth century, 70 percent of Beijing residents ate primarily coarse staples, for their costs were about half of the refined ones.[3] Great culinary creativity went into using wheat or coarse flour or a mixture of the two to make all kinds of steamed buns and pancakes with or without fillings, and noodles flavored with a wide variety of sauces, dumplings, and baked goods.

As mentioned, Beijing's nonstaple foodstuffs primarily included vegetables and animal and aquatic products, as well as cooking oils. The local climate allowed for the cultivation of a great variety of vegetables, with storage as the primary factor limiting their availability on the market. In the spring, spinach was available in large quantities, supplemented by wild vegetables such as shepherd's purse, dandelions, the tender new leaves of *Toona sinensis* (Chinese mahogany) and willows, fresh elm seedpods, and bamboo shoots. In the summer, people enjoyed a diet rich in vegetables—beans, squash, eggplant, bell pepper, lotus root, turnips, tomato, chives, fennel, garlic greens, amaranth, lettuce, mustard greens, celtuce (a type of lettuce), and other leafy vegetables. Although the wealthiest in the city could afford a variety of fresh vegetables year-round, most residents ate only potatoes, turnips, and bean sprouts, as well as dried and salt-pickled vegetables in the winter. Vegetables introduced from overseas, such as potato, onion, cabbage, and cauliflower were also consumed in Beijing.[4] In the early twentieth century, families there spent about 10 percent of their food budget on vegetables, and each person consumed about half a pound per day on average.[5] Cooking oil consumption stood at about 0.8 pounds per month for low-income families and 2 pounds per month for middle-income families.[6]

Pre-1949 Beijing had a well-established market system, serving approximately two million residents. In addition to a large number of traveling vendors, grain stores spread across the city in commercial centers and alleyways. The grain business constituted Beijing's largest category of commerce;[7] Dayou Grain Store, for example, was the biggest commercial establishment in the Chaoyang District.[8] In 1948–49, the nonstaple food sector made up about 20 percent of all businesses in Beijing and employed 42 percent of the city's employees, including twenty-five thousand vendors.[9] There were more street vendors than shops, and more small shops than large ones. Family shops with little capital constituted the majority, and they rarely employed outside workers. While the larger shops were concentrated in commercial centers, the small ones and vendors were deeply rooted in densely populated neighborhoods. They operated with great flexibility and extended business hours, allowing purchases on credit and providing delivery service. Many of the businesses had shops in the front and factories and residences in the back. Businesses competed to create winning flavors and trusted brands through careful scrutiny of ingredients, high quality, large selections, distinctive character, and extraordinary service, and many became known nationally and even internationally.[10]

These were the general contours of Beijing's food commerce that the new Chinese Communist Party government encountered on January 31, 1949, when it took control of the city. The years from 1949 to 1952 were a period of economic recovery. With the long-awaited arrival of peace after decades of war, the year 1951 was unprecedentedly prosperous for the Beijing market, and many of the city's merchants called it the "unforgettable . . . golden year"[11] in which "the supply of nonstaple foods was bountiful."[12] Things, however, soon took a sharp turn, starting with the Five-Antis Campaign in 1952 and followed by the state monopolization of purchasing and marketing in 1953, changes that first politically subdued Beijing's merchants and then imposed economic restriction on the city's commerce.

CONTROL OF FOOD THROUGH STATE MONOPOLY, 1953-55

The CCP was committed to building a society free of private property after 1949, and the Five-Antis Campaign during the Korean War was a turning point in the transformation to state ownership.[13] The campaign accomplished two functions at the same time: squeezing the private sector for funds to support China's involvement in the war and taming the capitalists. A large percentage of private business owners were fined, and some were prosecuted for "bribery, tax evasion, misappropriation of public property, cheating on labor and materials, and stealing state economic information," although the amount of illegal income was usually overestimated, as the government itself later acknowledged. Forced confessions, physical violence, and executions were prevalent, and suicides by capitalists occurred in many cities.[14] Following the momentum of this campaign, the state inaugurated its first Five-Year Plan and began to speed up structural changes to the economy. "The General Line for the Transitional Period," announced by the CCP in September 1953, outlined the plan to replace private ownership with state ownership. Beijing began to follow the new policies in late October, taking measures to move toward socialism.

The government first increased state orders to private enterprises to achieve a monopoly over purchasing and marketing in order to squeeze out of the market large private wholesalers who served as the linchpin between production and marketing. Through controlling the supply of raw materials and the distribution of products, the state gained power over these enterprises and integrated them into a nationally planned economy.[15] The number of private wholesalers declined significantly within half a year.[16] In the nonstaple sector, private wholesalers had been involved in dealing six main categories of foodstuffs: pork; beef and lamb; poultry, eggs, and aquatic products; local agricultural products; vegetables; and cooking oil. By August 1955, only a limited number of medium-sized and small food wholesalers remained.[17]

The state then imposed a series of monopolies over the procurement and distribution of staple and nonstaple foods; who could access grains and how much each person could get was now determined by the state. On October 31, 1953, the Beijing municipal government issued new policies that linked official household registration with food rationing: only a set amount of wheat flour was allowed to be distributed by state-run grain companies to each resident with official household registration in the city.[18] On December 1, it officially instituted a grain-rationing system, basing distribution on age and the physical intensity required by a person's job. The average allowance per person was about 372 pounds per year. In comparison, the average annual grain consumption per person was roughly 286 pounds per year in the Qing era, and the average grain allowance per person was 108–264 pounds per year when Japan occupied a large part of China in the 1940s, including Beijing.[19]

New policies were also adopted for the production of nonstaple foods, likely to alleviate the pressure of grain shortage. Without modern technology, nonstaple foods are difficult to preserve or transport. In 1953, the Beijing municipal government promoted the policy of "suburban agriculture serving the capital city" and called for increased production of vegetables, fruits, meats, eggs, and dairy products. Government bureaus determined the size of land allocated to growing vegetables, the volume to produce, and the prices for the products. In August 1954, the city government took over the management of all eighteen wholesale vegetable markets in the suburbs. All the vegetables that came on the market, whether produced by agricultural collectives or individual farmers, were purchased or managed through state-run vegetable stations. Those thus collected were distributed to enterprises, institutions, and vendors. The prices were determined uniformly, and trading outside of this system was banned.[20]

The volume of vegetables on the market did increase, and Beijing residents consumed more overall (270 pounds per person on average for 1957, or 0.8 pounds per day versus the 0.6 pounds per day before 1949). State control, though, created problems in their provision. The system worked better during shortages but faltered during times of abundance. As an easier route to filling their quotas, farmers now preferred to cultivate fast-growing vegetables such as bok choy and other leafy greens. But these vegetables were hard to preserve, and farmers were unwilling to store them. Since the vegetable stations had to accept everything they were sent, the farmers were not motivated to care about the quality of the vegetables or to pace the supply for the market. Large amounts of a single type of vegetable frequently flooded the market, and much ended up rotting in front of state-run vegetable shops, which had to sell these at deeply discounted prices, such as less than one yuan for a whole basket of tomatoes or ten cents for a pile of eggplants or cucumbers. Some shops allowed residents to take whatever quantity of vegetables they wanted for ten cents or even for free. The shops sometimes had to pay farmers to take the excess vegetables back to the villages to feed pigs or make fertilizer. In April, August, and September, however, there were barely any vegetables in the stores or only dried-up potatoes and onions.[21] The system was alternately wasteful and austere.

The meat consumed in the largest quantity in Qing-era Beijing was lamb, followed by pork, chicken, duck, and fish. Beijing had a wide variety of aquatic products, including freshwater fish from rivers and ponds and saltwater fish from Tianjin. In 1926, each family consumed about seven pounds of food from animal products per month, including pork, lamb, organ meats, fish, shrimp, and eggs.[22] The population of Beijing, the capital city of the newly founded PRC, doubled in less than a decade, from about two million regular residents before 1949 to just over four million by the end of 1957, and its composition changed as well, with the expansion of state institutions and an increasing number of residents from other parts of China.[23]

Pork consumption increased, and there was a shortage in its supply after 1953. The shortage was not caused simply by the population increase, which in itself created good business opportunities, but was largely a result of the state's monopolization of grain in 1953. Farmers worried about not being able to purchase feed grain and so slaughtered pigs in large numbers, including those not yet fully grown. To ensure Beijing's supply of pork, the government adopted a policy of assigning pig production quotas to villages in 1954. In 1955–56, the central government assigned Beijing a quota of sixty thousand pigs. Quotas were distributed to production groups, and pigs were purchased by state-run stations.

Farmers resented this policy, because they could not make their own decisions on how many pigs to raise, while each level of government took the liberty of increasing the quota. Other problems were the low prices for pigs at state-run stations and shortages of feed grain. In an effort to ease the tension, the state adjusted its policy and allowed private ownership of pigs, provided assistance to the farmers, and paid higher prices for state purchases. This policy adjustment resulted in a more stable pork market in 1957, but a sharp downturn quickly followed between 1958 and 1962.[24] Starting on December 1, 1957, pork, lamb, and beef could only be purchased with state-issued coupons, and the amount allowed was divided into five levels according to age and occupation, averaging roughly half a pound per person per month. Excluding a slight increase in the consumption of aquatic products, Beijing residents' level of protein consumption from animal products in 1957 was not significantly higher than in 1952 or in the years before 1949. In addition to meat, sugar was put under the coupon system, and in 1953, the state began to assert control over the market supply of eggs and bean noodles.[25] In 1954, the Beijing municipal government, following central government policy, abolished the private market for cooking oil and started rationing it.[26]

The state monopoly on procurement and distribution effectively severed the connection between private urban commerce and the countryside. Meanwhile, the government centralized purchasing by state institutions in major cities, thus taking large-scale trades away from private wholesalers. By October 1954, state-owned companies controlled about 95 percent of the wholesale operations in Beijing. The remaining wholesalers traded small handicrafts or highly specialized commodities, such as antiques.[27] Overall, by late 1954, the private sector was insignificant, and state-owned companies dominated the economy. The state was ready to push the Transformation further ahead.[28]

FOOD DISTRIBUTION UNDER STATE OWNERSHIP, 1956-57

The primary format for the Transformation was known as "public-private partnership" (*gongsi heying*). The Provisional Regulations on Public-Private Partnership were announced by the central government on September 2, 1954, and by November 1955, only a small percentage of industrial and commercial establishments in Beijing remained in private hands.[29] On January 4, 1956, led by Yue Songsheng of the Tongrentang Chinese medicine store, all Chinese medicine shops in the city applied for joint partnerships, and many other industries followed suit.[30] In the three-day period between January 11 and the evening of January 14, the values of seventeen thousand enterprises were determined, providing the basis for the calculation of payments to the owners. On January 15, two hundred thousand people celebrated the completion of the Transformation on Tiananmen Square, as described at the beginning of this article. By the end of 1956, the private element of the economy was negligible.[31]

The situation in the food industry mirrored the general process of the Transformation. During the "high tide of socialism" in 1956, vegetable farmers were all organized into agricultural co-ops. The vegetable industry, from production to distribution, was collectivized and put under even stricter control.[32] Businesses that traded in pork, beef and lamb, poultry and eggs, aquatic products, agricultural products, sugar, candies, baked goods, salt and condiments, soy products, and wine, as well as restaurants, were all placed under state ownership or direct state control.[33]

The Transformation changed what and where foods were available. Many smaller stores were eliminated or combined in a rush, especially those selling items that were needed for daily meals, such as salt, soy sauce, bean paste, cooking oil, and vegetables. All these changes made it inconvenient and time-consuming for residents to obtain basic foods. In the Fucheng Gate and Dongdan areas, for example, 233 vendors that had been scattered around the neighborhoods were combined into thirty-three clusters. The city saw an 11.4 percent decrease in the number of businesses in the food provision sector.[34] Food retailers continued to decline in number after 1956. In 1957, there were 4,705 points in the city where they gathered; in 1960, there were only 594.[35] As the population doubled, the number of businesses declined.

The Transformation reduced the number of small retailers but did not totally eliminate them, because the functions they performed had low efficiency and profit, and the state was unwilling to take them over or to assume the large responsibility of providing them with the stable salary and welfare understood to be guaranteed under socialism.³⁶ For the small vendors, the Transformation focused on commodity supply. Vegetable vendors were organized to purchase as collectives but continued to sell their goods individually. Food vendors and street stalls were often organized into collective dining halls, and vendors were required to join co-op stores if their businesses had become successful.³⁷ During yet another "high tide of socialist transformation" in 1957, a large number of vendors joined co-op stores; collective stores, in turn, came under joint ownership with the state. By the end of 1957, only 3 percent of all food retailers (not counting restaurants) were operating privately.³⁸

When the rural-urban flow of agricultural products was cut by the state's squeezing of wholesalers out of the market and banning of long-distance trade, shortages emerged in food provision. In the more relaxed atmosphere created by the Hundred Flowers Movement in 1956, the Beijing municipal government loosened its control of the rural market to increase food supply. The free market in agricultural products that had first emerged in the suburban agricultural areas expanded into the city in September 1956. The number of these markets increased to thirty-five by the end of the year, with eight in wholesale and twenty-seven in retail. The number of private vendors increased sharply, with five hundred of them selling vegetables. The more varied and higher-quality foods they offered were welcomed by consumers. Seeing a good business opportunity, some farmers slaughtered pigs and sold the meat on the market before they filled their state quotas. The prices for free-market vegetables were higher than those at the state-run markets, so farmers were unwilling to sign contracts with the state vegetable companies or even to honor those they had previously signed. The state, seeing that it could not continue its monopoly over procurement and distribution, once again reoriented its policy. In August 1957, when the Anti-Rightist Movement was raging, the central government reinforced the state's control over procurement and distribution: items such as pork and vegetables that were supposed to be purchased and distributed uniformly by the state were not allowed to circulate on the free market, which was closed.³⁹

LIUBIJU 六必居

The Transformation changed not only the everyday life of Beijing's residents but also the city's long-established culinary culture. This was best reflected in the experiences of the "old famous shops," such as Liubiju, a store specializing in high-quality pickled vegetables, founded in the seventeenth century,

FIGURE 8.1. Man making bean paste at a pickle factory in Baoding, a hundred miles southwest of Beijing, 1930s–40s. Courtesy of the Collection of Hedda Morrison Photographs of China, Harvard-Yenching Library.

in the early Qing dynasty (some believe it was founded in the late Ming).[40] Pickles were a daily necessity for many Beijing residents, and Liubiju's products were both valued by locals and sought after by tourists as gifts. The store's ability to achieve and maintain high quality was rooted in the economic system, time-tested business practices, and close connections with rural suppliers. All of these components were changed fundamentally by the Transformation, and the quality of its products declined as a result.

Liubiju had assured the quality of its products through a careful selection of ingredients. Before the state monopolized purchasing and marketing in 1953, Liubiju had its own suppliers for all its ingredients. The foundations for high-quality pickled vegetables are yellow bean paste and sweet-flour bean paste, which in turn depend on the quality of the soybeans and flour used. The soybeans Liubiju used came from Majuqiao in Fengrun County, Hebei, where the beans were larger and fuller, with thinner skins and higher oil content. Laishui County, west of Beijing, supplied wheat with a higher level of gluten that was more suitable for making paste, and Liubiju did its own milling at the shop.[41]

FIGURE 8.2. Man straining pickles at a pickle factory in Baoding, 1930s–40s. Courtesy of the Collection of Hedda Morrison Photographs of China, Harvard-Yenching Library.

Liubiju had purchased its vegetables from specific areas and farmers. For the pickled black melons, generations of farmer Wang Guangyi's family of Xiaohongmen Paifang Village in the Yongding Gate area south of Beijing had supplied Liubiju exclusively with the dark-skinned melons with eight black stripes. Han Wenliang and his father-in-law in Wanzi Village in the Taipingqiao area outside Guang'an Gate grew thick, green celtuce weighing about one pound each for Liubiju; the family had been in the business for decades. The garlic, each with six cloves covered in white skin, came from Li Village in Changxindian, where Li Yuan's family had been working with Liubiju for several generations. The Li family always harvested their garlic two or three days before the summer solstice and delivered it directly to Liubiju. The melons for making pickles were picked when they were 80 percent ripe, with seeds not yet fully formed, because they would have too little flesh if harvested too early or skin too thick and tough if harvested too late. Other vegetables were selected using standards just as high: six-inch-long autumn cucumbers from outside of Anding Gate, green beans from Fengtai, six-inch-long white radishes and broad-leaved chives from Haihui Temple in the southern suburbs. All these vegetables were contracted for delivery to Liubiju as soon as they were harvested, and pickled right away to achieve ideal flavor, color, and texture.⁴²

Liubiju's quality also resulted from following a strict production procedure, adjusted for different materials and weather conditions. For the yellow bean paste and sweet-flour bean paste, airing and adding water were the two most important procedures, and each had to be done at certain intervals. The early stage of making the bean paste required eight cycles of stirring every seven days. Once summer began, it needed ten cycles of stirring, seven times a day. When it was nearly ready, the stirring decreased to ten cycles, three times each day, but if the weather was hot, more stirring was necessary. These procedures guaranteed the proper fermentation of the bean paste. When the melons for making the pickles were about seven inches long and 80 percent ripe, the farmers would pick them in the early morning and deliver them to Liubiju before noon. Liubiju's staff washed the melons right away and then put them in a sauce of sixteen parts melon to one part salt for thirty-six hours. The melons were then pickled in bean paste for two days and two nights, dried in the sun for a day or two and turned several times in the process. Next, they were placed into a mixture of yellow and sweet-flour bean paste and stirred ten cycles, seven to eight times every day, following a strict schedule adjusted for different weather conditions. When the bean paste and pickles were being made, workers were assigned to night shifts. If it rained during the night, those on watch would wake up the night-shift workers, who would have to cover up the pickling vats within five minutes. These procedures were all supervised by the "master of production" (*zhangzuo*), and anyone who broke the rules would be warned or punished.⁴³

In the early 1950s, however, as a contemporary observer commented, "The quality of Liubiju's pickled vegetables has become awful, and it is deteriorating day by day.... Some customers have complained, 'How could these possibly be Liubiju's pickles?' and old residents of Beijing cannot help sighing when mentioning the quality of Liubiju's products."⁴⁴ The ownership of the store was transformed in January 1955, but the quality of their products did not improve. A study in 1956 identified four reasons for the decline in Liubiju's quality: material supply, pricing, wage structure, and management.

Liubiju lost its long-established system of material supply after the state placed all "primary commodities" under "planned supply." Instead of the high-quality soybeans it used to make bean paste, it received from the state suppliers soybean cakes left after oil was extracted (in 1954) and black beans instead of soybeans (in 1955). And instead of the high-quality flour it had previously used for its bean paste, Liubiju now received from the grain bureau a combination of low-quality flour and brans. The fresh, carefully timed, directly delivered vegetables of specific sizes were no longer available; the Beijing Municipal Vegetable Bureau supplied Liubiju with the same mixed vegetables it provided for the whole city. The six-to-seven-inch fresh cucumbers were replaced with a variety of substitutes, some with thick skin and some too overgrown and too big to pickle whole. The vegetables went through the market in hemp sacks or large baskets, leaving the cucumbers scratched, broken, and less flavorful. The pickles made with these cucumbers had unappealing colors and were not crunchy.[45]

Eggplants that have not grown to full size at frost do not taste good when eaten as fresh vegetables, but they are perfect for pickling, and Liubiju used to pay farmers a higher price for these. In autumn 1955, however, the store was unable to obtain any such eggplants. The Vegetable Bureau determined the price for eggplants according to their sizes for consumption as fresh vegetables, which meant that farmers could not make as much money if they sold the small "frost eggplants." These small, firm eggplants were so cheap that some of the farmers preferred to feed them to their pigs rather than sell them to Liubiju.[46] Only if the prices for these specialty vegetables were high enough would the farmers take the trouble to grow them. Since their purchase price was now set by the government, the farmers were unwilling to grow anything that required special care or that affected the harvests and thus lowered their income or their ability to meet the quotas set by the government.[47]

In order to solve these problems, the municipal administration agreed to supply Liubiju with better materials; for example, the store received a special supply of soybeans to improve the quality of its products, but the results of sampling one *jin* (equivalent to 16 *liang* at that time) of the soybeans they received on March 16, 1956, were as follows:

Good quality (big and round): 6 *liang*;
Small and dull: 8.1 *liang*;
Moldy: 0.5 *liang*;
Damaged by worms: 0.8 *liang*;
Dirty: 0.6 *liang*.

Therefore 1.9 *liang*, or 12 percent, of the soybeans could not be used, and extra labor was needed to sort the beans. Only 37.5 percent of the beans met Liubiju's standard.[48]

Changes in agriculture and the new urban-rural relations under the planned economy made the supply problem difficult to solve. The farmers who had supplied Liubiju with specialty vegetables had now joined agricultural co-ops and no longer had the right to decide what to grow, and their remuneration was determined by the work point system. Some of the lands that had produced vegetables for Liubiju were now urbanized. For instance, Liubiju had purchased crosnes tubers (also known as Chinese artichokes) from Daxiaojing Village outside of Guang'an Gate, but that land had been appropriated to build state government offices. The farmers who had once grown crosnes tubers were now reassigned to other jobs. A farmer named Wang, who had been famous for growing this crop, was now working as a custodian in one of the new buildings. In 1956, the supply of crosnes tubers dwindled to the point that there were only six pounds of crosnes tuber seeds left in Beijing. Liubiju considered using supplies from the northeast, but their quality could not be guaranteed because of the long transport distances.[49]

Liubiju's pickles had been relatively more expensive because their ingredients cost 10–20 percent more than the average market prices. The store also made sure to use a sufficient quantity of ingredients in its products, which further contributed to its higher production costs. After 1956, prices for commodities were all determined with the same formula—production cost plus a set percentage of increase regardless of the quality of the product. This policy consequently discouraged companies from producing specialty products that usually required complicated production processes. Prices were nominally determined by the industrial or commercial associations but were, in fact, controlled by the state administration.[50]

This system of pricing had the effect of forcing the manufacturers of higher-quality products to cut corners, since they were now competing with producers of inferior-quality products. Liubiju had been selling a special soy sauce that was produced by fermenting and then condensing juice from yellow bean paste. In the past, the price for one pound of this was equal to that of five pounds of yellow bean paste. Under the pricing system introduced in the 1950s, the store was not allowed to charge more than the cost of 1.6 pounds of yellow bean paste for this soy sauce. Unable to afford to sell the soy sauce at this price, the store began to blend it with other ingredients and sell this lower-quality product.

Furthermore, Liubiju's famous "pickled black vegetables" had been sold at one yuan per pound before the Transformation. The store improved the quality of this product after the Transformation but was only allowed to sell it at 0.8 yuan per pound. An economist commented, "It would have been reasonable if the original quality had been maintained while the prices had been lowered as a result of decreased production costs stemming from improvements in management and methods of production. But this is not the case with Liubiju's reduced prices; they are the result of administrative orders and regulations on uniformity. The policy forced Liubiju to use inferior ingredients, and the quality fell."[51]

The prices of Liubiju products were lowered anywhere from 8 to 50 percent (30 percent for most products) after the Transformation, in order to reduce what was now seen as overly high profits and in order to "serve the people."[52] The sales prices were determined according to the cost of production, which was calculated too low, because it excluded both the cost of equipment depreciation and of interest paid on credit transactions to obtain materials, partially made materials, and commodities. Consequently, the real profit for the store was now much lower than the gross profit predicted by the government. The state-set gross profit rate in 1955 forced the store to eliminate a number of its popular services, including lending containers and delivery. In the past, Liubiju's products had aimed at various profit levels, but now the differences between the gross profit rates of all products were set under 10 percent. The store lost the motivation to make specialty products. The old "division of labor" among the pickle stores, in which Liubiju specialized in high-quality products, was also disappearing. Lowering the quality of Liubiju pickles to that of other stores in fact negatively impacted the store's sales, just as it had hurt Liubiju's profit. Its 1955 profit dropped to one-tenth of its 1932 profit of 20,000 taels of silver.[53] In terms of accumulating capital for industrialization, the state would have gained more from Liubiju through taxation if the store had been allowed to continue its traditional, established practices.

Another factor contributing to the decline of Liubiju was that the new wage structure that had emerged after the Transformation, oriented toward egalitarianism at the cost of quality products. Differences in wage levels were small, and the workers who carried out the most important and demanding duty at the store—making the pickles—were paid less on average than the cooks in the cafeteria. In spite of his experience, skills, and responsibility, the wages of Dong Shunhe, the production master, were only 10 percent higher than those of the average worker. This wage system discouraged workers from doing more or improving their skills. Elements in the old wage system designed to reward the workers were abolished. For instance, in the process of making bean paste, the white mold on the bean cakes needed to be brushed off after the initial fermentation. The workers could then sell it and divide the profit. The cleaner the cakes were brushed, the better the flavor of the paste. This system thus benefited both the store and the workers, motivating them to continue creating high-quality products. But this practice was abolished in the 1950s, which both decreased the workers' income and adulterated the quality of the bean paste.[54]

The new wage structure also jeopardized the survival of the skills and traditions that Liubiju had developed over the past centuries. It took half a year to make one type of the pickles, and some other types were made only once a year, which made experimenting difficult and costly. These factors made it crucial to pass down acquired skills and knowledge. Traditionally, old masters kept their special skills secret and only passed them on to chosen and trusted disciples. After the Transformation, clear master-disciple relationships no longer existed, and there were no rules concerning nor any motivation for passing on a master's skills. Master-workers were not treated well enough in the new system to encourage them to pass on their skills. Meanwhile, young workers were paid well, earning almost as much as the old masters, and so did not have the motivation to work hard or to learn new skills, since there was not much room for their wages to go up, even if they learned more.[55]

In 1952, the central government decided that all enterprises should adopt the eight-hour workday, and so Liubiju abolished night shifts. Consequently, no one was available for the late-night and early-morning stirrings, resulting in lower-quality pickles. The new management system specified no clear chain of responsibility. The autumn of 1955 saw a few extraordinarily hot days, and extra stirrings were needed. But all the employees left after eight hours of work, and there was no policy on overtime. Dong Shunhe and few volunteer workers ended up doing extra work for several nights to save the pickles from spoiling. Because of the insufficient staffing, however, the pickles from that season were not as crunchy as they should have been.[56]

Before the Transformation, Liubiju operated on a system in which the production master was personally responsible for everything. He would assign work and supervise the employees, who would follow his words unconditionally because he controlled their employment, and his skill and experience won him respect. Besides, his personal connections with the workers, who often were his close or distant relatives, added to his authority. After the Five-Antis Campaign, however, the workers set up a supervisory system in the store and abandoned their unconditional respect for the master's orders. The master's functions were replaced by new "production group" leaders, who could not conduct business in the old way but had no new rules to follow and lacked the authority to discipline workers who did not take their jobs seriously.[57]

DONGLAISHUN 東來順 AND OTHER CASES

On February 5, 1956, in the more relaxed political atmosphere right before the Hundred Flowers Movement, the *People's Daily* published an article by reporters Wang Huiping and Fan Rongkang, raising the question of why the restaurant Donglaishun's lamb did not taste good anymore. They observed that the meat was not thinly sliced but rather came in lumps on the plate and in the pot, and it was hard to chew and swallow. The sauces did not taste right either: the soy sauce was no longer sweet, the sesame sauce stuck to the tongue, and the hot sauce was merely red pepper powder mixed with water and was not fried in sesame oil. The pickled garlic was no longer caramelized but instead was watery, spicy, and bitter. When old customers went to the restaurant, they first asked, "Is there good meat today?" before they took a seat, and the employees were saddened to see the lumps of inedible meat left on the table.[58] The reason for all of this was that the restaurant had begun to focus on lowering costs and prices and had to make do with whatever was available, because it interpreted its new function as serving the masses. Therefore, the quality of the materials was low, and the variety decreased.[59]

Donglaishun's problems started after it entered a public-private joint ownership in 1955. It had purchased its lamb directly from herders in Inner Mongolia in the past and later changed to buying from the more than 30 private butchers in Beijing, paying prices higher than the market average. After 1949, it was still able to purchase meats from some private butchers and some state-owned shops, choosing leg, sirloin, or neck meat and paying market prices. After the national monopoly on food started in 1953, and especially after Donglaishun entered the joint ownership in 1955, the lamb it needed was only supplied by one state-owned shop in Beijing, which also sent it goat, fresh as well as frozen meat, fatty as well as lean parts—whatever was available. The quality of Donglaishun's lamb hot pot sharply declined. At the state's request, the restaurant dropped its price for lamb twice, from 1.4 to 1.3 yuan per pound in October 1955 when it entered the joint partnership and then a further drop, to 1.1 yuan per pound, to equal the fixed price at other restaurants. This, in turn, forced Donglaishun to purchase lower-quality meat.

Changes in management practices also affected the quality. Donglaishun had a tradition of slicing its meat very thin, and a worker could slice 30–40 pounds of good meat per day. In seasons when there was a high demand for hot pot, the restaurant would hire temporary workers to slice meat. After the Transformation and the joint partnership, the representative of the state urged the workers to increase the amount of meat they sliced and stopped the restaurant from hiring temporary workers. The employees now sliced on average 60–70 pounds of meat every day and up to 110 pounds on Sundays. With this pressure to increase the volume of meat sliced and its low quality, the workers could only cut thick slices.[60]

According to the *People's Daily*, maintaining the quality of the lamb at Donglaishun had become a "political problem." The author said, "Donglaishun's lamb hot pot is the product of the working people's creativity. How can treasuring this culinary skill and developing this national heritage not be a political task? When Donglaishun's lamb does not taste good anymore, people will criticize not just one restaurant or one unit in the commercial administration but the party, the government, and the socialist system. How can this not be a political task?"[61] When the criticisms of Donglaishun's lamb reached the top leadership of the CCP, it became even more of a political problem. At a meeting of the State Council, Chen Yun, one of the top leaders of the CCP, used Donglaishun's lamb as an example to talk about quality problems, and then he commented on the duck at Quanjude: "In the past, it took about one hundred days to raise the ducks for Quanjude, starting from ducklings. Their feed consisted of mung beans and millet. Since the state monopolization of purchasing and marketing, Quanjude's ducks have come from labor camps, and the roast ducks do not taste good anymore."[62] With such attention from the top leadership, a solution to problems faced by Donglaishun and Quanjude emerged: the lamb and duck had to taste good to prove the superiority of the socialist system. Donglaishun was given special access to the best lamb available, and the grain bureau provided it with a special allowance of fine flour, green beans, sesame paste, sesame oil, high-quality soy sauce, mushrooms, and shrimp; three times as much pickled garlic; and pickled chive flowers from specialty stores. The restaurant was allowed to have flexibility on pricing, charging more for high-quality lamb.[63]

On January 31, 1956, Beijing's First and Third Bureaus of Commerce presented a report on the quality of products at famous old shops.[64] Among its findings were the following:

> According to our investigations at eleven stores, including Donglaishun Restaurant, Daoxiangchun Southern Foods Store, Liubiju Pickled Vegetable Store, Shengxifu Hat Store, and Wangfujing Department Store, all these businesses have seen decreases in the variety of their commodities and a deterioration in the quality of their products. Many of their long-established characteristics are disappearing. Daoxiangchun used to carry more than

one thousand types of products, and now it has only about six hundred types. Liubiju's bean cakes, Puliu soy sauce, and Qilin vegetables, and Tianyuan Pickled Vegetable Store's sugar-pickled mustard heads, pickled eggplants, and pickled walnuts have all been in short supply for a long time. The quality of the remaining varieties has declined severely. The lamb hotpot at Donglaishun, the roast duck at Quanjude, the fermented tofu at Wangzhihe, and the braised beef at Yueshengzhai have all dropped steeply in quality.[65]

The state's monopoly on commodities, the report admits, made it impossible to procure some of the materials that had been supplied from other regions. In addition, the reorganization of labor also harmed these stores. Shengxifu Hat Store had outsourced its production to families experienced in making high-quality hats. After these handcraft families were organized into production co-ops or combined into factories and some of the more skilled workers were assigned to new administrative jobs, they could no longer make hats of high quality in accordance with the shop's schedule.[66]

REFLECTIONS AND QUESTIONS

Liubiju, Donglaishun, and Beijing's food provision system are small-scale cases that embodied the issues at the heart of the establishment of "socialist commerce" in the 1950s. The newly founded People's Republic of China promised people a better life through socialism, and at the same time, it aimed at industrialization via rapid, state-driven capital accumulation. These two goals turned out to be conflicting in the way the CCP carried out its planned economy. Beijing's new food provision system gave everyone the same access to food at a level that was slightly higher than it was at the end of the nineteenth century and meaningfully higher than what people had in the 1940s during World War II, but just as many socialist systems around the world have demonstrated, the system did not sustain high productivity, and in the case of Beijing, it resulted in a stagnant level of food availability as well as fewer choices and a lower quality of food for both daily consumption and the specialty shops.

These consequences resulted from the very nature of this new planned economy. The national monopoly of procurement and distribution enforced in 1953 eliminated any alternative for both resourcing and marketing businesses, as illustrated through the examples of the supply of vegetables and grains and the pricing system for Liubiju's products. Nationalization in 1956 changed the ownership, management, and compensation structure of enterprises, which took away workers' motivation to be productive and created inefficient management. The CCP claimed to be transforming "capitalist industry and commerce" to socialism, but it is debatable in what sense the businesses of Beijing that on average had fewer than two employees were "capitalist" and in what ways theories of capitalism can be applied here. In his 1948 study of rural reconstruction, anthropologist Fei Xiaotong proposed that instead of state-driven accumulation, China should foster its bottom-heavy traditional economy and enable accumulation gradually.[67] Economist Barry Naughton similarly argues that "the rapid economic growth of Hong Kong and Taiwan during the 1960s and 1970s could be considered a continuation and vindication of the traditional economy. After all, these were regions within that economy that had followed a path of evolutionary growth from traditional beginnings and had relied primarily on small firms to jump-start economic development."[68] In other words, state-led, forced accumulation might not be the only possible or most efficient choice for economic growth and improving people's living conditions.

The new system also dealt a fatal blow to Beijing's cultural traditions. The flourishing of Beijing's food culture in the past depended on several crucial conditions. A close relationship between the city and the rural areas surrounding and beyond Beijing provided the city with grains, fresh vegetables, and other necessary foodstuffs. With the state's increasing control of rural China and its growing monopoly over procurement and distribution of grains and other agricultural products in the cities, the restaurants and the small mobile food vendors lost their diverse sources of supply. Under collectivization, the sense of pride in one's goods and the keen consciousness of upholding the standards of "old brands" were gone, as was the motivation for perfection and innovation that resulted from competition. In the past, private businesses operated with a strong sense of "identity" that nurtured familiarity and trust from the community. Now, instead of purchasing from private owners who were responsible for their own goods and reputations, consumers dealt with the abstract "government" or "collective." The loss of "identity" (and thus of "unique flavors") and the remapping and disappearance of retail as it once was eliminated much of the human connection and cultural dimension so central to the making and serving of food. The Transformation effectively created a disowned city by abolishing private ownership, leaving important lessons for today's Chinese cities that are trying to restore a sense of cultural identity.

NOTES

1. "Dashiji," in Beijing Juan Bianji Zu, ed., *Zhongguo zibenzhuyi gongshangye de Shehuizhuyi Gaizao (Beijing juan)* (henceforth *ZZGSG-BJ*). Beijing: Zhonggong Dangshi Chubanshe, 1991, 586.
2. The percentage of grain in food expenditures in Beijing was as follows: 80% in the early twentieth century, 47.55% in 1955, 31.32% in 1978, and 9.37% in 1997. See *Beijing zhi—Zonghe juan—Renmin shenghuo zhi* (henceforth *BZ-ZJ-RSZ*) (Beijing: Beijing Chubanshe, 2007), 189–91.
3. Yuan Xi, *Jindai Beijing de shimin shenghuo* (Beijing: Beijing Chubanshe, 2000), 55–56.
4. Yuan, *Jindai Beijing*, 59.
5. The average size of Beijing families then was 3.5–5.5 people in families with 100–1,000 yuan of income, and 1.1–2.3 people in families with 0–100 yuan of income. Yuan Xi, "Jindai Beijing chengshi renkou yanjiu," *Renkou yanjiu* 27, no. 5 (September 2003); *BZ-ZJ-RSZ*, 210–11.
6. Yuan, "Jindai Beijing chengshi renkou yanjiu,"; *BZ-ZJ-RSZ*, 204.
7. *Beijing zhi—Shangye juan—Liangyou shangye zhi*. Beijing: Beijing Chubanshe, 2004, 52–54.
8. Zhu Yingna, "Dayou liangdian de gongsi heying," in *ZZGSG-BJ*, 545.
9. Beijing Shi Di'er Shangye Ju Shizhi Bangong Shi, eds., Beijing Shi Di'er Shangye Ju Shizhi Bangong Shi, *Dangdai Beijing fushipin shangye* (Beijing: Zhongguo Caizheng Jingji Chubanshe, 1994), 2–3.
10. Beijing Shi Di'er Shangye Ju Shizhi Bangong Shi, *Dangdai Beijing fushipin shangye*, 5–6; *Beijing shangye sishi nian* Bianjibu, *Beijing shangye sishi nian* (Zhongguo Caizheng Jingji Chubanshe, 1989), 6–7.
11. *Beijing shangye sishi nian*, 50.
12. *Beijing shangye sishi nian*, 236.
13. *ZZGSG-BJ*, 82–84, 85–86, 87–89.
14. *ZZGSG-BJ*, 9–10. Christian Lamouroux and Dong Xiaoping, "Beijing Chengwenhou ge'an yanjiu: Zhuanxie Beijing shangye shi de ziliao, fangfa yu chubu jieguo," in Christian Lamouroux, ed., *Zhongguo jindai hangye wenhua yanjiu: Jiyi de chuancheng yu gongneng* (Beijing: Guojia Tushuguan Chubanshe, 2010), 319–20.
15. *ZZGSG-BJ*, 11.
16. *ZZGSG-BJ*, 168.
17. Beijing Shi Di'er Shangye Ju Shizhi Bangong Shi, *Dangdai Beijing fushipin shangye*, 34.
18. *BZ-ZJ-RSZ*, 196–97.
19. *BZ-ZJ-RSZ*, 193–95.
20. Beijing Shi Di'er Shangye Ju Shizhi Bangong Shi, *Dangdai Beijing fushipin shangye*, 22–24.
21. *BZ-ZJ-RSZ*, 212–13; Beijing Shi Di'er Shangye Ju Shizhi Bangong Shi, *Dangdai Beijing fushipin shangye*, 22–24.
22. *BZ-ZJ-RSZ*, 216.
23. *Beijing shangye sishi nian*, 28–29.
24. Beijing Shi Di'er Shangye Ju Shizhi Bangong Shi, *Dangdai Beijing fushipin shangye*, 21–22.
25. Beijing Shi Di'er Shangye Ju Shizhi Bangong Shi, *Dangdai Beijing fushipin shangye*, 30–31.

26 *BZ-ZJ-RSZ*, 205.
27 *ZZGSG-BJ*, 12; 168; 202–8; 237–43.
28 *ZZGSG-BJ*, 179–83.
29 *ZZGSG-BJ*, p. 18.
30 On Tongrentang, see Ding Yizhuang, "Minguo shiqi Beijing Tongrentang yaopu de jingying moshi: Youguan Tongrentang de koushu lishi," in Lamouroux, *Zhongguo jindai hangye wenhua yanjiu*, 294–318; and Sherman Cochran, *Chinese Medicine Men: Consumer Culture in China and Southeast Asia* (Cambridge, MA: Harvard University Press, 2006).
31 *ZZGSG-BJ*, p. 21.
32 *Beijing shangye sishi nian*, 202; Beijing Shi Di'er Shangye Ju Shizhi Bangong Shi, *Dangdai Beijing fushipin shangye*, 22–24.
33 Beijing Shi Di'er Shangye Ju Shizhi Bangong Shi, *Dangdai Beijing fushipin shangye*, 41.
34 *Beijing shangye sishi nian*, 78–80.
35 *Beijing shangye sishi nian*, 98.
36 Feng Xiaocai, "Shehuizhuyi de bianyuan ren: 1956 nian qianhou de xiaoshang xiaofan gaizao wenti," in Huadong Shifan Daxue Dangdai Shi Yanjiu Zhongxin, ed., *Zhongguo dangdai shi yanjiu*, 3 (Beijing: Jiuzhou Chubanshe, 2011).
37 *ZZGSG-BJ*, 12–13; 168.
38 Beijing Shi Di'er Shangye Ju Shizhi Bangong Shi, *Dangdai Beijing fushipin shangye*, 47–48.
39 Beijing Shi Di'er Shangye Ju Shizhi Bangong Shi, *Dangdai Beijing fushipin shangye*, 49–51; *Beijing shangye shishi nian*, 98–99.
40 *ZZGSG-BJ*, 482.
41 Lin Qing, *Zenyang huifu Beijing Liubiju jiangcai de youliangtedian* (Beijing: Beijing Caizheng Jingji Chubanshe, 1956), 2.
42 Lin, *Zenyang huifu*, 2.
43 Lin, *Zenyang huifu*, 5.
44 Lin, *Zenyang huifu*, 6.
45 Lin, *Zenyang huifu*, 6.
46 Lin, *Zenyang huifu*, 11–12.
47 Lin, *Zenyang huifu*, 8.
48 Lin, *Zenyang huifu*, 11.
49 Lin, *Zenyang huifu*, 12.
50 Lin, *Zenyang huifu*, 7.
51 Lin, *Zenyang huifu*, 7.
52 Lin, *Zenyang huifu*, 13.
53 Lin, *Zenyang huifu*, 14.
54 Lin, *Zenyang huifu*, 8.
55 Lin, *Zenyang huifu*, 18.
56 Lin, *Zenyang huifu*, 9.
57 Lin, *Zenyang huifu*, 17.
58 Wang Huiping and Fang Rongkang, *People's Daily*, February 5, 1956.
59 Yang Guanghui, *Beijing Donglaishun shuanyangrou de tedian shi zenyanghuifu de*. Beijing: Caizheng Jingji Chubanshe, November 1956, 9.

60 Yang, *Beijing Donglaishun*, 388.
61 Yang, *Beijing Donglaishun*, 388.
62 Chen Yun, *Chen Yun wenxuan (1949–1956)* (Beijing: Renmin Chubanshe, 1984).
63 Yang, *Beijing Donglaishun*, 11–13.
64 *ZZGSG-BJ*, 387–90.
65 *ZZGSG-BJ*, 387.
66 *ZZGSG-BJ*, 387–88; Kuang Rian, 16.
67 Fei Xiaotong, *Xiangtu chongjian* (Changsha, Hunan: Yuelu Shushe, 2012). Originally published in 1948.
68 Barry Naughton, *The Chinese Economy: Adaptation and Growth* (Cambridge, MA: MIT Press, 2018), 68.

9 ONE COUNTRY, TWO MATERIAL CULTURES

JACOB EYFERTH

MAO-ERA CHINA HAD NOT ONE BUT TWO DISTINCT MATERIAL cultures. On the one hand, there was the world of socialist commodities: Mao suits and Mao badges, Shanghai wristwatches, Hero fountain pens, propaganda posters, teacups inscribed with revolutionary slogans, bedsheets printed with smokestacks and tractors. These objects are best understood as belonging to the material culture of urban China. Rural China, except for a few wealthy areas near the major cities, had a material culture not just simpler and poorer but also qualitatively different, in at least four ways. First, most of the goods rural people consumed were their own products, grown on nearby land or fashioned from local resources. Second, they were use values, not commodities: they were made for direct consumption rather than for exchange. Third, as noncommodities, they were allocated in households or collectives based on need or merit, rather than bought and sold for cash. Finally, they were mostly allocated in raw, unprocessed form—husked grain rather than wheat flour, cotton lint rather than finished textiles—and had to be processed before being consumed, often in labor-intensive ways. China's rural economy was to a large extent demonetized and decommodified, and millions of rural people touched money and industrial commodities only very infrequently. Rural people lived in a different material world from urbanites, and different material realities translated into different social worlds.

This difference was not due to the survival of a self-sufficient peasant economy. Commodification had proceeded apace through the nineteenth and twentieth century, and the average farmer in the 1930s was deeply enmeshed in market exchange—more deeply, in fact, than the collective peasant under Mao. Nor was it the intended outcome of communist austerity policies. Maoism is known for its emphasis on plain living and self-sufficiency, and a countryside without commodity exchange may be seen as the realization of Maoist goals. Yet the Chinese Communists did not pursue austerity for its own sake; sacrifice and abnegation were valued only because they paved the way to future abundance.¹ In fact, in the early years of the People's Republic, leaders sought to reduce local self-sufficiency and to draw the countryside into exchange relations with the industrial cities. It was only after 1953–54, and for pragmatic rather than ideological reasons, that the state soured on rural-urban commodity exchange.²

A WORLD (ALMOST) WITHOUT COMMODITIES

According to Marx, the wealth of capitalist societies appears "as an immense collection of commodities."³ Isolated by divisions of labor, we are unable to observe the conditions under which other people live and work; it is only when we see the products of their labor displayed in the marketplace that we obtain a material representation of other people's work and begin to grasp the complex articulation of the societies we inhabit. This is true, with some qualifications, also for socialist societies: citizens of Brezhnev-era Moscow or Mao-era Beijing would have seen the interdependencies and hierarchies of their societies reflected in the material displays of markets and department stores. The difference in the price and cultural prestige of, say, a foreign transistor radio, a domestically produced bicycle, and a sack of cabbages from the countryside would have taught them object lessons about how their social world was structured.

People who do not participate in a commodity economy, or do so only marginally, cannot materially grasp social complexity, although they may understand it in abstract ways. For an urban factory worker in Beijing, social connections were embodied in the canned peaches from Guangdong or the White Rabbit candies from Shanghai that she occasionally consumed, and in the displays of shops and markets that she observed every day. Much of what was displayed may have been unaffordable to her, but the habit of handling money every day meant that she could imagine herself as a potential consumer of the goods displayed. By contrast, a peasant who was surrounded in his daily life by things grown or made in his village, who received most of his income in grain and other produce, whose cash income from collective work was in the range of 10–15 yuan *a year*,⁴ and whose shopping options were limited to Supply and Marketing Cooperative stores stocked with reject goods from the cities, had to work much harder to create a mental representation of "China" or "the socialist world." Such terms are of course always abstractions, but for the urban person, they had some tangible, physical content.

Ideology is most powerful when things, not words, do the talking: when the way people relate to things, and things relate to each other, confirms our basic convictions about how the world works. In urban China, commodities sent out signals that both reinforced and contradicted the state's explicit messages but on the whole encouraged identification with the system, if not necessarily with specific leaders or policies. Things did not speak in the same way to rural people—or rather, it was local objects that did the talking, and they spoke in a local idiom. One obvious difference is the greater presence in urban China of propaganda objects—porcelain figurines of model opera heroes, enamel cups emblazoned with Mao quotes, posters of revolutionary leaders, etc. If, on average, an urban person bought an enamel bowl every eight years and a thermos bottle every five years, while a rural person bought an enamel bowl every twenty years and a thermos bottle every 33 years, urban people were about two to six times more exposed to the political messages imprinted on these objects.[5] Being less able to rely on the language of commodities, state officials in the countryside depended more on verbal messaging: on meetings and shouted slogans, which may have been less persuasive than the whispers of commodities.[6]

More important than overt messages, however, were the implicit ones that result from being exposed to a logic of commodity exchange. Money itself is a powerful abstraction: by creating equivalence between dissimilar things, it relates different types of work and modes of life to one another. Money establishes an all-encompassing economy of claims and obligations through which social relations are organized. My money, however little it may be, gives me a claim on a corresponding portion of total social wealth, and thus indirectly a claim on other people's labor. In an imagined pure commodity economy, it is up to me which portion of social wealth I claim. Under socialism, many goods are only partly commodified: they may be sold for cash, but sale is restricted to specific groups defined by merit, need, waiting time, or some other criterion. In urban China, housing, healthcare, and education were largely decommodified; in addition, most consumer goods were rationed, with varying degrees of stringency. Urban people thus lived in a dual system, depending for their basic needs on a paternalistic state while satisfying other needs from the market. This did not dent consumers' appetites or their ability to fashion intricate hierarchies of distinction from limited materials. Nor should we expect that it did; after all, most capitalist societies supplement markets with forms of public provisioning, and this does not reduce the acquisitive instincts of their members.

Research on consumption in the West suggests that the totality of commodities functions as a semiotic system.[7] Distinctions between genders, classes, ethnic groups, generations, etc. are mapped onto commodities, so that, for example, fine wool, silk, denim, and printed cotton are seen as the appropriate apparel for elite men, elite women, male commoners, and female commoners, respectively.[8] Little work has been done on consumer semiotics in socialist China, but as research by historians Karl Gerth and Sun Peidong shows, Chinese consumers used commodities to signal status, wealth, and power in much the same way as consumers did elsewhere.[9] The fact that conspicuous consumption was discouraged does not mean that people did not use commodities to compete over status: there may have been no great display of luxury, but a Hero fountain pen in the breast pocket of a cadre suit signaled distinction as effectively as a silk tie or a Rolex watch. Such signaling is a basic cultural competence that people learn by growing up in a commodity economy. An inability to express oneself through commodities marks one as culturally incompetent, as a country bumpkin who is unable to navigate society's symbolic order.

Another fundamental difference between the rural and urban worlds of goods was that while urbanites purchased ready-made commodities, rural people obtained raw materials that had to be processed before consumption. The distinction is not absolute: urban people, too, bought cloth rather than ready-made garments and had it tailored into clothes. Yet by and large, it holds: while urbanites bought polished rice or noodles, rural people received grain that needed to be cleaned and milled before being cooked. Urbanites bought cloth or garments; millions of rural people made their clothes from raw cotton, which they cleaned, carded, spun, and wove into cloth. Urbanites burned coal in stoves or enjoyed central heating; rural people collected firewood or dried grain stalks from the fields. The work of preparing raw materials for consumption was mostly done by women, often after long shifts in the collective fields.

There is a stark difference between the experience of a person who derives use value from the soil and other resources, expending his or her physical strength, and that of a person who purchases a commodity in a store. According to sociologist Alfred Sohn-Rethel, the commodity in its pure form—the packaged object, displayed for exchange—is abstracted from all use, cut off from its past in production and its future in consumption. "As long as commodities are subject to exchange, that is, as long as they are on the market, they may not be put to use, neither by sellers nor by buyers . . . In the market place . . . things stand still, ready for only one kind of action: their exchange. A commodity marked at a definite price is subject to the fiction of total material immutability, and not only on the part of human hands. Even nature, we assume, holds her breath, as long as the price of the commodity is to remain the same."[10] According to Sohn-Rethel, the real abstraction of commodity exchange establishes the categories of abstract thought: notions of quality and quantity, of difference and value arise only in the context of commodity exchange. Outside that, there is no need for a general category of, say, iron; while there may be different manifestations, such as a lump of ore, a steel bar, or a rusty knife, iron as a thing with fixed qualities—measurable, categorically different from other things yet commensurate with them in value—exists only in societies habituated to commodity exchange. One does not have to follow Sohn-Rethel all the way to see that exposure to commodities—frozen in time, representing objective value—creates different habits of thought than a life supported by use objects that grow and change under the user's hands.

MATERIAL LIFE IN CENTRAL SHAANXI, 1949-83

How, then, did the material world of rural people differ from the more well-known world of urbanites? My description is based on interviews conducted between 2012 and 2017 in Zhouzhi and Xingping Counties, in Central Shaanxi's Wei River Valley. This area, also known as Guanzhong, is a fertile plain, distinct from the poor mountain areas to the south and the harsh Loess Plateau to the north. In terms of rural incomes, industrialization, and urbanization rates, it is close to the national average. It was spared the worst of the Great Leap famine and did not suffer any natural disasters in the Mao years. Agricultural productivity increased dramatically under the collectives, thanks to increased irrigation; living standards, however, did not improve until the adjustment of farm prices in the 1980s.[11] The three villages where I conducted interviews are now about two hours' bus ride from Xi'an. In the collective years, it would have taken most of a day to reach them, but they were linked by motor roads and were in no way considered remote. Interviews are supplemented with consumption statistics; where Shaanxi data are not available, I rely on national statistics.

FOOD
Food consumption in Guanzhong remained intensely local in the collective years; salt was the only "imported" item that all households bought. Here, as elsewhere in China, grain was the source of 80–90 percent of calories and the main portion of rural people's incomes.[12] Nationwide, rural grain consumption rose after land reform and reached a peak of 205 kg per person in 1957; after collectivization, it fell to levels around 170–90 kg, with the 200 kg level

only reached again in 1978. Average calorie intake throughout the Mao years remained below 1930s levels.[13] The diet in Guanzhong consists largely of noodles and leavened buns, made from wheat if available and from corn, barley, or sorghum if not. Wheat and millet were distributed in husked form (*yuanliang*); corn was distributed on the cob, to be dried and shucked at home. Coarse grains such as corn and millet made up 60 percent of grain consumption. The people I interviewed did not remember famine deaths, but they recalled constant scarcity and frequent hunger.

Cooking oil in Guanzhong was made from cotton seeds. Per capita distribution in Shaanxi was one to two *jin* (0.5–1 kg) per person per year. National statistics show an average rural consumption of 1.2 kg of oil per capita for the years 1957–80.[14] Since frying was impossible with such small amounts, people boiled or steamed their food; one interviewee remembered using an eyedropper to drip oil on dishes. Lard was a more important source of fat than oil, and most families raised two pigs at a time, slaughtering one each winter. People remembered selling half the pork they raised—either because they were required to or because pigs were a source of cash. With about 50 kg of meat (much of it fatback) per pig, a family might retain 25 kg, or about 5 kg per person, which corresponds to the rural average for the collective years. Eggs were another source of protein, but as with meat, people tended to sell them.[15] In 1980, when living standards in the Shaanxi countryside had begun to improve, average yearly consumption of eggs and poultry was 130 g and 150 g per capita, respectively; the Guanzhong average may have been twice as much. Given the shortage of land, production teams in the region did not grow vegetables; households used their small private plots to grow wheat and corn. The only vegetables that were widely grown (often in unused corners of the courtyards) were chives, garlic, chili, and gourds. People also ate wild greens collected from hills and riverbanks.

When asked about cash expenditures, most people described salt, vinegar, soy sauce, and baking soda (as leavening for steamed buns) as daily necessities. All of these were used sparingly; in times of scarcity, people would forgo soy and vinegar and buy grain instead. Sugar and alcohol were rare luxuries. In 1965 (a "good" year), average sugar consumption in Shaanxi was 200 g per person, used mostly as a strengthening tonic for children and the elderly. Average alcohol consumption was 150 g.[16] Most men smoked, and tobacco accounted for 3 percent of household spending,[17] but most of it was locally grown. Food purchased for cash also included fried dough twists (*mahua*), eaten on holidays, and candies, given out at weddings. Bean curd was generally available for those who could spend cash on food. In 1978, when rural markets had reopened and rural incomes were on the rise, 76 percent of the food consumed by rural households was self-produced.[18]

CLOTHING

It is perhaps no surprise that rural food was self-supplied; after all, farmers had always fed themselves. Not so with textiles: already in the 1860s, more than one-half of China's cotton cloth was distributed through the market.[19] This ratio increased with the advent of foreign yarn and cloth in the 1870s and the rise of a domestic cotton industry since the 1910s. When the CCP came to power, three-quarters of all Chinese yarn and one-quarter of its cloth were made in modern mills. Industrially produced cloth is typically the vanguard of capitalist development; historically, it was the first (and often only) industrial commodity that commanded a mass market, and it was often the desire for factory textiles that drove rural people toward commodity production. Lenin and Trotsky spoke of cotton textiles as the *smychka* or "link" that tied rural peasants to urban industry. According to Trotsky, the rural-urban link had to be understood as "endless ribbon of cloth which stretches between the town and the countryside ... a *smychka* without cloth has no content. It is merely an empty word."[20]

In 1949, CCP leaders decided to phase out rural handloom weaving and to concentrate textile production in the cities. Their motivation was twofold: first, with prices for raw materials and finished products determined by the state, textile production was enormously profitable. It was the cotton textile industry, more than any other sector, that funded China's development in the Mao years. Second, hand spinning and hand weaving are extremely time-consuming: a woman who clothed a family of five spent half of the year doing textile work.[21] Maoist development strategy relied heavily on labor mobilization in the countryside, and the fastest way to mobilize extra labor was to free rural women from household chores, including textile work.

Nonetheless, rural hand spinning and hand weaving survived into the 1980s. How many women continued to spin and weave and how many people continued to wear *tubu* (homespun) cloth is impossible to determine, since no data were collected. Based on interviews and archival documents, though, I believe that manual textile production remained widespread wherever rural people had access to cotton, that is, in most low-lying parts of China except the northeast and the south. I found output figures for handloom cloth only for the year 1964, when a report by the Chinese Supply and Marketing Cooperative estimated a rural handloom output of 566 million meters, amounting to 12 percent of China's 1964 cotton textile output.

Assuming that all of it remained in the countryside, this would have added 98 cm to each rural person's ration—not insignificant at a time when official rural per capita supply was four meters. If the estimates are reliable, handloom output was almost as high in 1964 as it had been at its prewar peak of 1936.[22]

People in Guanzhong remembered that until the 1970s, everybody apart from cadres and courting or newlywed couples wore *tubu* clothes. This was the case also in Qidong County, Jiangsu, a much wealthier and more developed area. Since 1954, cotton cloth was rationed, with rural rations half as much as urban ones. Nationwide, rural rations averaged 5.5 m per capita for the collective years, with a peak of 8.7 m in 1959 and a drop to 2.3 m in 1961.[23] Clothing minima are difficult to define, but based on interviews, I estimate that an adult (male or female) farmer in Guanzhong needed two unlined suits for summer and one padded suit for winter. In addition, one needed several pairs of cloth shoes and a headscarf for protection from the summer sun. Taking into account different replacement rates for these items, I calculate a physical minimum of 13 m for an adult who worked outdoors most of the year, and 9 m for the statistically average person, including children and old people. At this level of supply, clothes would be washed infrequently and not at all in winter, and patched and worn until they fell apart; lice would be inevitable. Falling below these minima would mean that a person could no longer go out in inclement weather and therefore could not fully participate in collective work. The long-term average of 5.5 m, then, fell dramatically short of replacement needs; a person who relied for her clothing entirely on ration cloth would have found herself in rags and almost naked after a few years. Moreover, my interviewees did not use their ration coupons. With few exceptions, they did not have enough cash to buy factory cloth; instead, they sold the coupons on the black market and used the extra cash to buy grain.

How then did rural people clothe themselves? They did so by theft and embezzlement at all levels of the administrative hierarchy. Procurement prices for cotton were set so low that most teams lost money on its cultivation, and farmers and collective leaders had no qualms about clawing back part of the harvest.[24] Team leaders hid cotton from the state and distributed it to households, pickers (usually women) stuffed cotton in their jackets, families sent children out to steal from the fields, and collectives allowed part of the harvest to spoil in the fields and distributed the "waste" cotton to its members. Despite aggressive attempts by the state to procure all cotton in the countryside, some 20 percent of the harvest remained in peasant hands, and much of it was transformed into cloth by rural women. Since women worked full shifts in agriculture, textile work had to take place in moments "stolen" from the collective, often at night when men and children were asleep.[25]

A brief note on hygiene in Guanzhong: while dirty clothing was frowned upon, it was common to dry-brush clothes rather than wash them in water. This was because people had few spare clothes, and those they had were in more or less constant use. Powder detergent was unknown before the 1980s, so people used soda, wood ash, or the pods of the Chinese honey locust (*Gleditsia sinensis*) instead. Rural consumption of laundry soap in the 1960s and '70s was one to two bars a year, about one-tenth of the urban level.[26] Toilet soap was practically unknown. Lindane powder (*liuliu fen*) was sprinkled onto the seams of clothes to keep the lice at bay. Personal hygiene was largely limited to washing hands and faces.

HOUSING

The one aspect where rural people could be said to be better off than urbanites was housing, at least in terms of square footage. Rural people were generally owners of their homes; new couples were assigned plots at the time of marriage and bought construction materials from the production team. Wherever possible, carpenters were recruited from within the team and compensated in work points. Most other work—laying foundations, tamping the earth, laying bricks, etc.—was performed by neighbors on the basis of reciprocity. Houses in Guanzhong were built from local mud and timber. Kiln-fired bricks and tiles were not used until the 1970s; walls were made from adobe bricks, and roofs were covered with wheat straw. Glass windows and concrete were not used for private houses until the 1980s.[27] In 1981, the average rural person in Shaanxi had 8.2 square meters of living space, of which 2.2 square meters were built using modern methods, with bricks used for door and window frames and for pillars to support the roof. Only 0.2 percent of rural housing in 1981 contained reinforced concrete.[28]

The only pieces of furniture that all households had were chests and boxes, typically provided by the groom's family as part of the betrothal gift. A typical set consisted of two chests, one box of drawers, and a jewelry box.[29] Tables were rare, high chairs almost unknown. People sat cross-legged on a *kang* (a heated brick platform) or squatted on the floor or on low stools. Beds were not much used; in winter people slept on the *kang*, in summer on reed mats in the courtyard. Bricks or polished hardwood blocks served as neck rests; to this day, old people prefer them to pillows. Kitchen stoves were made of adobe bricks, with the wok cemented in at the top. Leak-proof brick stoves and chimneys were introduced in the late collective period. Kitchen equipment consisted of a wok, a few knives and spatulas, and bamboo sieves and containers. Each household had a few earthenware jars of different sizes to store water, pickles, sauces, etc. Grain was stored in sacks or woven reed containers. Farm tools such as plowshares, shovel blades, and hoe blades were bought at local markets and fitted onto wooden handles at home. In the villages where I did my interviews, about one family in three had a loom, and every family had at least one spinning wheel. Looms were portable and freely shared with neighbors. All furniture and tools were made by village carpenters.

Store-bought implements included washstands, copper or enamel wash basins, hand mirrors, enamel bowls and cups, and thermos bottles. While every family had some of these, total consumption was limited; as mentioned above, out of a hundred rural people, three bought a thermos bottle and five an enamel mug in any given year.[30] Rural cooperative stores stocked rubber shoes, towels, paper, pencils, and matches, but none of these were sold in large quantities. Durable consumer items began to spread in the 1970s. In 1980, at a time when living standards were rising rapidly, one out of three households in rural Shaanxi had a bicycle, one out of four had a watch or clock, and one out of five had a sewing machine.[31]

FUEL AND LIGHTING

Fuel accounted for a surprisingly large share of the rural household budget: 7–9 percent, rising to 14 percent in the post-Leap crisis years. In 1978 (the first year for which I could find data), 68 percent of rural energy needs were self-supplied, indicating that farmers heated and cooked with biomass distributed by the collective or with grass and firewood collected in the hills. In 1980s rural Guanzhong, 50 percent of household energy consumption came from agricultural biomass (grain stalks supplied for a fee by the collective), 25 percent from wood, 17 percent from reeds and grasses, and 8 percent from coal.[32] I haven't seen evidence for an explicit ban on coal use in rural areas, but it appears to have been available only in mining areas. Electricity reached most Guanzhong production teams in the late 1970s, though this does not necessarily imply that homes were connected; initially, electrification (as well as other infrastructure, such as roads, canals, and water wells) was geared toward collective needs rather than domestic consumption. Electricity powered irrigation pumps before it lit rural homes; wells were dug in the fields before piped water reached the villages. Electricity was rationed: each married couple was allowed one 25-watt lightbulb; broken bulbs had to be returned before they could be replaced.[33]

ACCUMULATION, UNDERCONSUMPTION, AND WOMEN'S OVERWORK

Why did a socialist state perpetuate a situation in which millions of rural people were locked into time-consuming and backbreaking work? The activities detailed above were, after all, spectacularly inefficient. Already in the 1930s, a single worker in a mechanized spinning mill replaced the output of eighty hand-operated spinning wheels; the ratio for PRC factories must have been higher.[34] The same applies to the milling of flour, the collection of firewood, and many other tasks. Having women spend time on household chores meant that their labor was unavailable for intensive agriculture, where it was needed if the state were to meet its ambitious development goals. Second, why did a party ideologically committed to eradicating the "three big inequalities" (between agriculture and industry, city and countryside, and mental and manual labor) tolerate blatant inequality in material supplies?[35] And finally, why did the socialist state hesitate to tap into latent rural demand for consumer goods? As mentioned above, Lenin and Trotsky saw the exchange of rural products for urban-industrial commodities as the main motor of socialist development.[36] Since the state controlled prices at both ends, profit was guaranteed: in the textile sector, state planners set the price for cotton so low, and that for finished cloth so high, that state-owned cotton mills broke even in the first year of operation.[37] Why, then, not profit from rural-urban trade and benefit the countryside at the same time?

We can, I think, safely exclude Maoist utopianism as a motivating factor for the shortage of commodities in rural areas. For a few brief months in 1958, Mao and other leaders seem to have convinced themselves that communism was within reach, that social relations in the new people's communes were no longer governed by the money-form, and that people could be supplied according to their needs, without the intervention of money or a work-point system. As cultural historian Laurence Coderre has shown, this conviction did not last. Already in November 1958, Mao criticized unnamed leftists who wanted to do away with socialist commodity production and commodity exchange, and reaffirmed Stalin's verdict that "commodity production must not be identified with capitalist production" because commodity production and the money economy are designed, under socialism, "to serve the development and consolidation of socialist production."[38]

It is important to clarify what the CCP meant by commodity, but the party's internal debates are as likely to obscure as to clarify the issues. Party leaders discussed commodities in two different contexts: in theory debates on the nature of the socialist economy, and in pragmatic planning contexts.[39] In both contexts, the term was sometimes used in the familiar sense of a consumer good that is bought and sold on the market. However, "commodity" could also refer to an object whose production and distribution was governed by price calculation, rather than by material-balance planning. Material-balance planning uses physical units (tons of steel, bales of cotton, sacks of flour, etc.) rather than prices to track supplies as they move through the system. This was considered the more advanced, more socialist method of planning, and was prevalent in state industry. Debates about the role of the commodity under socialism were often less concerned with consumption (even less with consumerism) than with drawing appropriate boundaries between a truly socialist sector governed by material-balance planning and a semisocialist sectors that still relied on prices—albeit prices that were set by the state. "Commodity" in these debates carries no connotation of free consumer choice or equivalent exchange; it is simply a good whose supply is managed with the aid of prices. For example, grain purchased and distributed by the state was known as commodity grain (*shangpin liang*)—even though grain was allocated to consumers through the state grain bureaucracy, rather than bought and sold in the market.

Paradoxically, in this logic it is the countryside that is the realm of the commodity, despite the fact that it was largely deprived of commodities in the sense of consumer goods. Stalin's justification for the continued existence of commodities was that collective farmers were unwilling to part with their grain for anything but cash: "At present the collective farms will not recognize any other economic relation with the town except the commodity relation—exchange through purchase and sale."[40] Only if the urban state sector and the rural collective sector could be merged into a single system, only if state administrators could identify all resources and needs in the country and match them to each other, would commodities and money disappear. This view prevailed also in the PRC. After the Great Leap Forward, not even leftists argued for the inclusion of the countryside in a system of state ownership and direct allocation—perhaps indeed because rural people would not have it, or more likely because such a step would have opened the door to rural demands for inclusion in the urban welfare regime.

The fact that state planners conceived of the relationship between urban industry and agrarian countryside as a commodity relation (that is, a relationship of exchange rather than allocation) helps explain the scarcity of commodities in the countryside. In urban industry, the individual firm was not a locus of value realization; no profit was made by stinting a plant of raw materials, reducing its wage bill, or depressing prices for its products. Or, more precisely, these acts shifted profit from one unit in the system to another, but this was irrelevant from an overarching perspective, since all units passed on their profits and losses to the state. The countryside, by contrast, was outside the state-owned sector. If economic relations inside state industry resembled those between cost-sharing and profit-sharing units of a multifirm conglomerate, relations with rural collectives were like those between a conglomerate and its dependent subcontractors. Changing the terms of trade between urban industry and rural agriculture could and did generate profits for the state, in a very direct way.

This is just another way of restating the well-known fact that capital accumulation in the PRC relied on mandatory, unequal exchange between urban and rural sectors. The logic here is simple: a large agrarian country with a small industrial sector cannot achieve rapid industrialization by relying on the routine reinvestment of industrial profits, which will then generate more profits; it needs to systematically extract surpluses from the agrarian and light-industrial sector and channel them to heavy industry. The mechanism to achieve this is "scissors pricing": the state buys grain, cotton, tea, oilseed, and other agricultural products at depressed, state-mandated prices; processes them in state industry; and sells them back at prices that are high enough to guarantee a profit to the state. The countryside, in other words, functions as an internal colony: it provides the raw materials needed in urban industry, and absorbs urban industry's finished products.[41] However, this still does not explain why state planners chose to undersupply rural China rather than trying to set in motion a virtuous cycle, in which an increasingly wealthy rural population would absorb the growing output of factories, to the benefit of both. I see three overlapping answers: scarcity, inflation fears, and a tacit realization that rural women could be made to fill the commodity gap at no cost to the state.

First, scarcity: given its unfavorable land-population ratio, China could not produce great surpluses of agricultural products. Demand outpaced supply for most items, not only in the cities, where workers expected better food and clothing, but also on the world market, where China sold agricultural products to earn the export dollars needed to buy advanced machinery. The need for foreign currency was such that China sold cotton cloth, tea, and other products below domestic prices—in other words, domestic consumers were made to subsidize state exports.[42] State planners prioritized export and urban needs over rural demands, and systematically undersupplied rural markets.

Second, inflation fears: one result of the state's arm's-length relations with the countryside was that money became a problem in a way it was not in urban areas. Urban workers received monthly wages, and their cash expenditures were steady and predictable. In the countryside, the state disbursed huge quantities of cash seasonally at harvest time. As historian Matthew Lowenstein has shown, this was a problem because sudden cash injections in the countryside led to seasonal spikes in the demand for commodities, which interfered with the supply of goods in urban areas; they also fueled the black-market trade and threatened to trigger inflation.[43] Throughout the collective years, the state sought to keep cash out of the hands of farmers. It did so by increasing the supply of commodities at harvest time in order to mop up excess liquidity in rural areas,[44] by promoting rural saving schemes, and by capping the amounts that agricultural production teams could pay out to their members. These policies were successful: as mentioned above, per capita payout to collective members hovered between 10 and 15 yuan a year. The shortage of liquid cash in the countryside goes a long way to explain low commodity consumption.

Third, capitalizing on rural women's unpaid labor: One fundamental difference between rural and urban life was that in the countryside, there was no sharp division between work and domestic life, production and reproduction. Urban work units could schedule overtime but could not extend their operations into the families and households of their workers—not only because regulations forbade it but because shop floors and homes did not form a technological continuum. In the countryside, by contrast, homes blended into fields, in ways that created conflict between farm households and the state. On the one hand, state investment in agriculture was in constant danger of being diverted to household use. Fertilizer destined for the collective fields might end up on private plots, collective trucks were used for private travel, and people took time off from collective work to do private chores. On the other hand, rural labor times were not regulated by the clock, and collectives could extend shifts at will. Most importantly, state and collectives could extract extra labor from rural women by undersupplying basic needs. By extracting the lion's share of the cotton harvest and selling back insufficient quantities of textiles, the state shifted the responsibility for clothing the countryside onto rural women, forcing them to scavenge for leftover cotton and process it into homespun textiles. The same logic applies to other products, where resource extraction and commodity shortages combined to force men and women to work longer hours in the fields, and women to work longer hours at home, in order to substitute for missing grain, biomass, cotton, fuel, etc. It is this logic of substitution that underpinned accumulation in socialist China and explains rural China's impoverished material culture.

NOTES

1 See chapter 7 of this volume.
2 Shue, *Peasant China in Transition*, 195–245; Perkins, *Market Control and Planning*.
3 Karl Marx, *Capital*, vol. 1 (London: Penguin, 1976), 125.
4 Nongmuyuye Bu Jihuasi, *Nongye Jingji Ziliao: 1949–1983* [Materials of the agricultural economy, 1949–1983] (henceforth *NYJJZL*) (Beijing: no publisher, 1983,), 511, 517. Lardy and Ash independently arrive at even lower estimates. See Lardy, *Agriculture*, 161, 243n11; and Ash, "Squeezing the Peasants, 988, table 11.
5 Jeffrey Taylor, *China Consumer Demand Statistical Update* (Washington, DC: Center for International Research, Bureau of the Census, US Department of Commerce, 1987), 92, 94.
6 Chapter 5 in this volume documents the intensity of explicit propaganda messaging in the countryside.
7 See Roland Barthes, *The Fashion System* (New York: Hill and Wang, 1967); Pierre Bourdieu, *Distinction: A Social Critique of the Judgement of Taste* (Cambridge, MA: Harvard University Press, 1987).
8 Marshall Sahlins, *Culture and Practical Reason* (Chicago: University of Chicago Press, 1976), 182.
9 Gerth, *Unending Capitalism*; Sun, *Shishang yu zhengzhi*.
10 Sohn-Rethel, *Geistige und körperliche Arbeit*, 47 (my translation). Sohn-Rethel—friend of Bloch, Benjamin, and Adorno—is relatively unknown in the English-speaking world, perhaps due to the poor translation of his work.
11 Vermeer, *Economic Development*.
12 Lardy, *Agriculture*, 154.
13 *NYJJZL*, 538; Lardy, *Agriculture*, 147–48.
14 *NYJJZL*, 539.
15 Guojia tongjiju nongcun chouyang diaocha zongdui, *Ge sheng, zizhiqu, zhixiashi nongmin shouru, xiaofei diaochayanjiu ziliao huibian* [Compilation of survey materials, peasant incomes, and expenditures in all provinces, autonomous regions, and province-level cities] (Beijing: Zhongguo Tongji Chubanshe, 1985), vol. 2, 120.
16 Guojia Tongjiju, *Ge sheng*, Vol II, 120.
17 Chang Mingming, *Zhongguo nongjia shouzhi wenti yanjiu, 1949–1956* [Investigation into the incomes and expenditures of Chinese rural families, 1949–1956] (Beijing: Zhongguo Shehui Kexue, 2015), 110 (national data, 1954).
18 Guojia Tongjiju, *Ge sheng*, vol. 1, 40 (national data).
19 Xu Dixin and Wu Chengming, eds., *Chinese Capitalism, 1522–1840* (London: MacMillan 2000), 170–75.
20 Chris Ward, *Russia's Cotton Workers and the New Economic Policy* (Cambridge: Cambridge University Press, 1990), 7.

21 "Ma Tinghai Nongye Shengchan Hezuoshe shi zenyang fadong funü canjia shengchan de" [How the Ma Tinghai Agricultural Production Cooperative mobilizes women to participate in production], *Renmin ribao*, February 2, 1954, 2.
22 Xu Jianqing, "Mianhua tonggou, mianbu tonggou tongxiao zhengce yu shougong mianfangzhiye" [The policy of unified purchase of cotton and unified purchase and marketing of cotton cloth and the handicraft textile industry], *Dangdai Zhongguoshi yanjiu*, no. 2 (2010): 27–34; Xu Jianqing, "Zhidu bianqe yu shougong mianfang zhiye: 1954–1965" [System transition and handcraft cotton weaving: 1954–1965], *Zhongguo jingjishi yanjiu*, no. 4 (2009): 73–75.
23 Yu Zongxian and Zhao Gang, *Zhonggong fangzhiye zhi fazhan jiqi dui woguo fangzhipin duiwai maoyi zhi yingxiang* [The development of the textile industry of Communist China and its impact on our external textile trade] (Taibei [Taipei]: Xingzhengyuan Jingjianhui, 1965), 105.
24 Thomas Wiens, "Poverty and Progress in the Huang and Huai River Basins," in *Chinese Rural Development: The Great Transformation*, edited by William L. Parish (Armonk, NY: M. E. Sharpe, 1985), 82. Wiens's calculation of labor returns in an Anhui commune shows that cotton had the lowest return per workday among eleven crops, one-fourth lower than for rice and less than half that for wheat.
25 Hershatter, *The Gender of Memory*, 45–48, 191–92, 186, 259–60.
26 Taylor, *China Consumer Demand*, 91.
27 Danbei interviews, August 25, 2012.
28 Guojia Tongjiju, *Ge sheng*, 122.
29 Most women owned at least one silver or pewter hairpin; some also had earrings and bracelets.
30 Taylor, *China Consumer Demand*, 92, 94 (averages for the 1970s).
31 "Shaanxi sheng tongji ju, Shaanxi sheng tongji nianjian 1986" [Shaanxi statistical yearbook 1986] (Xi'an: Shaanxi Renmin Chubanshe, 1986), 322.
32 Zhonggong Shaanxi Shengwei Nongcun Zhengce Yanjiushi, *Shaanxi sheng nongcun shehui jingji diaocha* [Socioeconomic investigations of the Shaanxi countryside] (Xi'an: Shaanxi Renmin Chubanshe, 1986), 343. Data are by weight, not energy content.
33 Wu Xiujie, *Ein Jahrhundert Licht: Eine technikethnologische Studie zur Beleuchtung im chinesischen ländlichen Alltag* (Wiesbaden: Harrassowitz, 2009), 66–70.
34 Yan Zhongping, *Zhongguo mianfangzhi shigao* [Draft History of China's Cotton Textile Industry] (Beijing: Shangwu Yinshuguan, 2011 [1955]), 335.
35 I follow Karl Gerth in translating *san da chabie* as "three big inequalities," rather than "differences."
36 Selden and Ka, "Original Accumulation."
37 Chao, *Development of Cotton Textile Production*, 250.
38 Coderre, "Necessary Evil," 31.
39 Coderre, "Necessary Evil," 27–28.
40 Stalin, *Economic Problems of Socialism*, 16, cited in Coderre, "Necessary Evil," 32.
41 The notion of rural China as an internal colony is associated with agricultural economist Wen Tiejun. For a discussion, see Alexander F. Day, *The Peasant in Postsocialist China: History, Politics, and Capitalism* (Cambridge: Cambridge University Press, 2013), 98–102.

42 Kaoru Sugihara, "International Circumstances surrounding the Post-War Japanese Cotton Textile Industry," in Douglas A. Farnie and David J. Jeremy, *The Fibre that Changed the World: The Cotton Industry in International Perspective, 1600–1990s* (Oxford: Oxford University Press 2004), 535–36.
43 Matthew Lowenstein, "Return to the Cage: Monetary Policy in China's First Five-Year Plan," *Twentieth-Century China* 44, no. 1 (2019): 53–56.
44 Dorothy Solinger, *Chinese Business under Socialism* (Berkeley: University of California Press, 1987), 286.

10 THE MAKINGS OF CHINA'S COLD WAR MOTOR CITY

COVELL F. MEYSKENS

IN SEPTEMBER 1969, CHINA'S DEFENSE MINISTER, LIN BIAO, ordered the Second Auto Works (or the Works) to manufacture five hundred trucks for Hubei's National Day parade in 1970. When this directive was received, some employees argued it was unrealizable, since construction of the factory had begun in 1965 and had advanced only slightly before the Cultural Revolution threw the project into disarray.[1] Regional leaders nonetheless insisted that production targets be met. Border clashes had erupted with the Soviets in March 1969, and Moscow's million soldiers along the frontier could push into Chinese territory at any moment. The United States also had nearly a half million troops in Vietnam and had China firmly fixed in its geopolitical crosshairs. Faced with the threat of war, laborers at the Works tried to accomplish production quotas by making up for a lack of machinery by using hand tools. In the end, only twenty trucks were completed in time. Project leaders knew they were not roadworthy, and so workers were assigned to run out and push them if needed. While the trucks did not stall in front of the viewing rostrum, they broke down further along the parade route.[2]

On the surface, it might seem most appropriate to chalk up this militarized rush to produce trucks as another example of Maoist China's failed economic policies. In this chapter, I bracket the question of whether the Works was a failure. Instead I argue that its construction was the product of a material regime that had three main facets, all of which show how the contradictions of international and domestic politics became embedded in material culture in Mao's China.[3] The first feature of this material regime was a militaristic approach to the construction of space, which resulted from the Works inclusion in the CCP's Third Front campaign to establish a secret heavy-industrial base in inland China in preparation for war with the Soviets or Americans. To protect Chinese industry, the party allocated roughly forty percent of the national capital construction budget to building the Third Front between 1964 and 1980, and it required that its nearly two thousand projects be dispersed and hidden in mountains, out of sight of enemy bombers.[4] In this way, the CCP's concerns about Cold War rivals penetrating Chinese territory became imprinted in its industrial geography. While these security parameters determined the Works' general placement, its final whereabouts became a subject of political strain, with some pushing for a more spread-out, covert location while others favored a more developed, central site. When Sino-Soviet border skirmishes made war appear imminent in 1969, the party center settled the debate, asserting that the only acceptable location was deep in the mountains.

A second prominent facet of the Works' construction was a spartan, productivist approach to the materiality of everyday life. The Second Auto Works had to, as the contemporary party slogan said, "produce first and live later," by which the government meant suppressing investment in nonproductive matters, such as housing and urban services.[5] This policy of austerity was designed to not only save scarce material resources for increasing heavy industry, which the government judged necessary for China's defense and development, but also advance the socialist goal of reducing differences between the material conditions of manual and mental labor *and* urban and rural areas. This developmental method resulted in what historian Hou Li has characterized as "industrialization without urbanization."[6] While some project participants attest in archival documents, memoirs, and oral interviews to finding meaning in helping build an industrial China, many express discontent with the material privation of everyday Maoism. Project leaders tarred critics as betraying Maoist China's spartan developmental path with their bourgeois capitalist penchant for higher consumption and the Soviet preference for big buildings.

The final feature of the material regime underpinning the Works was a war-inspired approach to the use of science and technology. Maoism's approach to technoscience emerged in "the revolutionary 'cradle' of Yan'an," where CCP leaders decided in the 1940s that they should not depend on China's limited foreign-made machines and technical experts to fight the Guomindang and Japan's more powerful militaries.[7] The party had to be self-reliant and stress native practices and mass mobilization. In accordance with this view, party leaders thought that the most expedient way for China to industrialize in the face of growing Soviet and American hostility in the 1960s was to emulate how the CCP dealt with resource scarcity in its wartime base areas. Work units had to mobilize domestic and especially local resources in militarized campaigns to compensate for shortages of machinery and technicians.[8]

When employees at the Works warned that relying on local resources would yield poorly constructed buildings and trucks, they were reproached for trying to make China follow in the footsteps of the Soviet Union, where bureaucrats and technicians had putatively orchestrated a capitalist resurgence that normalized their material privileges.[9] No one not employed at the Works was supposed to know about this or any other event at the factory, since, as a Third Front project, it was a national secret. When trucks were brought to the National Day parade in Wuhan, Works' newspapers celebrated this accomplishment; the national press, however, made no mention of the factory's existence until 1979, because absolute secrecy was regarded as the only way to safeguard the Third Front from the military dangers of the Cold War.[10]

GATHERING TREASURES FOR A COLD WAR FACTORY

China's geopolitical position in the Cold War became particularly risky in the early 1960s. Not only did Moscow turn from a friend into an enemy after the Sino-Soviet split, but Washington also increased its support for anticommunist forces in Vietnam. International tensions between Beijing and its Cold War enemies sparked the Third Front campaign to industrialize China's interior after Washington responded to a supposed North Vietnamese attack on an American navy vessel in the Tonkin Gulf on August 4, 1964, by deploying airplanes to bombard North Vietnam.[11] Worried that US aggression might spill over the border, CCP leaders divided the country into three war zones: a First Front along the coast and in the northeast and northwest, a Second Front behind coastal provinces, and a Third Front in Central China. In the last region, the party demanded the building of a large military industrial complex.[12]

The immediate cause of this defensive spatial arrangement was Beijing's mounting tensions with Washington. Its historical origins, however, lay in the CCP's understanding of the wars of the early twentieth century. According to Mao Zedong, the Third Front was a response to Stalin and Chiang Kai-shek not moving enough industry into rear areas before World War II and then having to industrialize the interior amid the heat of battle. Mao also connected the Third Front's physical layout to the CCP's waging of guerilla warfare against the Guomindang and Japanese from mountain hideouts, a military strategy that CCP leaders considered to be still applicable to China's defense during the Cold War.[13]

During discussions about which projects to incorporate into the Third Front, CCP leaders decided that China needed to expand automobile

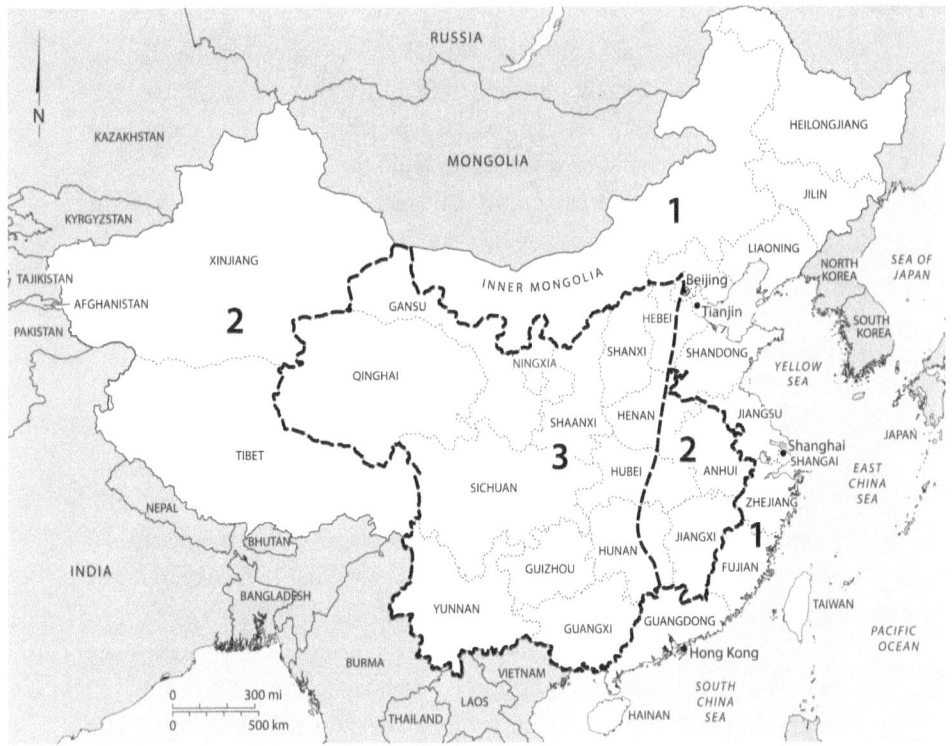

MAP 10.1. The First, Second, and Third Fronts, 1964–80. Courtesy of Covell Mesykens.

production. The First Auto Works had been built in the 1950s and begun manufacturing vehicles. Factories in Beijing, Shanghai, and Nanjing made auto parts, and a few other factories produced buses and motorcycles.[14] And yet China's auto industry was still underdeveloped. In line with CCP leaders' productivist proclivities, what they wanted were not small automobiles, which were geared toward consumers, but heavy-duty trucks, which served the collective objective of raising national output of producer goods. To put more trucks onto China's roads, Mao decreed that it was "time to build a Second Auto Works."[15]

Placed in charge of this endeavor was Rao Bin, a man who had led a revolutionary base area in Shanxi and after 1949 was assigned leading positions in the automotive industry. One of his colleagues remembers being shocked when Rao informed him that "the Second Auto Works is going to pursue a road of self-reliance and . . . self-plan a factory with an annual production capacity of one hundred thousand trucks." His colleague wondered how such a mammoth project was possible when China did not even have enough resources for the First Auto Works to achieve its initial goal of manufacturing thirty thousand trucks per year. When Rao was asked how he planned to realize this lofty objective, he replied that he was going to "gather treasures" from Chinese and foreign industry, by which he meant mobilizing both material and ideational resources to build the Works.[16]

One foreign treasure Rao and his colleagues sought to imitate was the Stalin Automobile Plant, which in the 1930s had dealt with systemic material scarcity by pooling resources from Soviet factories and technical institutes to make industrial designs, train labor, provide equipment, and supervise production. Following this developmental example, the First Machine-Building Ministry, which oversaw China's auto industry, commanded the First Auto Works to manage the whole project, the Shanghai Auto Factory to head up construction, the Wuhan Auto Factory to make truck parts, and the Nanjing Auto Factory to create vehicle designs. Every single work unit involved also had to send some staff to the Works, as well as train technical school graduates to fill out the factory's ranks. The First Auto Works, for its part, transferred a third of its labor force.[17]

According to Third Front policy, if domestic resources were inadequate to build a project, the supervising ministry could request foreign materials.[18] The First Machine-Building Ministry took advantage of this bureaucratic possibility and imported two American trucks—one from the American company Dodge and another from the now-defunct American company International. Both trucks were purchased from Canada, since Washington had instituted an embargo on China in 1950 during the Korean War.[19] Upon receiving the trucks, First Auto Works' technicians reverse-engineered and modified their designs according to leading officials' specifications.[20]

Defense considerations took precedence, because military leaders had complained that troops either "had guns and no trucks or . . . several guns and only one truck."[21] To address this material deficiency in China's force structure, the general staff demanded the annual manufacture of 45,000 trucks. The Metallurgy Ministry also called for more trucks for mining ventures, since the current fleet could not provide enough mineral products to fulfill manufacturing quotas. In the past, shortages were handled by importing 160,000 trucks. This policy had reduced funding for domestic development, since truck imports had cost three times more than investment in the automobile industry between 1949 and 1966. To make Chinese mining less dependent on imports, the First Machine-Building Ministry directed the Works to make 55,000 mining trucks annually. To help realize this massive undertaking, the ministry purchased 195 pieces of foreign equipment, and it ordered hundreds of domestic factories to produce 21,000 pieces of equipment.²²

SEARCHING FOR SPATIAL SECURITY

All these materials were not sent to a centrally located city whose existing industrial base and urban infrastructure would have facilitated constructing the Works. This geographic decision followed from the security logic behind Third Front policy, which required that all factories not be located in big cities, because they could be easily annihilated by enemy aircraft or, as Mao remarked, "with just one hydrogen bomb."²³ To keep Third Front industry out of enemy planes' view, the party mandated that all projects had to be constructed in "mountainous, dispersed, [and] hidden" locations.²⁴

In January 1965, Rao Bin and a few high-ranking officials from the First Auto Works went to survey twenty counties in central and western China in search of a secure site for the Second Auto Works. At first, the survey group drove and hiked through the mountains, looking for a suitable spot along the projected path of the Chengdu–Wuhan railroad. Next, surveyors examined locations in northern Guizhou and northeast Sichuan.²⁵ Surveyors collected data on so many places that the Works became known as a "briefcase company," named after the documents that project leaders carried around on their alpine treks.²⁶

After inspecting many sites, the survey team determined that the best way to safeguard the factory was to split it into several workshops, place each in a valley, and conceal important ones inside caves.²⁷ While project planners thought that military considerations should be given their due, they recognized that economic factors could not be ignored. The Works had to be near a big water source, since the factory would require ample amounts, and a railway had to be nearby, so that supplies could be shipped in and trucks could be moved out.²⁸

In the end, the factory's location was decided not by the survey team but by Deng Xiaoping, who said in November 1965 that the factory should be placed along the route of the Xiangfan–Chongqing railroad, which was soon to be built between Sichuan and Hubei as part of the Third Front.²⁹ Northwest Hubei was chosen as the most fitting location because the Han River could provide water, and the Danjiangkou hydropower station could deliver electricity.³⁰ After a year of surveying, opinions coalesced around two main options. One group maintained that the Works should be placed in the small town of Shiyan, where high mountains would obscure its location. Another group argued that security measures had to be complied with more strictly and that the factory should be divided up into workshops of no more than a thousand square meters. The First Auto Works' assistant chief engineer, Meng Shaonong, found this design idea preposterous, asking at a meeting whether "these cadres have ever seen a factory," since their plan would necessitate cutting the factory up into a hundred pieces.[31]

In October 1966, central party officials sided with the Shiyan group and designated a two-hundred-square-kilometer area as the works' location. Their word should have been final, and construction should have begun in 1967. However, by then the factional conflicts during the Cultural Revolution had led to workers abandoning their posts and dragging project leaders back to the First Auto Works for struggle sessions.[32]

Some laborers who remained behind formed a rebel faction that appealed to the planning commission to change the factory's location, because of the current designs' impracticality and inadequate security arrangements. They asserted that the designs of the Shiyan plan were not viable because its industrial geography was "too dispersed, so even when [the factory] is built, it won't be possible to produce" any vehicles. Also, there was only one road into the area. If it were to be bombed, then the factory "would be kaput." Ten nearby reservoirs posed dangers too. If one collapsed, "that would be end of the Second Auto Works."[33] Rebels contended that these issues could be avoided if the factory were placed at a more central location, near the medium-sized town of Xiangfan. What the rebels did not say, but likely thought, is that they preferred to live in the more developed and less remote area surrounding Xiangfan.

When another faction averred that the rebels' suggested site would be too militarily exposed, they retorted that such a large factory could never be hidden.[34] In response to rebel demands, the planning commission organized a survey in 1967, which concluded that the factory should stay in Shiyan. The rebels then declared past designs invalid because they were performed by bourgeois intellectuals, who sought to direct China onto a capitalist road and were engaged in industrial projects not for the collective good but in pursuit of personal fame. The only factory designs the rebels considered politically legitimate and properly socialist were those signed by a collective entity like their own.[35]

In 1968, provincial authorities moved to implement the party center's order to bring factional struggles under control by putting the military in charge. The Hubei government dispatched a thousand soldiers to the Works to ensure that factional politics did not further hinder construction.[36] The

Works could no longer exist only on paper. The factory had to be materialized. To further the construction process, ministerial and provincial officials commanded the rebels at the First Auto Works to allow project leaders to return within two weeks. Other laborers were given ten days to come back and participate in bolstering China's industrial defenses against American and Soviet aggression.[37]

COLD WAR TENSIONS AND MATERIAL AUSTERITY

Knowing that even when all employees returned to the Works that available machinery would be insufficient to complete its construction, the State Council implemented the Maoist policy of substituting huge inputs of manual labor for a much smaller number of machines, ordering the mobilization of tens of thousands of additional workers.[38] Nearby counties recruited around twenty thousand people and dispatched them to automotive factories nationwide to receive technical training.[39] The First Machine-Building Ministry brought in another 12,082 cadres and 10,235 technicians from factories in Changchun, Shanghai, Nanjing, and Wuhan, and the ministry assigned 4,469 technical school graduates to be industrial workers. Construction teams in Beijing and at the Daqing oilfield, meanwhile, transferred thirty thousand people, and Hubei mobilized sixty thousand rural militia members to perform manual labor.[40]

When this sudden influx of labor arrived at the Works, project leaders did not respond by building apartment blocks. They did not do so due to industrial design rules laid out by Planning Commission Director Li Fuchun at the start of the Third Front campaign. According to Li, Third Front projects should not follow the Soviet model and build "big and complete" industrial enterprises with "large administrative buildings, a large social service sector, and nonproductive buildings whose standards are excessively high." Instead, Third Front administrators had to follow Maoist methods of development, "make do with what is available," and only furnish industrial enterprises with "rammed-earth housing" and basic social services, so that more resources could go into productive pursuits.[41] Works' leaders summarized this policy with a simple slogan: "First build the factory and afterward housing."[42]

Some factory personnel argued that the building priorities should be flipped. When the assistant commander of the Wuhan Military Region, Kong Qingde, learned of their complaints, he told them that they could leave but would no longer be paid, nor given a letter of introduction for another job. Since such a letter was required to be hired anywhere in China, Kong's command was effectively a sentence of permanent unemployment. Kong told workers that they had to implement Mao's order to "engage in a race against time with American imperialism and Soviet revisionism" and swiftly expand Chinese truck production.[43] With war on the horizon, China's limited resources had to go into constructing factory workshops, which would raise military readiness, not into "nonproductive buildings," such as housing, offices, or cultural centers.[44]

Upon arriving at the Works, laborers made do and moved into any available buildings. Some rented rooms in local peasant homes. Others lodged in stables, chicken coops, mills, and schools.[45] Still others slept outside on thatched mats. Frequent rains made living outside long-term not viable, so some sought shelter underneath machinery.[46] Whether someone slept inside or out, the party allocated every worker four kilograms of cotton to make a blanket. Still cold, some people crammed into the same bed head to toe to keep warm, a practice which some workers remember leading to homosexual relations.[47] Laborers also scoured the area for sticks and grass to assemble their own peasant-style residences.[48] No buildings constructed were permitted to have flush toilets. If someone transgressed this design dictate, they risked being castigated as bourgeois and violating the party line.[49]

EXPERIENCING MAOIST MATERIALITY

Official guidelines presented the spartan character of material culture at the Works in a favorable light, portraying its ruggedness as way to "inculcate Mao Zedong Thought into workers" and "construct a revolutionary labor force patterned after the People's Liberation Army."[50] In their everyday life, workers would experience the socialist principle of "overcoming selfishness and developing a public spirit."[51] This facet of the factory's materiality was especially important for reforming intellectuals who "had to work hard to overcome bourgeois individualism."[52] To achieve this goal, administrators and technicians were ordered to not work in office buildings or live in special accommodations, thereby shrinking the spatial divide between mental and manual labor. Managerial and technical personnel had to instead "eat, live, and work alongside the masses" at construction sites. The Works' austerity was also designed to help materialize the socialist objective of lessening the urban-rural divide by giving factory employees living standards comparable to those in the countryside.

As historian Felix Wemheuer has noted, people in China viewed the socialist project in multiple ways, "from optimistic hopes and dreams to disillusion and . . . apathy."⁵³ How different people experienced the Works' materiality is a case in point. One of the more avid supporters of building the factory was its director, Rao Bin. According to his wife's memoir, Rao wrote her a letter in which he described his living conditions. There was no electricity, only a kerosene lamp, whose light he nightly labored under, preparing the next day's work. All he had for a bed was a hard plank, and all he had to eat was rice porridge. Despite this asperity, Rao did not "think that life is hard" since he felt "a kind of intimacy with this sort of simple living," which reminded him of CCP life during "the war against Japan."⁵⁴ In this regard, Rao was akin to other longtime CCP members who sublimated their own suffering and viewed it as part of being "a surrogate of the revolution," as political scientists David Apter and Tony Saich have shown in their study of Yan'an-era leaders.⁵⁵

Some project participants recall regularly affirming their support for austere living at public events. One way they did so was by singing "Chairman Mao's Soldiers Are the Most Loyal to the Communist Party," a contemporary song in which people declared that they would emulate the military's stoic determination and make their "home wherever there is difficulty."⁵⁶ A Shanghai recruit similarly declared in a public meeting that although "building the [factory] would be difficult," his colleagues should take it as a challenge to surmount by "going all-out."⁵⁷ When war came, the factory would also be there to contribute its products to national defense, thanks to their efforts. Another recruit from the First Auto Works remembers his coworkers "holding a deeply established conviction" of the importance of "contributing to building an automotive industry" for China, while a younger recruit recollects having "only one desire" at the time: "answering Chairman Mao's directive" to build the Second Auto Works, a phenomenon that Anita Chan has demonstrated to be prominent among youth in the 1960s and 1970s.⁵⁸

Other employees viewed the material culture of Shiyan more negatively. People complained about a lack of paved roads, such that when it rained, they did not hold their umbrellas upright but rather pointed them downward to avoid being covered in mud.⁵⁹ Some worried that while they were at work their roommates would steal their belongings. Another source of anxiety was the flammability of thatched-hut residences, which several times led to workers' possessions being incinerated.⁶⁰ Some recruits were used to urban material comforts and could not adjust to living in makeshift housing, drinking slimy water, eating pickled vegetables, and working so much every day that their whole body hurt.⁶¹ One employee from the First Auto Works wryly noted that the only way "people from big cities like us" could adapt to living in a "poor mountain ravine" was because of "the power of revolutionary optimism to take strong-willed people and concentrate them in a valley."[62] Other employees thought that they had no choice but to stay, since they could not receive an official job transfer. Some, however, were so distressed by the material stringency of daily life that they fled to big cities.[63]

According to central planners, Shiyan was projected to become a large city. In reality, it was somewhere in between an urban and rural area. Project leaders regarded this liminal state as a way of moving the needle closer to realizing the socialist project of unifying the city and countryside into a single egalitarian whole. They thus permitted some peasant households to remain distributed amid factory workshops rather than be relocated elsewhere. Another five thousand rural residents were resettled. Project leaders aided some of them with setting up fruit orchards and dispatched agricultural experts from Wuhan to teach peasants the latest scientific techniques in vegetable cultivation. Both these measures aimed to boost local support for the Works' construction by increasing rural revenue.[64] The factory further stimulated rural finances by having peasants engage in other remunerated pursuits, such as gathering rocks, bamboo, and sand to assist with building the Works.[65]

Despite government aid, local peasants still grumbled to project leaders, criticizing the factory for occupying "our land, so we had to make our home in the riverbed" and entering "into valleys, so we had to move onto mountainsides."[66] Workers also held disparaging views of local peasants, which were rooted in specific material objects. Some laughed at those trying to sell stones as coal and sweet potato leaves as vegetables.[67] Other employees worried about peasants taking advantage of the lack of a wall around the complex and stealing factory and personal property.[68] As these examples illustrate, the CCP's attempt to eliminate the urban-rural divide, while closing material gaps in some respects, simultaneously generated new material points of tension.[69]

A MILITARIZED INDUSTRIALIZATION DRIVE

The source of tension that pushed the building of the Works into high gear was the intensification of Soviet military pressure on China in 1969. The key party leaders urging accelerated construction were Mao Zedong and Zhou Enlai. Mao thought quickening the building of the Third Front was so crucial to national defense that he personally told the Wuhan Military Region's commander, Zeng Siyu, to engage in a race against time to complete Third Front projects before the outbreak of war with the Soviets or Americans.[70] Zhou Enlai similarly emphasized the Works' importance to the Wuhan Military Region's assistant commander, Kong Qingde, stating that its trucks were critical to solving the military's shortage of all-terrain vehicles at a time when the Soviet Union was engaging in border clashes with China, and the United States and its allies had the country nearly surrounded.[71]

Regional military leaders responded to Mao and Zhou's orders to expedite Third Front construction by commanding the Works to implement a policy known as "the Four Simultaneities," according to which the factory's design and construction should be done at the same time as installing machinery and beginning production.[72] In accordance with this policy, workers of every rank were told not to wait until enough trucks arrived to transport supplies. They had to make do with local resources and immediately use handcarts, baskets, and shoulder poles to lug in stones and sand from nearby mountains and riverbeds, as well as steel, cement, and machinery dropped off at a dock dozens of kilometers away.[73] Twenty thousand people were also mobilized to carry power lines to the Works from the Danjiangkou hydroelectric station nearly a hundred kilometers away.[74]

Laborers were also ordered to make workshops from rammed earth to save sparse resources, such as cement and iron, for other industrial endeavors.[75] Some technicians cautioned against this policy, arguing that workshops had to be made of reinforced concrete to be stable. Otherwise, vibrations could cause dirt buildings to crack and collapse.[76] Regional military leaders rejected these critiques and admonished technicians for not following the Maoist principle of self-reliance. China had to depend on its own resources, not subscribe to a "slavish comprador philosophy" that praised Soviet "revisionist designs" and the Soviet habit of building big factories.[77] China had to instead pursue its own developmental way and construct small, inexpensive factories with locally obtainable materials.[78]

Factory planners deployed several resource-saving strategies to achieve these goals.[79] One tactic was making open-air factory workshops that had no roofs or walls. Other methods included reducing the cement in building foundations, not firming up the ground underneath railroads, and not using antirusting agents on underground wires. Electrical lines were also not laid, and safety lights were not included.[80] All these building strategies had the opposite effect than intended. Instead of hastening construction, they slowed it down. Electrical lines had to be installed. Railway tracks became lumpy. Dirt walls fell apart and were replaced with reinforced concrete. Building foundations subsided because they could not hold heavy machinery. Peasants walked into workshops and took tools, so walls were erected to keep them out.[81]

Other very costly measures were undertaken to shield the Works from military danger. Not only was the factory located in the mountains, but it was also divided into twenty-seven workshops, each of which was ensconced in a valley and attributed a number to conceal its function.[82] To further secure the factory, 350 air-raid shelters were dug out, so that every workshop had at least one. In total, air-raid shelters were big enough to hold ten football fields underground.[83] These security measures had nefarious effects. Machinery oxidized in damp caves. Workshops were flooded during every hard rain, and torrents of water rushed through valleys. So that workshops were not regularly subject to the vagaries of weather, walls were erected to prevent mudslides, and ditches were shoveled to divert rainwater.[84]

Initial efforts in 1969 to manufacture trucks at the Works were marred by problems too. Rao Bin and a few other project leaders at first opposed orders from Defense Minister Lin Biao to produce five hundred trucks for the next year's National Day parade in Hubei.[85] Regional military leaders were not swayed. As Kong Qingde told his colleagues at a factory meeting, the Soviets had a million soldiers, a thousand planes, and ten thousand tanks on the border, ready to strike. Chairman Mao had called for the speeding up of Third Front construction to ready the country for war, and everyone had to strive their utmost to realize his command. Anyone who did otherwise was insufficiently concerned about national security.[86] Although workers were able to gather auto parts from around China to manually assemble twenty trucks, they were seriously flawed. Laborers made light of the faulty results of this militarized drive to hurriedly cobble together trucks to defend China against its Cold War foes, saying that while each truck "looked fierce, its head and tail bobbed back and forth when it drove fast, and when it stopped, it spewed out oil and water."[87]

THE SECOND AUTO WORKS AND CHINA'S THIRD FRONT

It is undeniable that the first set of trucks that the Second Auto Works made had severe problems, and that the process of building the Works was not an entirely coherent endeavor, in which all the elements involved fit together into a cohesive whole. Quite to the contrary: the Works' establishment was riddled with contradictions. These incongruities were the result of international and domestic political tensions becoming ingrained in the material regime underlying the Works' construction. Of utmost importance was the geopolitical conflict between China, the United States, and the Soviet Union, which led to military concerns having an overriding influence over the Works' construction. In prioritizing military matters, Mao's China was not following a rationality unknown in other countries. It was adhering to a well-established pattern in the history of modern state-making. As historical sociologist Charles Tilly famously remarked of modern Europe, "War made states, and states made war."[88] This adage also applies to Maoist China. In response to rising military tensions with the United States and the Soviet Union in the early 1960s, the CCP leadership made strengthening China's industrial defenses into a top national priority.

Leaders made this policy decision based on the lessons they learned from the wars of the mid-twentieth century. In their view, Stalin and Chiang Kai-shek had both not established enough heavy industry in rear areas prior to World War II. Due to their inadequate military preparations, the Soviet Union and China both had to develop inland regions while simultaneously trying to fight off invading enemy forces. To avoid this perilous military position, CCP leaders endorsed the construction of a huge military industrial complex in the Chinese interior. Knowing that a large truck fleet would be required in any future military contingency, the party center ordered the establishment of the Second Auto Works. Like for other Third Front projects, party leaders drew on their experience of guerilla warfare when choosing where to place the Works, designating locations scattered in the mountains, like the party's former revolutionary base areas, as the most secure. The Third Front's clandestine layout not only had roots in the CCP's military past. It was also a product of the Cold War, echoing the American and Soviet practice of obscuring the material existence of parts of their national security apparatus to ensure their safety and survivability.

Military tensions were also embedded in the building methods used to construct the Works. So that the factory could sooner contribute trucks to defending China from Cold War threats, construction schedules were compressed, parts of the factory were judged unnecessary to build, local handicrafts were swapped for manufactured goods, human muscles took the place of machinery, and local unskilled labor was mobilized to make up for a shortage of technical personnel. The inspiration for this approach to building a factory was once again the CCP's experience of guerilla war. Some people involved in the Second Auto Works pushed back against these militaristic methods of quickening the factory's completion. However, they were criticized for abandoning the Maoist developmental way and calling for China to act like its enemies: giving technicians the last word in construction plans and favoring the use of machines and machine-made products.

For military reasons, the CCP also required austere material conditions at the Works, so that more resources could be funneled into expanding China's military-industrial base. Project leaders accused anyone who urged better living standards of neglecting national security, forsaking Maoism's spartan collective ethic, and endorsing the bourgeois, individualistic, consumerist ways of China's adversaries in Moscow and Washington. People responded in several ways to the material lack that followed from this policy of privation. While some young people and party members viewed material sacrifice as an expression of their devotion to China's revolution, many people could not adjust to the harsh material conditions of their everyday lives. Conflicting viewpoints also emerged around the party's attempt to close the gap between the city and countryside, with industrial workers holding negative opinions of their rural neighbors and countryfolk condemning the factory for taking their land. In all these instances, Cold War China's industrial war machine came to embody the contradictions of the country's insecure geopolitical position and domestic political disagreements over the material culture of Maoist developmentalism.

NOTES

1 Qiu Dongshan, "Dongfeng qiche zong shejishi Wang Rushi," in Hubei Sheng, *Shiyan wenshi di 14 ji xia*, 75.
2 Liu Lijun, "Raobin qiche danxin pu," in Hubei Sheng, *Shiyan wenshi di 14 ji xia*, 180; Chung-Yuk Shamus Mok, "China's Motor Cities: Industrialization and Urban Development Under State Socialism, 1948–90" (PhD diss., Michigan State University, 1994), 196–97.
3 I take the material regime concept from chapter 9 in this volume.
4 Naughton, "The Third Front." For more on the Third Front, see Meyskens, *Mao's Third Front*.
5 Hou, *Building for Oil*, 29–62. On Maoist asceticism, see Maurice Meisner, *Marxism, Maoism, and Utopianism: Eight Essays* (Madison: University of Wisconsin Press, 1982), 118–31.
6 Hou, *Building for Oil*, 4, 94. On Maoist urbanization, also see Liu, "Making a New World."
7 Schmalzer, "Self-Reliant Science," 79.
8 On militarized labor, see Shapiro, *Mao's War against Nature*, 70–75.
9 On the idea of a capitalist restoration in the Soviet Union, see Roderick MacFarquhar, *The Coming of the Cataclysm, 1961–1966* (New York: Oxford University Press, 1997), 362–64.

10 The first mention of the Second Auto Works in the national press is in "Di erqi zhizao cahng niuzhuan changqi kuisuan jumian," *Renmin ribao*, October 30, 1979, 5.
11 Mark Bradley, *Vietnam at War* (Oxford: Oxford University Press, 2009), 111. Defense Secretary Robert McNamara admitted that the August 4 incident never happened, but an earlier incident on August 2 did (*The Fog of War*, directed by Errol Morris [Los Angeles: Sony Pictures Classics, 2003]).
12 Naughton, "Third Front," 351.
13 "Mao Zedong tingqu Yu Qiuli huibao 'sanwu' jihua he sanxian jianshe wenti shi de qianghua," January 23, 1965; and Mao Zedong, "Yao yanjiu Sitalin he Jiang Jieshi de chetui," November 26, 1964, both in *Zhongguo gongchandang yu sanxian*, edited by Chen Donglin (Beijing: Zhonggong Dangshi Chubanshe, 2015), 135, 119–20; and M. Taylor Fravel, "Shifts in Warfare and Party Unity: Explaining China's Changes in Military Strategy," *International Security* 42, no. 3 (Winter 2017/2018): 53–59.
14 Xu Bingjin and Ou Yangmin, *Zhongguo qiche shihua* (Beijing: Jixie Gongye Chubanshe, 2017), 39–46, 63–75.
15 Zhang Mao, *Rao Bin zhuanji* (Beijing: Huawen Chubanshe, 2003), 192–93.
16 Huang Jiemin, "Jiang qiche bi jiang siren," in Hubei Sheng, *Shiyan wenshi di 14 ji xia*, 348.
17 Li Zizheng and Ge Bangning, "Qiche jie de lao geming," in Hubei Sheng, *Shiyan wenshi di 14 ji xia*, 228; Xu and Ou, *Zhongguo qiche*, 47.
18 Guowuyuan Sanxian Jianshe Tiaozheng Gaizao Guihua Bangong Shi Sanxian Jianshe Bianxie Zu, *Sanxian jianshe* (Beijing: Guowuyuan Sanxian Jianshe Tiaozheng Gaizao Guihua Bangong Shi Sanxian Jianshe Bianxie Zu, 1991), 22.
19 Dongfeng Qiche Congsi Shizhi Bangongshi, *Di er qiche zhizao changzhi, 1969–1983* (Shiyan: Dongfeng Qiche Congsi Shizhi Bangongshi, 1986), 21–22. On the American embargo, see Zhang Shu Guang, *Economic Cold War: America's Embargo Against China and the Sino-Soviet Alliance, 1949–1963* (Stanford, CA: Stanford University Press, 2001), 1–3.
20 Dongfeng Qiche, *Di er qiche*, 146–47.
21 Guojia Jihua Weiyuanhui, "Guanyu di er qiche chang jianshe qingkuang he wenti de huibao tigang," January 27, 1968, in *Erqi jianchang zhongyao wenjian huibian*, edited by Di Er Qiche Zhizao Chang Changzhi Bianzuan Weiyuanhui Bangongshi (Shiyan: Di Er Qiche Zhizao Chang Changzhi Bianzuan Weiyuanhui Bangongshi, 1984), 67.
22 "Guowuyuan pizhuan yi jibu junguanhui guanyu jiasu di er che chang jianshe de baogao," October 28, 1969, in *Zhongguo gongchandang yu sanxian*, edited by Chen Donglin (Beijing: Zhonggong Dangshi Chubanshe, 2015), 249–50; Dongfeng Qiche, *Di er qiche*, 239.
23 Mao Zedong, "Zai tiqu XX bu huibao de zhishi," February 17, 1965, in *Panzhihua kaifa jianshe shi wenxian ziliao xuanbian*, edited by Zhonggong Panzhihua Shi Dangshi Yanjiushi (Panzhihua: Zhonggong Panzhihhua Shiwei Dangshi Yanjiushi Bian, 2000), 8.
24 Guowuyuan, *Sanxian jianshe*, 21.
25 Jiang Jiyan and Li Xueshi, "Wo canjia le san ci xuan changzhi," in Hubei Sheng, *Shiyan wenshi di 14 ji shang*, 60–61.
26 Dongfeng Qiche, *Di er qiche*, 8

27 Zhang, *Rao Bin zhuanji*, 192–93.
28 Ou Yangmin, *Shuiyuan di: Nan shui bei diao zhongxian gongcheng* (Beijing: Renmin Chubanshe, 2010), 214–15.
29 Huang Zhengxia, *Jiannan licheng* (Beijing: Xinhua Chubanshe, 2007), 57.
30 Dongfeng Qiche, *Di er qiche*, 67.
31 Zhang Guodian, "Qunzhong yu lingdao xiang jiede de chengguo: Huiyi erqi changzhi fangan queding de jingguo," in *Erqi jianshe shiliao*, vol. 1 (Shiyan: Erqi Changzhi Bianji Shi, 1984), 6.
32 Li and Ge, "Qiche jie de lao geming," 229.
33 Xu and Ou, *Zhongguo qiche*, 60.
34 Qu and Zheng, *Yidai jiang xing*, 453; Dongfeng Qiche, *Di er qiche*, 67–68. Interview with automobile workers, Shiyan, January 2012.
35 Qiu, "Dongfeng qiche zong shejishi Wang Rushi," 75.
36 Qu and Zheng, *Yidai jiang xing*, 453.
37 Hubei Sheng Shiyan Shi Weiyuanhui Wenshi He Xuexi Weiyuanhui, *Shiyan wenshi di 14 ji xia*, 408.
38 "Guowuyuan pizhuan yi jibu," 249.
39 Shiyan Shi Difangzhi Bianzuan Weiyuanhui, *Shiyan shi zhi* (Beijing: Zhonghua Shuju, 1999), 167.
40 Shiyan Shi, *Shiyan shi zhi*, 167.
41 Li Fuchun, "Zai quanguo jihua huiyi shang de jianghua," September 21, 1964, in *Zhongguo gongchandang yu sanxian*, edited by Chen Donglin (Beijing: Zhonggong Dangshi Chubanshe, 2015), 88.
42 Qu and Zheng, *Yidai jiang xing*, 456.
43 Qu and Zheng, *Yidai jiang xing*, 451; Mao Zedong, "Zai tingqu changyuan guihua shexiang huibao shi de zhishi," January 23, 1965, in *Panzhihua kaifa jianshe shi wenxian ziliao xuanbian*, edited by Zhonggong Panzhihua Shi Dangshi Yanjiushi (Panzhihua: Zhonggong Panzhihhua Shiwei Dangshi Yanjiushi Bian, 2000), 7.
44 "Kong Qingde tongzi de jianghua," undated, circa 1969, Hubei Provincial Archive, S299-6-74, 23.
45 Xuan Min, "Jianku chuangye jian checheng," in Hubei Sheng, *Shiyan wenshi di san ji*, 2; Cai Yongchun, "Dui erqi jianshe chuqi shenghuo de huiyi," in *Erqi jianshe shiliao*, vol. 2, 18.
46 Interview with automobile workers, Shiyan, January 2012.
47 Yang Yujin, "Erqi jian chang chuqi de 'liu zi,'" in Hubei Sheng, *Shiyan wenshi di 14 ji shang*, 278.
48 Liu Qingxiang and Cui Minfan, "Yi dixia shi jianshe er san shi," in Hubei Sheng, *Shiyan wenshi di san ji*, 22–23.
49 Liu Lanqing, "Yi zuo weida de "qiaoliang,'" in Hubei Sheng, *Shiyan wenshi di 14 ji xia*, 315.
50 Di Er Qiche Zhizao Chang Choubei Chu, "Di er qiche zhizao chang jianshe fangzhen shisi tiao," November 20, 1966, in *Erqi jianshe shiliao*, vol. 2 (Shiyan: Erqi Changzhi Bianji Shi, 1984), 2.
51 "'Erqi' chengtao shebei zhanyi huiyi xuanchuanshu," December 15, 1966, in *Erqi jianshe shiliao*, vol. 1 (Shiyan: Erqi Changzhi Bianji Shi, 1984), 15.

52 The quotes in the rest of this paragraph are from this source. Di Er Qiche Zhizao, "Di er qiche zhizao chang," 3–4.
53 Wemheuer, *Social History of Maoist China*, 7.
54 Zhang Mao, "Rao Bin yu erqi," in Hubei Sheng, *Shiyan wenshi di 14 ji xia*, 286.
55 David Apter and Tony Saich, *Revolutionary Discourse in Mao's Republic* (Cambridge: Harvard University Press, 1994), 145.
56 Ma Fude, "Jianku fendou jian erqi: Zhazha shishi xue daqing," in *Shiyan wenshi di ba ji*, edited by Hubei Sheng Shiyan Shi Weiyuanhui "Shiyan wenshi" Bianji Weiyuanhui (Shiyan: Hubei Sheng Shiyan Shi Weiyuanhui "Shiyan wenshi" Bianji Weiyuanhui, 2008), 181.
57 "Yi jibu Shen Hong tongzhi zai 'wu yi wu' huiyi shang de Jianhua," May 15, 1969, in *Zhonggong zhongyang Guowuyuan Hubei shengwei jixie gongye bu lingdao tongzhi guanyu erqi jianshe zhongyao zhishi he jianghua huibian, 1966–1984*, edited by Zhonggong Erqi Zhizao Chang Zhangzhi Bianzuan Weiyuanhui Bangongshi (Shiyan: Zhonggong Erqi Zhizao Chang Zhangzhi Bianzuan Weiyuanhui Bangongshi, 1984), 9.
58 Li Huimin, "Erqi jianchang shiwu nian zhounian jinian," in Hubei Sheng, *Shiyan wenshi di 14 ji xia*, 109; Ma Youyi, "Wode rensheng jiazhi," in *Jiqing suiyue*, edited by Han Gaohong (Beijing: Zhongguo Shehui Chubanshe, 2004), 134; Anita Chan, *Children of Mao Personality Development and Political Activism in the Red Guard Generation* (Basingstoke, UK: Palgrave, 1985).
59 Xuan, "Jianku chuangye jian checheng," 4.
60 Cai, "Dui erqi jianshe chuqi shenghuo de huiyi," 28.
61 Ma, "Jianku fendou jian erqi," 182.
62 Chen Renqiu, "Wo yu qiche shengchan zhunbei gongzuo de qingyuan," in *Jiqing suiyue*, edited by Han Gaohong (Beijing: Zhongguo Shehui Chubanshe, 2004), 150–51.
63 Ma, "Jianku fendou jian erqi," 182.
64 He Chengzhi, "Yi jianshi chuqi de caihuo gongzuo," in Hubei Sheng, *Shiyan wenshi di san ji*, 137; Liu and Cui, "Yi dixia shi jianshe er san shi," 23.
65 Xuan, "Jianku chuangye jian checheng," 5–6.
66 Xuan, "Jianku chuangye jian checheng," 5–6.
67 Xuan, "Jianku chuangye jian checheng," 4. The latter were less common in urban diets.
68 Chen Zutao, *Wode qiche shengya* (Beijing: Renmin chubanshe, 2005), 167.
69 For a monograph on this point, see Jeremy Brown, *City Versus Countryside in Mao's China: Negotiating the Divide* (New York: Cambridge University Press, 2012).
70 Qu and Zheng, *Yidai jiang xing*, 473–74.
71 Qu and Zheng, *Yidai jiang xing*, 450.
72 Liang Wangrui, "1969 nian 5 yue huiyi xianqi erqi jianche rechao," in Hubei Sheng, *Shiyan wenshi di 14 ji shang*, 151.
73 Liu Lanqing, "Erqi jianshe touchan de yi ci huizhan," in Hubei Sheng, *Shiyan wenshi di 14 ji shang*, 421. Interview with automobile worker, Shiyan, January 2012.
74 Ou, *Shuiyuan di*, 222.
75 "'Di er qiche zhizao changzhi' bianzuan weiyuanhui, *Di er qiche zhizao changzhi 1969–1983*, 78.
76 Interview with automobile workers, Shiyan, January 2012.
77 Chen Zutao, *Wode qiche*, 165.

78 "Zhao Xiu tongzhi zai quansheng qiche tuolaji chang huizhan xinchang hui shang de jianghua," 1970, Hubei Provincial Archive SZ 107–5-33, 6–7. The quote is on p. 7. The document is undated, but on p. 1, it states that the Cultural Revolution has been going on for four years, so I have dated the speech as being from 1970.
79 Liu, "Raobin qiche danxin pu," 183.
80 Xu and Ou, *Zhongguo qiche*, 62.
81 Chen Zutao, *Wode qiche*, 166–68; Zhang, "Rao Bin yu erqi," 289.
82 Interview with automobile worker, Shiyan, January 2012.
83 Shiyan Shi Difangzhi Bianzuan Weiyuanhui, *Shiyan shizhi* (Beijing: Zhonghua Shuju Chubanshe, 1999), 914.
84 Erqi Jianshe Zong Zhihui Bu, *Baogao wenxue ji* (Shiyan: Erqi Jianshe Zong Zhihui Bu, 1972).
85 Qiu, "Dongfeng qiche zong shejishi Wang Rushi," 75
86 Liu, "Raobin qiche danxin pu," 180.
87 Qiu, "Dongfeng qiche zong shejishi Wang Rushi," 76.
88 Charles Tilly, "Reflections on the History of European State-Making," in *The Formation of National States in Western Europe*, edited by Charles Tilly, Studies in Political Development (Princeton, NJ: Princeton University Press, 1975), 42.

AFTERWORD

Material Culture and the Socialist Uncanny in Mao's China

JONATHAN BACH

THE GRAND SOCIALIST EXPERIMENTS OF THE TWENTIETH CENTURY turn on the question of radically altering the relationship between people and things, subjects and objects, materiality and spirit, in order to redeem them from the condition Marx famously laid out: once things become commodities, they appear as if magically detached from their makers while, conversely, their makers—now workers—come more and more to resemble objects. Both things and humans become suspended in a kind of trance under the spell of the commodity, living in a dreamworld from which, as the 1920s Soviet Constructivists put it, a new, wide-awake socialist world must arise to shake off the misty boundary that separates human from thing: "Our things in our hands," declared Aleksandr Rodchenko, "must be equals, comrades."[1] This call epitomizes one of twentieth-century socialism's central challenges: how to exorcise fetishism from commodities as they continue to circulate under socialism, and thereby restore the agency to both thing and human that capitalism disguises and drains? Could the new socialist projects realize a new form of economy that does not deny humanity, that can have the commodity without fetishizing it?

The chapters in this volume trace, among other things, state socialism's attempts to control and transcend the capitalist construction of the commodity as alienating and exploitative. Across the chapters, the Mao period's fear of capitalist residue and the threat it posed to the socialist project is palpable—one could say, perhaps, that a certain inverted spectrality was taking place. If, for Marx and Engels, communism was the spirit haunting bourgeois society, then historical socialism (conceived as a transitory phase with an adapted form of commodity economy) had its own problem with ghosts. In twentieth-century socialism, the spirit of communism, which, as Derrida reminds us, was always yet to come, had not fully materialized, which is to say, the cycle of repetition that Marx critiqued in *The 18th Brumaire* had not fully ended.[2]

Put differently, capitalism was not fully dead. But it was partially dead, and things that are neither fully dead nor alive are particularly spooky. The ghost, or that which haunts, arrived both from the inside (namely, in the persistence of bourgeois attitudes carried over from the prerevolutionary era) and the outside (namely, the contemporaneous capitalist West). This apparition, or counterconjuration, is multiply ambiguous; sometimes it becomes hard to tell in the essays who is haunting (or hunting) whom.[3] This is by no means to imply that capitalism is in some sense an unending "real" underneath a dissimulating veneer of socialist rhetoric.[4] Rather, it is to observe how the essays collected here highlight different ways in which socialism confronted, and was confronted by, the spectrality of capitalism and how it navigated this uncanny situation.

In the Freudian sense, uncanny contradictions are less problems amenable to a solution than aporias.[5] Insofar as they are unresolvable, however, they are also productive, because denial, repression, and displacement (the standard reactions) are all strategies that ensure that whatever else happens, the contradictions are always only provisionally resolved but don't really go away. Instead, they reappear as pathologies, often in that quintessentially uncanny form of the double. Indeed, throughout this volume, variations on doubles keep appearing: socialist subjects are haunted by their evil twin, the "bad element," while rural socialist movie teams are shadowed by their "capitalist tail" of hawkers. The socialist brick becomes set against the capitalist brick, while frugality is encouraged by conjuring a simulacrum of abundance. Domestic commodities mimic those produced abroad while also condemning them as treacherous poison.

Each chapter calls forth its own specifics of doubling, of uncanny encounters with—and of—materiality as the government seeks to defetishize the commodity form. Drawing from them, I wish to highlight three forms of doubling—the model, the prosthetic, and the simulacrum of sacrifice—that undergird what we might provisionally call the socialist uncanny. All three are called into being by the task of awakening people and things from the capitalist trance and thus restoring agency: the model restores agency by "becoming political," the prosthetic by fusing bodies and objects into entangled subjects, and the simulacrum by regulating desire through its abnegation. Ultimately, they all work toward the Marxian vision of transcending the mystical aura of the commodity through new forms of production, by performing the ultimate sleight of hand: to reap the benefits of commodities without their fetishism and thus to extract capital without surplus value, in order to build socialism.

BECOMING POLITICAL THROUGH THE MODEL

In Marxism, an object "becomes" socialist when it is relocated within social relations, correcting the bourgeois misrecognition that places them outside. For this, objects need to be animated with a new life. Humans, too, need to be marked anew as having agency, since bourgeois society treats them too as objects, as tools, as means to an end. The high socialist period, in China as elsewhere, sought to operationalize this renewal of agency for things and people through the catch-all concept of "becoming political." In practice, this entailed adopting the "correct" political perspective as much as taking ownership of the means of production. This is because material objects and humans alike were thought to contain a kind of latent socialist immanence that could be made legible and actionable through the correct interpretation and interpellation. For material objects, whether natural materials or consumer items, this meant their essence had to be first liberated before their full potential could be realized by all, not just by the few.[6] For example, bamboo, as Jennifer Altehenger shows in chapter 1, had to "become political if it was to serve the people"—its political quality needed to be coaxed out "correctly" in order to make bamboo legible to the masses. This coaxing, in turn, sheds light on the importance of "models" in socialism, specifically how the narrative possibilities inherent in the model gives both objects and workers agency.

Socialist models draw their power, as Denise Ho notes, from being "both representative and real," combining both behavior (virtuous attitudes) and action (technical know-how) within a temporal frame that connects past and present with the future perfect.[7] As Altehenger shows in chapter 1, coaxing the "correct" political quality out of bamboo involved turning a real-life bamboo craftsman, "Zhang the man," into the larger-than-life "Zhang the model." These doubles take on different narrative lives, with the success of Zhang the model eventually making the conditions increasingly difficult for Zhang the man to continue his craft, which required relative rural isolation.[8] This doubling points to a fundamental (and familiar) tension: true craft is shown as resulting from individual effort, but as it is lionized by the party and becomes the model for mass production, its quality inevitably weakens. In response, there always need to be new models and new forms of knowledge production and transfer. These models mediate between the spiritual needs of the party for ideological validation and the economic needs of the country for new materials and techniques to overcome real shortages and shortcomings.

The socialist model thus becomes a key site for "becoming political," whether for bamboo or for what might seem like its opposite, the brick. Unlike bamboo, the brick does not possess a hidden quality that requires correct handling to be made visible. Rather, as Cole Roskam shows in chapter 2, it requires a renarration of its value to turn it into a socialist object. Bridging the otherwise divergent examples of bamboo and brick is the model worker who serves as the mediating force of narration connecting the ordinary worker and the object. Both bamboo and bricks encounter increasing tension as craft and technique morph into technical expertise: the more knowledge has to be standardized, codified, and transferred to others, the more tension emerges between the artisan and the factory, between the increasing importance of expertise versus the "simple values" of the people. The technical proficiency of new brick technology, Roskam shows, introduced just these kinds of tensions between worker and expert as they shaped, and were shaped by, the elements of their construction. This tension took the form of inequities between laborers and experts, thus reproducing inequalities and reintroducing hierarchies even while models were promoted as a way to overcome them.

The more a given model was harnessed to ideological or nationalist purposes, the more its mass implementation seemed to lead to the undermining of its seeming purity of purpose. As Christine Ho shows in chapter 3, a tenacious "tug-of-war over vernacular nationalism and economic priority" accompanied the development of PRC design and handicraft, in which the notion of a "national design" was promoted to assert China's agency in and beyond the socialist world, yet it found itself floundering under collectivization and centralization, which led to "the erasure of the same histories that designers sought to maintain." The model, by endowing its objects and workers with political agency, also created a kind of doppelgänger, which often seemed to work at cross purposes.

POLITICAL PROSTHETICS

Becoming political through the model and its diffusion engendered one form of doubling surrounding the restoration of agency to objects and workers. Another is what we might call political prosthetics, an approach that sutures the body and materiality in an attempt to break down the barriers between subject and object. If model making requires a hermeneutics of materiality—a process of making the hidden potential of materials such as bamboo, bricks, or handicrafts legible and interpretable—political prosthetics requires the prop. Props in theater, as the performance scholar Andrew Sofer argues, have long embodied a double role: demystification (because they are usually ordinary objects), and resacralization (because they appear as other, marked by their appearance on stage).[9] In Mao's China, the prop takes this one step further to mediate between social worlds, especially between urban and rural China, as Emily Wilcox shows in chapter 4, where props also mediate among types of value, stages of consciousness and development, and between classes as well as China and the world. The prop in Maoist dance extends the trace of rural folk performance into the urban (echoing the role of handicrafts in the creation of national design in chapter 3), but also brings the urban to the rural in the form of traveling performances and movie versions. In the process, the prop and the performer become a new kind of double, an entangled subject, seeking to embody the principle that neither objects nor persons exist outside of social relations.

The political prosthetic of the prop is extended by technology in Jie Li's account, in chapter 5, of mobile cinemas that turned their projectionists into different kinds of mediators: physical and spirit mediums. Like the dancers, they fused their bodies with the objects of performance, but their props, however, were often the very opposite of the fans, drums, swords, and lanterns used by dancers. They supplemented the official showings with objects not meant to function as stage props per se: projectors, power generators, cables, speakers, and screens (even if these certainly prop up, in the literal sense of support, the cinematic performances). Appropriating "backstage" props, the projectionists told stories and disciplined audiences through bamboo clappers, lantern slides, microphones, and radio sets, and adjusted the speed of the film to keep audiences engaged; in short, they used technological infrastructure as a prop, and turned their bodies into cyborgs. The projectionists' stories related by Li recall the uncanny qualities of early cinema, where its impact on audiences lay initially in the disorienting distortions of time and image, and then in the possibilities for its appropriation. As they mixed technical information, entertainment, and political education, their seemingly magical powers supplemented and enhanced the projectionists' ecclesiastical roles, as Li describes, as missionaries and priests from the central authority and ventriloquists for the state's voice.

Educated and urban, projectionists represented new temporalities, new imaginations, and new possibilities, but they could also trigger resentment for these very same qualities. This disjuncture between the projectionists and their villager audiences put them into a different role than the dance performers in chapter 4, whose controlled choreography left little room for appropriation. In the projectionists' wild choreography of rural cinema, it was all about appropriation, because the movies were secondary to the performative effect of showing them, which amounted to the power of the wily projectionists to control their audiences. Left largely to their own devices (literally), the projectionists used materiality to enact their own agency but also set something else in motion: a utopian vision in the double sense of new technology and communist ideology.

At first, the technology in particular was unfamiliar and astonishing to many villagers, as in the anecdotes that Li recounts of villagers who prepared food for the comrades on the screen or tried to light their pipes at the glowing filament of the projector bulb. Yet, as Tom Gunning argues about new technologies, once the unfamiliar becomes familiar, as happened quickly in the villages, the original astonishment wears off, only to linger as a kind of excess. The "imagined future, whether catastrophic or utopian or both, can never completely disappear; it can only be to some degree forgotten."[10] This forgotten imagined future returns as the uncanny throughout modern China in various forms. Today it is arguably infrastructure—new roads, high-speed trains, or Taobao villages embedded in e-commerce and server farms—that appears as the new marvel as early cinema once did, functioning as props and sites for ecclesiastical and magical performances of transformation.

SACRIFICE AND THE SLEIGHT OF HAND

Along with the ideological and technological doubling of "becoming political" through models, and the entanglement of bodies and objects through props, we find an even more classic form of doubling in the form of the simulacrum in the service of ritual sacrifice. In Mao's China, as in cognate cases, the quasi-religious imperative of performing self-sacrifice raised sacrifice to a literal embodiment of ideological commitment. As theorists of sacrifice from Mauss to Freud to Girard argue, sacrifice requires substitution that involves a dizzying dance of doubling: the person who is sacrificing something (sometimes themselves) is at the same time a victim (in that they pay the price), but they also stand for the deity in question, whether a god or a political or economic system. For Freud, victims are driven to sacrifice by a contradiction between a sense of personal guilt and a desire to identify with the authority figure. The act of sacrifice thus both alleviates *and* perpetuates guilt. For Girard, ritual sacrifice is a way to rechannel violence away from the actual victims by a double movement: first a scapegoat is sacrificed (for example, landlords, capitalist roaders, etc.) to ritually stand in for the unmarked victims, and then, when these are no longer available for whatever reason, a surrogate takes the place of the scapegoat and becomes a ritual substitute (for example, struggle sessions, etc.).[11]

This dynamic draws together the Maoist state and its subject, connecting the state (the sacred) and the individual (the profane) through the ritual of self-abnegation of material desire. This ritual can be conveniently practiced and performed at different levels and scales. Covell Meyskens shows in chapter 10 how it was performed amid chaotic Third Front industrialization, during which Mao's motto to "make do with what's available" and the prioritizing of "building the factory before housing" cultivated a ferocious energy based on total sacrifice. The new zone/city of Panzhihua was crudely conjured into existence for a number of official reasons—military strategy, industrial development, and distributing industry to the interior—but it also served as a site to create and perform sacrifice through the mantra of "overcoming selfishness," even at the expense of efficiency and production itself. Thus even the pressing national goal—the pursuit of industrialization at any cost—became something to be sacrificed to the spirit of sacrifice. The language of war that permeated even infrastructure, where each blast furnace was "just one battle victory," turned the Maoist materiality of industrialization into not just a metaphorical altar but a physical reality upon which lives and limbs were sacrificed.

Hardships were often an officially articulated and acknowledged form of sacrifice for urban workers sent to remote rural areas to build factories, where they slept under machinery or in chicken coops. Back in the cities and larger towns, however, the reliance on commodities created the need for a different kind of sacrifice: that of doing without. There were two kinds of things that one could do without: necessities and desires. Doing without necessities, for example, basic foodstuffs or material for clothing, was its own form of sacrifice, a proxy for strength, commitment, and, above all, competition—for doing without also meant finding ways to get. This pitted the ingenuity of those who could scrape together enough ration coupons or black-market items against vigilantes and antispeculation offices, creating countless scapegoats and surrogates for ritual sacrifice through humiliation and punishment.[12] Yet there was another category of commodity that proved even more difficult, complicated, and ultimately productive for the party: doing without things that one wanted. Since want is elastic, and need is relative, there is in principle no end of desire for commodities, especially when they serve as social markers.

These two kinds of doing without—basic foodstuffs and objects of desire—come together in poignant ways in Denise Ho's account in chapter 6 of small packets (known more generally in the West as care packages) of food and goods shipped to the mainland from Hong Kong, especially during those most lean years following the Great Leap Forward and into the Cultural Revolution. Ho recounts one woman remembering a classmate who, after her family received a suitcase brimming with food, "didn't dare touch the food. No one dared to touch it either. All of us said we would rather suffer along with the rest of the country." Ho's evocative examples suture together two of the most important themes of the book: how objects of different kinds became political, and how representations of material plenty work together with actual scarcity to produce a culture where sacrifice is valorized. Everyday objects sent from Hong Kong—pens, tinned food, spittoons—became "sugar-coated bullets" sent by the enemy. Marked as dangerously political because they were from the "outside," they acquired a kind of negative, anti-socialist agency.

Those same kind of objects, however, when viewed from the "inside," would be political in a different way, as objects to be proud of as symbols of national achievement, even if they existed largely in propaganda. This tension led to the imperative of producing socialist consumer goods on the inside. If successful, this production would solve many problems: it would highlight the ability and quality of socialist production, be a step toward fulfilling the Marxist dictum of providing for each according to their need, counter the seduction of socialism by outside goods, and even enable limited exports to other socialist countries or beyond. Most of all, it would allow for control over latent consumer desire that threatened the system. But attempts to control consumer desire through socialist production became a central contradiction of the Mao era (and arguably a fatal contradiction for the Soviet bloc, which China was able to later avoid by a stunning ideological reversal during its period of "reform and opening").

The creation of socialist consumer products thus appears as a kind of trap: the more consumer items were mass-produced, the greater the stoking of desires and exacerbation of the kinds of inequalities that the 1949 revolution was supposed to curtail in the first place, because material goods inscribe hierarchies and invite comparisons, and because desire is a slippery slope. To prevent socialist consumption from being possessed by the spirit of capitalism, the party had to resort to an upside-down solution: in addition to regulating the market for goods through central planning, it sought to also regulate consumption, that is, desire. And the control mechanism for regulating desire lay in calibrating self-sacrifice.

This is a tricky situation. Wanting to insure material plenty for the masses and repress commodity fetishism at the same time stoked desire as a form of excess.[13] And excess, as Georges Bataille famously wrote, has to be spent, gloriously or catastrophically.[14] The excess produced by the disjuncture between demand and desire thus became what the party struggled to control, displace, redirect, tame, or harness. Laurence Coderre shows in chapter 7 how the key form of expenditure was derived from moral rather than economic excess, emerging from the attempts to regulate consumption, and thus desire. This regulation was not, as Coderre convincingly argues, primarily to control access to a limited supply of goods (even if at times supplies were limited). Rather, it was an attempt to regulate the ideological dangers of consumption itself. Coderre's point is essential for understanding the contradictions at the heart of Maoist material culture: communism did not assume scarcity as a natural condition, and certainly not as a goal—on the contrary, communism's very appeal relied on the promise of plenty for all. Thus it needed to demonstrate abundance, whether real or promised, and at the same time distinguish it from consumerist excess, which it both invites and resembles. The boundary to be constantly negotiated was thus not between supply and demand but between "material bounty" and its "ideological dangers."

With exceptions of famine and other moments of upheaval or disaster, Maoist China did not consistently face a material lack of given items per se, though it certainly faced problems of production and distribution, and a resulting lack of diversity. Whether products were available or not, material plenty was elevated to a kind of magical thinking, a fantasy world existing temporally in the present (if spatially usually elsewhere), which simultaneously compelled individual restraint to avoid the trap of commodity fetishism. This fantasy world consisted both of representations and the deployment of mass delusion, such as during the early Great Leap Forward when, as the writer Yu Hua describes, reports about inflated or even nonexistent harvests assumed fantastic dimensions: "Pigs, it was said, now topped the scales at more than eleven hundred pounds; their heads were the size of large wicker baskets, and there was as much meat on them as on three pigs in the old days; a pot three feet tall and three feet wide was not big enough to cook one of these jumbo-sized porkers—why even with a pot six feet across, you could cook only half a pig!"[15]

In less mad times, the images of plenty circulated more conventionally through cinema, photography, and other forms of propaganda. It was through these, Coderre shows, that the privileging of self-sacrifice (a theme from the Long March on) was combined with the promise of plenty to justify and politically instrumentalize real, existing scarcity and to discipline cadres; as a 1963 report put it, despite poor production, "the problem of excessive eating and drinking is also very severe and is also prominent among cadre members."[16] Put differently, self-abnegation—the denial or postponing of gratification—became elevated as a personal virtue and a political necessity. Similar to the logic that drove the hungry schoolgirl in Denise Ho's example to forgo touching the food sent from Hong Kong, desire was to be curtailed out of ideological commitment. In Coderre's example in chapter 7 from the film *Delivering*, the protagonist Mother He *can* buy everything she desires and yet she refrains from doing it. This virtuousness connects sacrifice to the act of becoming political and thus turns everyday objects—quilt covers, Dacron shirts, or chicken—and everyday desires for them into a way to "mark an individual's progress" through the "willingness to sacrifice." In a kind of neoliberal move avant la lettre, this also shifted the burden of scarcity from the regime's responsibility to provide to the individual's willpower to resist temptation.

Sacrifice is thus a kind of doubling that redirects the excess produced by the contradiction of wanting material abundance without commodity fetishism. In the process, "the operation of ritual sacrifice depends," as anthropologists Brian Smith and Wendy Doniger put it, "on a kind of sleight of hand or self-deception, a shell game of displacement and replacement."[17] Coderre shows how it is not the actual existence of plenty that produces virtuous self-restraint in response but rather the need for virtuous self-restraint that produces the simulacrum of plenty, which then makes it possible to mimic and valorize self-abnegation in one's daily life. In psychoanalytic terms, the regime requires the performance of ritual sacrifice to show fealty to the big father. Thus, something must be created that can be sacrificed, and in a complex sleight of hand, the literally fictional commodity of the simulacrum of abundance created through propaganda functions as a material referent to allow the ritual of self-sacrifice as interpreted locally. In turn, this ritual marks the individual or community as politically safe.

This abundance is not only virtual—the result of propaganda—but, as Madeleine Yue Dong shows in chapter 8, it actually existed for some, particularly top cadres, such as those who conspicuously dined at the legendary Beijing restaurant Donglaishun. It became a model restaurant after top cadres granted it exceptions for special access and allowances for ingredients and pricing. Yet it was not a model in the way encountered earlier, like Zhang the model bamboo artisan or the model brick workers. If it were like these, Donglaishun would have been a model to emulate, to herald the extension of its excellence to the masses. Rather, and quite the opposite, the Donglaishun model was to serve as a representation, a simulacrum, a stand-in for what should be and yet is not available: "the lamb and duck had to taste good to prove the superiority of the socialist system." Within the logic of ritual sacrifice, this seemingly cynical contradiction had the ironic effect of marking the well-fed top cadre as politically superior precisely because they were able to consume *without* the need to sacrifice. Yet outside the logic of sacrifice, Donglaishun nakedly embodies how reliant state socialism was on special favors and limited access for an elite, showing not what socialism could achieve but precisely what it could not. By embodying the problem even as it occupied a space of aspiration, Donglaishun turned socialism itself into a fetish.

ACCUMULATED CONTRADICTIONS

The negotiation of material culture, markets, and agency—notably through the pursuit of consumption without commodity fetishism—appears throughout this volume as a key site for the material contradictions of the Mao era, in both senses: as contradictions inherent in material encounters, and as the relevant or central contradictions of the era. Socialism, ideally, would achieve accumulation without relying on the market to determine social relations, to achieve growth without surplus value. In practice, many attempts to pursue this generated only more contradictions, as when Jacob Eyferth shows in chapter 9 how the socialist state perpetuated a "spectacularly inefficient" system when it came to rural-urban trade, ignoring latent rural demand and failing even to efficiently develop a kind of classic dependency system that, at least, could have reduced poverty and improved resource allocation without sacrificing central power. The exacerbation rather than amelioration of rural-urban differences rested on an inverted theory of accumulation, whereby the commodity was no longer seen as that which was bought and sold in the market and mediated by price but as a product that was managed by the state, which used price as a lever. In Eyferth's rural examples, but also in the cities, when the commodity was removed from consumption behavior, it seemed to displace fetishism on to politics, where economic problems (such as poor lamb quality) became reframed as political problems.

Ironically, and tragically, as Eyferth argues, when capital accumulation was recast as a perverse kind of unequal exchange between urban and rural, it effectively decommodified and demonetizied rural areas, making them poorer, disproportionately reliant on women's unpaid labor, and often with less access to goods than before 1949, further disconnecting them from urban areas and compounding existing inequalities. The party also stretched the concept of capitalism itself, as Dong's chapter 8 painfully conveys, when small merchants with fewer than two employees on average were labeled as capitalist despite hardly being owners of the means of production. If economic growth was the goal, Dong argues, it would have been far more successful, even within a socialist framework, without the kind of forced accumulation imposed by the state, perhaps something more along the lines of Hungary's "goulash communism" (aka Kádarism) after 1956. But, at least until 1979, whenever the government was faced with the dilemma of reconciling political with economic goals, the scales were often tipped to the political.

How to understand these accumulated contradictions? In 1957 Mao wrote an essay entitled "On the Correct Handling of Contradictions among the People." In it, he identified two types of contradictions: those that come from the inside, from "among the people themselves," and those from the outside, "between ourselves and the enemy." Without the "correct handling and resolving," he wrote, both these kinds of contradictions pose an existential danger to the country.[18] There is an unintended echo of Freud's characterization of the uncanny here, which for him existed as a kind of logical contradiction that appears threatening to the psyche precisely at the intersection of two kinds of appearances: internal, when the repression of childhood memories falters, and external, when premodern animism intrudes into our modern world.[19] For Freud, the uncanny is that which cannot be placed, and the essays collected here suggest that capitalism played such a role in the Mao era, haunting it as that which should no longer exist because it belongs to the past, and yet recurs as a threat from both repressed capitalist desires inside and anachronistic atavism outside. Socialist consumption sought to transcend commodity fetishism, and socialist production sought to transcend surplus value, and yet both of these struggled to ritually rechannel the very ghosts that were declared exorcised, or not fully acknowledged in the first place. Capitalism seems here to haunt socialism as an excess that cannot be placed, adding one more layer of spectral complexity to the conjuring and counterconjuring that Derrida laid out in *Specters of Marx*.[20]

Mao's call to acknowledge and "correctly handle and resolve" contradictions gained new dimensions after 1979, when the sacrifice economy of the Mao years was turned on its head. During the period of reform and opening, radical class struggle was repudiated and expertise revalued, vernacular nationalism became wholly compatible with economic priority, and the burden of responsibility for material lack was completely inverted, since today one *must* consume for the good of the nation, not refrain from consumption through self-abnegation. In April 2020, as the global health and financial crisis of that year deepened, the party's Central Committee and the State Council issued new guidelines to follow "market rules, market pricing, and market competition" in an attempt, as the Xinhua news agency framed it, to let "the market rather than the state decide where resources should go."[21] It would be too easy, however, to see this as a resolution of contradictions rather than a new version of an older uncanny situation, one where the temporalities and spatialities of commodities and their fetishism are even more prone to contradictions and symbolic unmooring. Among the specters haunting both capitalism and China's socialist market economy now, again, is the contradiction of growing inequality amid plenty and its accompanying hungers, both metaphysical and literal.

NOTES

1 For a discussion of this famous quote see Kiaier, *Imagine No Possessions*. See also Kravets, "On Things and Comrades."
2 Jacques Derrida, *Specters of Marx* (New York: Routledge, 1994), especially chapters 4 and 5.
3 On haunting and hunting, see Derrida, *Specters*, 140–41.
4 This is a criticism levied against Karl Gerth in Fabio Lanza, ed., "PRC History Roundtable: Karl Gerth, *Unending Capitalism: How Consumerism Negated China's Communist Revolution* (Cambridge University Press, 2020)," *The PRC History Review* 5, no. 1 (October 2020): 1–25.
5 Cf. Sigmund Freud, *The 'Uncanny'* (1919), Collected Works, Standard Edition, vol. 17 (1917–19), 217–56.
6 The term "object" admits a number of Chinese language variants; see the extensive discussion in Michael Schoenhals, "Objects that Mattered: An Essay" in Jennifer Altehenger, ed., *The Mao Era in Objects* (London: King's College Digital Lab), https://maoeraobjects.ac.uk/objects-that-mattered-an-essay.
7 The word *model*, Ho points out, is both noun and verb. Ho, *Curating Revolution*, 90, 92.
8 For the arc of the story into the post-Mao era, see also Ian Johnson, "A Chinese Folk Artist's Descendants Are Split by the Government's Use of Their Family's Legacy," *New York Times*, December 15, 2015.

9   Sofer, *Stage Life of Props*, 59.
10 Gunning calls this "re-enchantment through aesthetic de-familiarization" (47). Gunning, "Re-Newing Old Technologies," 59.
11 For a discussion of sacrifice as a form of substitution, see Smith and Doniger, "Sacrifice and Substitution. For classic texts see Sigmund Freud, *Totem and Taboo*, in James Strachey, *The Standard Edition of the Complete Psychological Works of Sigmund Freud*, vol. 13 (1913–14) (London: The Hogarth Press and the Institute of Psycho-Analysis, 1955), 1–255; and René Girard, *Violence and the Sacred* (New York: Continuum, 2005). For the Chinese case, see, inter alia, Ter Haar, "China's Inner Demons"; and Lee, *The Stranger*, especially chapters 5 and 6, dealing with internal and external enemies, respectively.
12 See, for example, the first-person account in Yu Hua, *China in Ten Words* (New York: Anchor, 2011), 149–50.
13 In the process, new social values arose around products, gender norms changed, divides between rural and urban markets grew, and lives were reshaped by products and consumption. See Gerth, *Unending Capitalism*. Note also that the discussion both in Gerth and in this volume is primarily about consumption among the general population, not the high elite cadres, or the *nomenklatura*, who sometimes had greater access to goods of all sorts (though see chapter 8 in this volume). For an interesting discussion of how the Soviet elite sought to reconcile their practices with socialist rhetoric, see Fitzpatrick, "Becoming Cultured." One could fruitfully compare her theorization of *kul'turnost'* with the Chinese discourse of *wenming*, for example as discussed in Anagnost, *National Past-Times*.
14 Georges Bataille, *The Accursed Share: An Essay on General Economy* (New York: Zone Books, 1998), 24.
15 Yu Hua, *China in Ten Words*, 116.
16 Solomon, *Revolution*, 52.
17 Smith and Doniger, "Sacrifice and Substitution," 189.
18 Solomon, *A Revolution*, 126.
19 Freud, *The 'Uncanny.'*
20 Derrida, *Specters*.
21 "China Vows to Unleash Deep Market-Oriented Reforms in New Policy Directive as Economic Uncertainty Grows," *South China Morning Post*, April 10, 2020.

CHINESE CHARACTER GLOSSARY

Bai feng chao yang 白凤朝阳
Bao liandeng 宝莲灯
beizhan beihuang wei renmin 备战备荒为人民
bengbengxi 蹦蹦戏
bu hudie 捕蝴蝶

caicha deng 采茶灯
caicha pudie 采茶扑蝶
Caidie fenfei 彩蝶纷飞
changgu 长鼓
chou wu 绸舞

daoju 道具
Dayuejin 大跃进 (1958–60)
dazhonghua 大众化
dianying fangying dui 电影放映队

erren zhuan 二人转

Fang Xiuchun 方秀春
Feige 飞鸽
Fenghuang 凤凰
Fuzhou Zhucai Gongyi Shiyanchang 福州竹材工艺实验厂

Gao Yishui 高依水
gongxiaoshe 供销社

gongyi meishu gongzuozhe 工艺美术设计工作者
guanmo huiyan 观摩会演
guwu 鼓舞

He Dama 何大妈
Hongchou wu 红绸舞
hongmu 红木
huadeng wu 花灯舞
huandeng 幻灯
huazu wudao 化组舞蹈

jian wu 剑舞
jianku fendou 艰苦奋斗
jianku pusu 艰苦朴素
jianshe 建设
jianzhu 建筑
jingjilin 经济林
jiudi qucai 就地取材

kongque wu 孔雀舞
kuaibanshu 快板书

lao san da jian 老三大件
Liang Sicheng 梁思成
lianhuanhua 连环画
Lin Jianqing 林鉴清
Liu Sijiu 刘四久
long wu 龙舞

mangmu chongbai waiguo huo 盲目崇拜外国货
minjian 民间
minjian yiren 民间艺人
minzu wudao 民族舞蹈
minzu xingshi 民族形式
mofan 模范

nianhua 年画

paolü 跑驴
puzhang langfei 铺张浪费

Qiangti Gaige 墙体改革 (1973–76)
qinjian jieyue 勤俭节约
qizhuangong 砌砖工

renao 热闹

san 伞
san da chabie 三大差别
san da jian 三大件
sanxian jianshe 三线建设
shan wu 扇舞
shehui zhuyi yuanjing jiaoyu 社会主义远景教育
shiyong jiaju 实用家具
shizi wu 狮子舞
Songhuo lushang 送货路上
Su Changyou 苏长有

Taiping gu 太平鼓
tongbao 同胞

tongxingzheng 通行证
tu dianying 土电影
tufa 土法

Wenhua Dageming 文化大革命 (1966–76)

xia xiang 下乡
xian chansheng hou shenghuo 先生产后生活
xiang minjian xuexi 向民间学习
xiangfeizhu 湘妃竹
Xiao Lan 小兰
xiaobao youjian 小包邮件

Yongjiu 永久

Zhang Shuiquan 章水泉
Zhongguo gudianwu 中国古典舞
Zhongguo minzu minjian wu 中国民族民间舞
Zhongguo wu 中国舞
Zhonghua Renmin Gongheguo 中华人民共和国 (1949–)
Zhongnan Zhucai Liyong Yanjiu Weiyuanhui 中南区竹材利用研究委员会
zhongxin gongzuo 中心工作
zhuan 砖
zhuanyao 砖窑
zili gengsheng 自力更生
zou lian chuan 走莲船

SELECTED BIBLIOGRAPHY

This selected bibliography includes theoretical works and monographs most central to each chapter and the collection as a whole. Some primary sources of relevance to the entire volume have also been included. For full citations of other sources, please see the endnotes of each chapter.

Abel, Richard, and Rick Altman, eds. *Sounds of Early Cinema*. Bloomington: Indiana University Press, 2001.
Ah Cheng. *The King of Trees: Three Stories by Ah Cheng*. Translated by Bonnie S. McDougall. New York: New Directions, 2010.
Anagnost, Ann. *National Past-Times: Narrative, Representation, and Power in Modern China*. Durham, NC: Duke University Press, 1997.
Ash, Robert. "Squeezing the Peasants: Grain Extraction, Food Consumption and Rural Living Standards in Mao's China." *China Quarterly* 188 (December 2006): 959–98.
Auslander, Leora. "Beyond Words." *American Historical Review* 110, no. 4 (October 2005): 1015–45.
Bach, Jonathan. *What Remains: Everyday Encounters with the Socialist Past in Germany*. New York: Columbia University Press, 2017.
Bennett, Jane. *Vibrant Matter: A Political Ecology of Things*. Durham, NC: Duke University Press, 2010.
Betts, Paul, and Katherine Pence, eds. *Socialist Modern: East German Everyday Culture and Politics*. Ann Arbor: University of Michigan Press, 2008.
Bren, Paulina, and Mary Neuburger, eds. *Communism Unwrapped: Consumption in Cold War Eastern Europe*. Oxford: Oxford University Press, 2012.
Brown, Bill. *Other Things*. Chicago: University of Chicago Press, 2015.
Brown, Jeremy, and Matthew D. Johnson, eds. *Maoism at the Grassroots: Everyday Life in China's Era of High Socialism*. Cambridge, MA: Harvard University Press, 2015.
Chao, Kang. *The Development of Cotton Textile Production in China*. Cambridge, MA: Harvard University Press, 1977.
Chen Donglin. *Sanxian jianshe: Beizhan shiqi de xibu da kaifa*. Beijing: Zhonggong Zhongyang Dangxiao Chubanshe, 2003.
Chen Donglin, ed. *Zhongguo Gongchandang yu Sanxian*. Beijing: Zhonggong Dangshi Chubanshe, 2015.
Chen Mo. *Huaji fangying: Shaanxi nüzi fangyingren*. Beijing: Zhongguo Dianying Chubanshe, 2014.

Chen, Tina Mai. "The Human-Machine Continuum in Maoism: The Intersection of Soviet Socialist Realism, Japanese Theoretical Physics, and Chinese Revolutionary Theory." *Cultural Critique*, no. 80 (Winter 2012): 151–81.

———. "Propagating the Propaganda Film: The Meaning of Film in Chinese Communist Party Writings, 1949–1965." *Modern Chinese Literature and Culture* 15, no. 2 (Fall 2003): 154–93.

Ci, Jiwei. *Dialectic of the Chinese Revolution: From Utopianism to Hedonism*. Stanford, CA: Stanford University Press, 1994.

Clark, Paul. "The Triumph of Cinema." In *Art, Politics, and Commerce in Chinese Cinema*, edited by Ying Zhu and Stanley Rosen, 87–97. Hong Kong: Hong Kong University Press, 2010.

Coderre, Laurence. "A Necessary Evil: Conceptualizing the Socialist Commodity under Mao." *Comparative Studies in Society and History* 61, no. 1 (January 2019): 23–49.

———. *Newborn Socialist Things: Materiality in Maoist China*. Durham, NC: Duke University Press, 2021.

Crowley, David, and Susan Emily Reid, eds. *Pleasures in Socialism: Leisure and Luxury in the Eastern Bloc*. Evanston, IL: Northwestern University Press, 2010.

Davis, Deborah, ed. *The Consumer Revolution in Urban China*. Berkeley: University of California Press, 2000.

DeMare, Brian James. *Mao's Cultural Army: Drama Troupes in China's Rural Revolution*. Cambridge: Cambridge University Press, 2015.

Dikötter, Frank. *Cultural Revolution: A People's History, 1962–1976*. New York: Bloomsbury Press, 2016.

———. *Things Modern: Material Culture and Everyday Life in China*. London: C. Hurst and Company, 2007.

Dobrenko, Evgeny. *Political Economy of Socialist Realism*. Translated by Jesse M. Savage. New Haven, CT: Yale University, 2007.

Eyferth, Jacob. "Craft Knowledge at the Interaction of Written and Oral Cultures." *East Asian Science, Technology, and Society: An International Journal* 4, no. 2 (2010): 185–205.

———. *Eating Rice from Bamboo Roots: The Social History of a Community of Handicraft Papermakers in Rural Sichuan, 1920–2000*. Cambridge, MA: Harvard University Press, 2009.

———. "Liberation from the Loom? Rural Women, Textile Work, and Revolution in North China." In *Maoism at the Grassroots: Everyday Life in China's Era of High Socialism*, edited by Jeremy Brown and Matthew D. Johnson, 131–53. Cambridge, MA: Harvard University Press, 2015.

Farquhar, Judith. *Appetites: Food and Sex in Post-Socialist China*. Durham, NC: Duke University Press, 2002.

Fehérváry, Krisztina. "Goods and States: The Political Logic of State-Socialist Material Culture." *Comparative Studies in Society and History* 51, no. 2 (April 2009): 426–59.

———. *Politics in Color and Concrete*. Bloomington: Indiana University Press, 2013.

Finnane, Antonia. *Changing Clothes in China: Fashion, History, Nation*. London: Hurst, 2007.

Fitzpatrick, Sheila. "Becoming Cultured: Socialist Realism and the Representation of Privilege and Taste," In *The Cultural Front: Power and Culture in Revolutionary Russia*, 216–37. Ithaca, NY: Cornell University Press, 1992.

Flath, James. *The Cult of Happiness: Nianhua, Art, and History in Rural North China.* Vancouver: University of British Columbia Press, 2004.

———. "'It's a Wonderful Life': 'Nianhua' and 'Yuefenpai' at the Dawn of the People's Republic." *Modern Chinese Literature and Culture* 16, no. 2 (Fall 2004): 123–59.

Gerritsen, Anne, and Giorgio Riello, eds. *Writing Material Culture History.* London: Bloomsbury, 2015.

Gerth, Karl. *Unending Capitalism: How Consumerism Negated China's Communist Revolution.* Cambridge: Cambridge University Press, 2020.

Goldstein, Joshua, and Madeleine Yue Dong, eds. *Everyday Modernity in China.* Seattle: University of Washington Press, 2006.

Goscilo, Helena. "Luxuriating in Lack: Plenitude and Consuming Happiness in Soviet Paintings and Posters, 1930s–1953," In *Petrified Utopia: Happiness Soviet Style*, edited by Marina Balina and Evgeny A. Dobrenko, 53–78. London: Anthem Press, 2009.

Guangxi Film Distribution and Exhibition Company. *Guangxi dianying faxing fangying shi.* Guilin: Guangxi Film Company, 1995.

Gunning, Tom. "Re-Newing Old Technologies: Astonishment, Second Nature, and the Uncanny in Technology from the Previous Turn-of-the-Century." In *Rethinking Media Change: The Aesthetics of Transition*, 39–60. Cambridge, MA: MIT Press, 2003.

Hershatter, Gail. *The Gender of Memory: Rural Women and China's Collective Past.* Berkeley: University of California Press, 2011.

Ho, Denise Y. *Curating Revolution: Politics on Display in Mao's China.* Cambridge: Cambridge University Press, 2018.

Holm, David. *Art and Ideology in Revolutionary China.* Oxford: Clarendon Press, 1991.

———. "Folk Art as Propaganda: The *Yangge* Movement in Yan'an." In *Popular Chinese Literature and Performing Arts in the People's Republic of China, 1949–1979*, edited by Bonnie McDougall, 3–35. Berkeley: University of California Press, 1984.

Hou Li. *Building for Oil: Daqing and the Formation of the Chinese Socialist State.* Cambridge, MA: Harvard University Press, 2018.

Huadongshifandaxue Zhongguo Dangdaishi Yanjiu Zhongxin, ed. *Zhongguo dangdaishi yanjiu* [Research in the history of contemporary China]. Beijing: Jiuzhou Chubanshe, 2011.

Huang, Yu, and Xu Yu. "Broadcasting and Politics: Chinese Television in the Mao Era, 1958–1976." *Historical Journal of Film, Radio and Television* 17, no. 4 (1997): 563–74.

Hubei Sheng Shiyan Shi Weiyuanhui Wenshi He Xuexi Wenyuanhui. *Shiyan wenshi di 14 ji shang.* Wuhan: Changjiang Chubanshe, 2015.

———. *Shiyan wenshi di 14 ji xia.* Wuhan: Changjiang Chubanshe, 2015.

———. *Shiyan wenshi di san ji.* Wuhan: Zhengxie Hubei Sheng Shiyan Shi Weiyuanhui Shiyan Wenshi Bianji Weiyuanhui, 1999.

Hung, Chang-tai. "The Dance of Revolution: *Yangge* in Beijing in the Early 1950s." *China Quarterly*, no. 181 (March 2005): 82–99.

———. *Mao's New World: Political Culture in the Early People's Republic.* Ithaca, NY: Cornell University Press, 2011.

Judd, Ellen. "Prelude to the 'Yan'an Talks': Problems in Transforming a Literary Intelligentsia." *Modern China* 11, no. 3 (July 1985): 377–403.

Kiaier, Christina. *Imagine No Possessions: The Socialist Objects of Russian Constructivism.* Cambridge, MA: MIT Press, 2005.

Kinzley, Judd. *Natural Resources and the New Frontier: Constructing Modern China's Borderlands*. Chicago: Chicago University Press, 2018.

Ko, Dorothy. *The Social Life of Inkstones: Artisans and Scholars in Early Qing China*. Seattle: University of Washington Press, 2017.

———. "Stone, Scissors, Paper: Thinking through Things in Chinese History." *Journal of Chinese History* 3, special issue 2 (July 2019): 191–201.

Kopytoff, Igor. "The Cultural Biography of Things: Commoditization as a Process." In *The Social Life of Things: Commodities in Cultural Perspective*, edited by Arjun Appadurai, 64–92. Cambridge: Cambridge University Press, 1986.

Kornai, János. *The Socialist System: The Political Economy of Communism*. Oxford: Oxford University Press, 1992.

Kravets, Olga. "On Things and Comrades." *Ephemera* 13, no. 2 (2013): 421–36.

Laing, Ellen Johnston. *Selling Happiness: Calendar Posters and Visual Culture in Early-Twentieth-Century Shanghai*. Honolulu: University of Hawai'i Press, 2004.

Lardy, Nicholas. *Agriculture in China's Modern Economic Development*. Cambridge: Cambridge University Press, 1983.

Larkin, Brian. *Signal and Noise: Media, Infrastructure, and Urban Culture in Nigeria*. Durham, NC: Duke University Press.

Latour, Bruno. *Reassembling the Social: An Introduction to Actor-Network-Theory*. Oxford: Oxford University Press, 2005.

Lee, Haiyan. *The Stranger and the Chinese Moral Imagination*. Stanford, CA: Stanford University Press, 2014.

Li, Jie. *Utopian Ruins: A Memorial Museum of the Mao Era*. Durham, NC: Duke University Press, 2020.

Litzinger, Ralph A. *Other Chinas: The Yao and the Politics of National Belonging*. Durham, NC: Duke University Press, 2000.

Liu Zexian. "Making a New World and a New People: Cold War, Maoist Austere Architecture and the 'Rammed-Earth Campaign,' 1966–1976," *Journal of Contemporary Chinese Art* 4, no. 2–3 (September 2017): 269–85.

Lu, Hanchao. *Beyond the Neon Lights: Everyday Shanghai in the Early Twentieth Century*. Berkeley: University of California Press, 1999.

Ludwig, Andreas. "Übereinstimmung, Teilhabe und Zufriedenheit—Die sozialistische Lebensweise." In *Alltag: DDR: Geschichten, Fotos, Objekte*, edited by Andreas Ludwig, 277–81. Berlin: Christoph Links Verlag, 2012.

Meisner, Maurice. "Utopian Goals and Ascetic Values in Chinese Communist Ideology." *Journal of Asian Studies* 28, no. 1 (November 1968): 101–10.

Meyskens, Covell. *Mao's Third Front: The Militarization of Cold War China*. Cambridge: Cambridge University Press, 2020.

Mullaney, Thomas. *The Chinese Typewriter: A History*. Cambridge, MA: MIT Press, 2017.

Naughton, Barry. "The Third Front: Defence Industrialization in the Chinese Interior." *China Quarterly* 115 (September 1988): 351–86.

Oushakine, Serguei Alex. "'Against the Cult of Things': On Soviet Productivism, Storage Economy, and Commodities with No Destination." *Russian Review* 73, no. 2 (April 2014): 198–236.

Pan Weilin, ed. *Jindai Zhongguo de wuzhi wenhua*. Shanghai: Shanghai Rare Book Press, 2016.

Pang, Laikwan. "Colour and Utopia: The Filmic Portrayal of Harvest in Late Cultural Revolution Narrative Films." *Journal of Chinese Cinemas* 6, no. 3 (2012): 263–82.
Pence, Katherine, and Paul Betts. *Socialist Modern: East German Everyday Culture and Politics*. Ann Arbor: University of Michigan Press, 2008.
Perkins, Dwight. *Market Control and Planning in Communist China*. Cambridge, MA: Harvard University Press, 1966.
Qu Deqian and Zheng Zhubin, eds. *Yidai jiang xing: Kong Qingde*. Beijing: Jiefangjun Chubanshe, 2001.
Reid, Susan E., and David Crowley, eds. *Style and Socialism: Modernity and Material Culture in Post-War Eastern Europe*. Oxford: Berg, 2000.
Rubin, Eli. *Synthetic Socialism: Plastics and Dictatorship in the German Democratic Republic*. Charlotte: University of North Carolina Press, 2008.
Schmalzer, Sigrid. *Red Revolution, Green Revolution: Scientific Farming in Socialist China*. Chicago: University of Chicago Press, 2016.
———. "Self-Reliant Science: The Impact of the Cold War on Science in Socialist China." In *Science and Technology in the Global Cold War*, edited by Naomi Oreskes and John Krige, 75–106. Cambridge, MA: MIT Press, 2014.
Schoenhals, Michael. *Doing Things with Words in Chinese Politics*. Berkeley, CA: Center for Chinese Studies, 1992.
Selden, Mark, and Chih-ming Ka. "Original Accumulation, Equality, and Late Industrialization: The Cases of the People's Republic of China and Taiwan." In *The Political Economy of Chinese Development*, by Mark Selden, 109–36. Armonk, NY: M. E. Sharpe, 1993.
Shapiro, Judith. *Mao's War against Nature: Politics and the Environment in Revolutionary China*. New York: Cambridge University Press, 2001.
Shu Changxue. "From the Blue to the Red: Changing Technology in the Brick Industry of Modern Shanghai." In *Proceedings of the Fifth International Congress on Construction History*, vol. 3, edited by Brian Bowen, Donald Friedman, Thomas Leslie, and John Ochsendorf, 313–20. Chicago: Construction History Society of America, 2015.
Shue, Vivienne. *Peasant China in Transition*. Berkeley: University of California Press, 1980.
Smith, Brian K., and Wendy Doniger. "Sacrifice and Substitution: Ritual Mystification and Mythical Demystification." *Numen* 36, no. 2 (1989): 189–224.
Sofer, Andrew. *The Stage Life of Props*. Ann Arbor: University of Michigan Press, 2003.
Sohn-Rethel, Alfred. *Geistige und körperliche Arbeit: Zur Theorie der gesellschaftlichen Synthesis*. Frankfurt a. M.: Suhrkamp, 1973.
Solomon, Richard H. *A Revolution Is Not a Dinner Party*. New York: Anchor, 1978.
Stalin, Joseph. *Economic Problems of Socialism in the U.S.S.R.* Peking: Foreign Languages Press, 1972.
Sun, Peidong. *Shishang yu zhengzhi: Guangdong minzhong richang zhuozhuang shishang (1966-1976)* [Fashion and politics: Everyday clothing fashions of the Guangdong masses]. Beijing: Renmin Chubanshe, 2013.
Ter Haar, Barend J. "China's Inner Demons: The Political Impact of the Demonological Paradigm." In *China's Great Proletarian Revolution: Master Narratives and Post-Mao Counternarratives*, edited by Woei Lien Chong, 27–68. London: Rowman & Littlefield, 2002.
Verdery, Katherine. *What Was Socialism, and What Comes Next?* Princeton, NJ: Princeton University Press, 1996.

Vermeer, Eduard. *Economic Development in Provincial China: The Central Shaanxi Plain since 1930.* Cambridge: Cambridge University Press, 1988.

Wang Hui. "Local Forms, Vernacular Dialects, and the War of Resistance against Japan: The 'National Forms' Debate." In *The Politics of Imagining Asia*, edited by Theodore Huters, 95–135. Cambridge, MA: Harvard University Press, 2011.

Weber, Max. *The Protestant Ethic and the Spirit of Capitalism.* Hoboken, NJ: Routledge, 2001.

Wemheuer, Felix. *A Social History of Maoist China: Conflict and Change, 1949–1976.* Cambridge: Cambridge University Press, 2019.

Werner, Jake. "Global Fordism in 1950s Urban China." *Frontiers of History in China* 7, no. 3 (2012): 415–41.

Werret, Simon. *Thrifty Science: Making the Most of Materials in the History of Experiment.* Chicago: University of Chicago Press, 2019.

Wilcox, Emily. "Beyond Internal Orientalism: Dance and Nationality Discourse in the Early People's Republic of China, 1949–1954." *Journal of Asian Studies* 75, no. 2 (May 2016): 363–86.

———. "Dynamic Inheritance: Representative Works and the Authoring of Tradition in Chinese Dance." *Journal of Folklore Research* 55, no. 1 (January–April 2018): 77–111.

———. *Revolutionary Bodies: Chinese Dance and the Socialist Legacy.* Oakland: University of California Press, 2019.

———. "When Folk Dance Was Radical: Cold War *Yangge*, World Youth Festivals, and Overseas Chinese Leftist Culture in the 1950s and 1960s." *China Perspectives*, no. 1 (March 2020): 330–42.

Yao Daigui and Wang Huangsheng. "Miandui 'yuefenpai': 1950 niandai de Zhongguo xin nianhua" [Facing "yuefenpai": New Year Prints of the 1950s]. In *Zai jiedu: Dazhong wenyi yu yishixingtai (zengding ban)*, edited by Tang Xiaobing, 154–75. Beijing: Beijing Daxue Chubanshe, 2007.

Yu Hua. *China in Ten Words.* New York: Anchor, 2011.

Yu Shuishan. *Chang'an Avenue and the Modernization of Chinese Architecture.* Seattle: University of Washington Press, 2012.

Zakharova, Larissa. "Le quotidien du communisme: Pratiques et objets." *Annales. histoire, sciences sociales* 68, no. 2 (April–June 2013): 305–14.

CONTRIBUTORS

JENNIFER ALTEHENGER is associate professor of Chinese history and Jessica Rawson Fellow in modern Asian history at the University of Oxford and Merton College. She is the author of *Legal Lessons: Popularizing Laws in the People's Republic of China, 1949–1989* (Harvard University Press, 2018).

JONATHAN BACH is professor of global studies at The New School. He is the author of *What Remains: Everyday Encounters with the Socialist Past in Germany* (Columbia University Press, 2017) and coeditor of *Learning from Shenzhen: China's Post-Mao Experiment from Special Zone to Model City* (University of Chicago Press, 2017) and *Re-Centering the City: Global Mutations of Socialist Modernity* (UCL Press, 2020).

LAURENCE CODERRE is associate professor of East Asian studies at New York University. She is the author of *Newborn Socialist Things: Materiality in Maoist China* (Duke University Press, 2021).

MADELEINE YUE DONG is professor of history at the University of Washington. She is the author of *Republican Beijing: The City and Its Histories* (University of California Press, 2003).

JACOB EYFERTH is professor of Chinese history at the University of Chicago. He is the author of *Eating Rice from Bamboo Roots: The Social History of a Community of Handicraft Papermakers in Rural Sichuan* (Harvard University Press, 2009).

CHRISTINE I. HO is associate professor of East Asian art history at the University of Massachusetts Amherst. She is the author of *Drawing from Life: Sketching and Socialist Realism in the People's Republic of China* (University of California Press, 2020).

DENISE Y. HO is associate professor of twentieth-century Chinese history at Yale University. She is the author of *Curating Revolution: Politics on Display in Mao's China* (Cambridge University Press, 2018).

JIE LI is professor of East Asian languages and civilizations at Harvard University. She is the author of *Shanghai Homes: Palimpsests of Private Life* (Columbia University Press, 2014) and *Utopian Ruins: A Memorial Museum of the Mao Era* (Duke University Press, 2020).

COVELL F. MEYSKENS is associate professor of history at the Naval Postgraduate School. He is the author of *Mao's Third Front: The Militarization of Cold War China* (Cambridge University Press, 2020).

COLE ROSKAM is associate professor of architectural history at the University of Hong Kong. He is the author of *Improvised City: Architecture and Governance in Shanghai, 1843–1937* (University of Washington Press, 2019) and *Designing Reform: Architecture in the People's Republic of China, 1970–1992* (Yale University Press, 2021).

EMILY WILCOX is associate professor of Chinese studies at William & Mary. She is the author of *Revolutionary Bodies: Chinese Dance and the Socialist Legacy* (University of California Press, 2018) and coeditor of *Corporeal Politics: Dancing East Asia* (University of Michigan Press, 2020).

INDEX

Page numbers in *italics* refer to figures.

Adam, Leonhard, *Primitive Art*, 70
Ah Cheng, on propaganda film screenings, 106
Ai Weiwei, 58
Altehenger, Jennifer, 42, 221
amateur practice: *Bamboo Animal Toys* (Zhuzhi dongwu wanju), 32, *33*; "how to" manuals for bamboo, 31–32; Lin Jianqing's advocacy of, 29; official advocacy of, 39n57; and propaganda murals, 78; stage performances in the socialist era, 112. *See also* handicrafts and handicraft skills
Anti-Rightist Campaign (1957): architectural production during, 52; handicraft production during, 76; material concerns animated during, 4; urban-rural flow of agricultural products during, 168
Apter, David, 209
architecture: China's socialist building production, 51; crisis of meaning, 52–53; the Fuzhou Bamboo Craft Experimental Factory, 35; housing construction in Shaanxi, 191; scholarship on Chinese architectural production after 1949, 41–42; sophisticated methods of production, 56–57. *See also* bamboo; bricks and brickmaking; rammed earth; steel
asceticism: Farquhar on moralist denial within Maoism, 150; larger goal served by, 14, 152, 160n19; Meisner on Chinese socialist ascetic values, 151; poverty and lack as meaningful and temporary, 148–49, 157, 160n19; promise of abundance invoked by, 183–84; Weber's views on, 151. *See also* austerity; sacrifice

austerity: bodily sacrifice of mobile projectionists, 103, 104–6, 115–17; model stories emphasizing thrift and frugality, 31, 155–56, 228; productivist convictions advocating, 8, 14; Soviet shortages and, 13–14, 149; of "suburban agriculture serving the capital city," 164–65; of the Third Front campaign, 15–16, 225; by urban workers sent to remote rural areas, 225; at the Works, 15, 201, 207–8, 211, 214
automobiles: production expansion associated with the Third Front, 202–3; Rao Bin's leadership of industry in China, 203–4, *205*, 212; Shanghai Auto Factory, 204; Stalin Automobile Plant, 204; used by mobile projectionists, 102, 116, 117; Wuhan Auto Factory, 204. *See also* First Auto Works; Second Auto Works (the Works)

Bach, Jonathan, on appropriation, 36n4
bamboo: as a "hinge material," 21–22, 34–35, 42; "how-to" manuals and, 31–32; in socialist construction, 9, 21, 24–26, 32–35, *35*, 221; social life of, 20; sofa chairs created for Mao Zedong and Zhou Enlai, 30; toy-making instruction, 32–33, *33*; urban-rural experiences of owning objects made from, 23, 35; Wu Zhonglun's *How to Plant Bamboo* (Zenyang zhong maozhu), 31–32. *See also* Fuzhou Bamboo Craft Experimental Factory
Bao'an County, 131
Bao'an News (Bao'an bao), 140

243

Bataille, Georges, on excess, 227
Beijing: "exchange meetings" (*jingyan jiaoliu hui*) held in, 48; food habits during the Qing, 162; Hubei Hall in the Great Hall of the People, 24; impact of policies on "foodscape" of, 14–15, 165–66; material displays of markets and department stores, 184; *Red Silk Dance* premiered in, 95. *See also* Donglaishun; Liubiju (Pickled Vegetable Store)
Beijing Film Studio productions, 152–53
bodies: bodily sacrifice of mobile projectionists, 103, 104–6, 115–17, 119; bricks linked to laboring, 42, 59; displacement of, by Hong Kong wind, 141; "physicality" cinema, 102–3, 118–19; and study of material culture, 7; urban-rural gap reflected in clothing, 5. *See also* dance; dance-props (*daoju*); famine; projectionists
bricks and brickmaking: aesthetic and structural capacity of, 52–53; in architectural modernism in the West, 44; bricks as neck rests, 191; in contemporary Chinese architectural production, 59; featured in the Zhongnanhai compound, 40, *41*; during the Great Leap Forward, 11, 53–55, *54*; in imperial-era building treatises, 43; in the Mao era, 43, 56; during Republican-era China, 45; rural housing built with, 191; semiotic potential of, 40, 42–43, 44, 46, 52, 57–59; Soviet-originated technologies, 50–51; Su Changyou's model construction practices, 46–48, *48*, 52; Taylorist bricklaying practices, 44, 47; in *Treatise on Architectural Methods or State Building Standards* (Yingzao fashi; 1103 CE), 43; in Vietnam, 60n8

capitalism: "capitalist tails" (*ziben zhuyi weiba*), 117, 220; China's aspiration to match rivals, 9, 51, 57, 151–52; class-based hierarchies of, 48, 56–57; excess associated with, 52, 155–56, 230; foreign products associated with, 132; and industrially produced cloth, 189; Marx and Marxism on capitalist societies as

"collection of commodities," 184, 219; in 1990s China, 150–51; resurgence in the Soviet Union, 202; role of material culture in development of, 8–9, 184–87; values of, and Cultural Revolution, 56, 117, 133, 140, 150, 206, 219–20, 230
Central Academy of Craft and Design: debates over oversight of, 68–69, 75, 76; establishment of, 11; intellectual heritage of, 69–70. *See also Decoration* (*Zhuangshi*)
Chan Anita, 209
Chen Mengjia, 69
Chen Yi, *41*
Chen Yun, 177
Chen Zhifo, 67, 81n29
Chiang Kai-shek: international famine relief encouraged by, 141; military preparations of, 202, 213
China Pictorial (Renmin huabao): images of retail abundance featured in, 146–48, *147*, *148*, 159n4; national dance culture reported on in, 87, 89, 93, 99n7
China Travel Service, transmission of small packets facilitated by, 126, 134, 136, 138
Chinese Communist Party (CCP): and automobile production, 202–3; and commodities, 193–95; and construction methods, 55–56; and material governance, 20–21; Nationalist regime contrasted with, 3; objects and workers as political agents, 23–26, 37–38n34, 221–22; organization of handcraft families by, 178; *Red Flag* (Hongqi) review of *Delivering*, 153; success of, measured by what could be held, felt, and tasted, 14; urban-rural divide addressed by, 3–5, 13, 208–10. *See also* Mao era; socialist construction
Ci Jiwei, 160n19
cinemas: construction of, 49; open-air, 102, 103, 106–9, 117, 118–19. *See also* dance—films; *Delivering Goods on the Road* (*Songhuo lushang*); films and film production; projectionists
class: bad labels, 4–5; and expertise, during the reform era, 231; and hierarchical relationship between design and designers, 72, 76; hierarchies of capitalism

based on, 48, 56–57; "materialist dialectics" associated with by Mao Zedong, 3, 11–12; mediation by dance props, 96–97, 223; mobile projectionists viewed as privileged, 118

class struggle: films emphasizing, 115, 119–20; repudiated during the reform era, 231

cloth and clothing: Dacron shirts, 153–54, 228; guidelines for travelers visiting China, 130; homespun (*tubu*), 5, 189–90, 196; ideological agency of textile mills, 49, 189; mass sensitivity to design identified in fabric patterns, 72; nylon stockings confiscated and resold, 132; rationing of cloth, 190; state-controlled prices, 193; textile manufacturing in Shanghai, 45, 67; textiles made from bamboo, 34; textile work by rural women, 189–91, 196; urban-rural gap reflected in, 5, 183, 186; used, as gifts, 131

Coderre, Laurence, 193, 227, 228

Cold War era: border control during, 128, 201; circulating material exchange during, 65; and Maoist developmentalism, 202, 212–14

collectivization: agricultural, 4, 114, 164–65, 167–68, 179, 187–88; and architectural production, 40, 52–53; and Beijing's food culture, 179; and brick production, 42, 46–50, 56–57; as central to socialist construction, 7, 10; of the handicraft industry, 11, 28, 76–77, 222; promotion of, by mobile film screenings, 114; and raw cotton allocation, 183, 186. *See also* massification (*dazhonghua*)

commodities: discussed by the CCP, 193–95; and gender, 185–86; Marx and Marxism on capitalist societies as collection of, 184, 219; socialist, inscribed with revolutionary slogans, 183; Stalin on, 193, 194; urban-rural divide reflected in access to, 5, 8, 15, 16, 183–85, 193–97; urban-rural exchange, 184–86, 193–94, 229. *See also* conspicuous consumption

commodity fetishism, vs. consumption, 148, 219–21, 227–31

commodity grain (*shangpin liang*), 194

communes: brick-production facilities in, 52–53, 55; economics of, depicted in *Delivering*, 153–56; film screenings at, 106, 113, 115, 118; newsletters describing life in, 138–39; processing of cotton by rural, 190, 198n43; vegetables from, featured in *China Pictorial*, 147, *148*

conspicuous consumption: dining by cadres at Donglaishun, 228–29; as a focus of *Delivering*, 154–57, 160n25; and status in socialist China, 186

Cooke, Edward S., 37–38n34

cotton: bags sewn by projectionists, 104; cooking oil made from seeds, 188; labor returns, 190, 198n24; Lenin and Trotsky on textiles, 189, 193; printed fabrics, 72, 74; as a material for socialist construction, 9, 20, 74; processing by rural women, 196–97; raw, allocation of, 183, 186; shortages of, 139; state-controlled "scissors pricing," 190, 193, 195. *See also* cloth and clothing

Cultural Revolution (1966–76): bricks and brickmaking during, 56; cinema as propaganda during, 106, 114–15; displaced urban youths (*zhiqing*) during, 107–8, 116, 117–18, 117–18; household possessions of workers during, 1–2; material concerns during, 1, 4; as "ten years of turmoil," 4; vilification of outside objects during, 137, 140

customs: border control, 127; food items with low duties, 142; guidebooks for visitors, 130; regulations outlined in *Xinwanbao*, 130–31

Czechoslovakia, 75, 129

dance: in *China Pictorial* (Renmin huabao), 87, *89*, *93*, 99n7; and embodiment of characters, 97; folk, documented in *Zhongguo minzu minjian wu jicheng*, 101n51; *Red Silk Dance* (Hongchou wu), 88–90, *90*, *93*, 95; trial performances (*guanmo huiyan*), 86; *yangge*, 94–95, 96, 97–98

—films: *Magic Lotus Lantern* (Bao liangdeng), 91, *92*; *Red Flowers Blossoming Everywhere* (Hong hua biandi kai), 91–92

dance: (*continued*)
—individual dance styles: dragon dance (*long wu*), 88, 97; lion dance (*shizi wu*), 87, 97; peacock dance (*kongque wu*), 87; silk dance (*chou wu*), 87, 93 (*see also* dance: Red Silk Dance [Hongchou wu]); sword dances (*jian wu*), 88, 90, 92; tea-picking dance, 88–89, *89*
—props (*daoju*): and embodiment of characters, 96–97, 223; ideological function of, 98–99; as integral to Chinese choreography, 12, 84–88, 92–97; in Mao-era films, 90–93; silk and bamboo fans, 85, 86–88, 90, 96–97

Dance News (Wudan tongxun): Fan Dance featured in, 95–97; pedagogical tools for dancers in, 93–97; trial performances (*guanmo huiyan*) featured in, 95–96

Decoration (Zhuangshi): bamboo featured in, 22, 30; inaugural cover of, 77–78, *78*; and visual identity of socialist Chinese design, 77–79

Delivering Goods on the Road (*Songhuo lushang*): conspicuous consumption as a focus of, 153, 156–57; protagonist Mother He (He Dama), 153–56, 228

Deng Xiaoping, selection of site for Second Auto Works, 205

Derrida, Jacques, 219–20, 230

design: and class, 72, 76; Eastern European, 75; French and German, 67, 70; furniture, from Ming and Qing dynasties, 23; of handicrafts, 11, 27–29; Japanese, 67, 69; Liu Jiakun's, 59; nativist models of artistic, 11, 58, 69–72, 76–78; socialist, and propaganda, 67–68, 78; studies of, in New China, 63–66, 69–70; studies of, in Republican period, 66; Wu Lao's, 71. *See also* Central Academy of Craft and Design; *Decoration* (Zhuangshi); *Organization of Design, The* (Tu'an de zuzhi); Pang Xunqin

diaspora: "Bamboo Curtain" traversed by overseas Chinese, 13, 129; and "mailbag rush," 126–27, 137; as "overseas connections" (*haiwai guanxi*), 126, 137; and relief packages, 126, 134, 136, 138.

See also Hong Kong; Macau; outside objects; Taiwan

Dobrenko, Evgeny, and socialist realism, 158–59

Dong, Madeline Yue, 230

Donglaishun: conspicuous dining by cadres at, 228–29; impact of Socialist Transformation on, 161, 176–77

Doniger, Wendy, 228

Eastern Europe: consumer culture in, 14–15; and handicraft design, 75; power generators imported to China from, 104; and trade in the socialist world economy, 6; and trade within Eastern bloc, 126, 129

ethnic minority groups: dances of, 100n24; in *Nationality Pictorial* (Minzu Huabao), 146, 159n1; reanimation of traditions of, 64; Tibetans, 104. *See also* handicrafts and handicraft skills—folk-national handicraft

excess: capitalism associated with, 52, 155–56, 230; and commodity fetishism, 148, 227–28; of nonstaple foods, 164–65

exhibitions: border controls relaxed for, 128–29; handicrafts in, 22, 28, 30, 65, 75, 79; Hubei Provincial Industry and Agricultural Exhibition, 24; of middle and primary school manual work, 29; National Handicraft Exhibitions, 75; Panama-Pacific Exhibition, 24. *See also* films and film production

Eyferth, Jacob, 229–30

famine: and airdrops of food parcels to mainland China by the Nationalist regime, 141; following the Great Leap Forward, 3, 4, 5, 125; and relief packages sent to mainland China, 125–26, 131–33, 134, 135–37, *136*, 140–42, *141*, 226, 228

Fang Lizhi, 56

fans, as dance props, 85, 86–88, 90, 96–97

Farquhar, Judith, on moralist denial within Maoism, 150

Film Projection magazine, 108, 114, 115

films and film production: Beijing Film Studio productions, 152–53; "capitalist tails" (*ziben zhuyi weiba*) and wares at screenings, 117, 220; class struggle emphasized in, 115, 119–20; exhibition network in the PRC, 102, 106–7, 112; film reels likened to "precious scrolls," 109–10, 119; Jiang Qing's model works (*yangbanxi*), 106; Mao-era, as "physical and spirit medium," 12, 102–3, 119–20; Mao-era, as political shamanism, 114–15; props in Mao-era dance, 90–93; "red treasure" (*hong bao pian*), 110; revolutionary mobilization of, 106, 153; screenings of foreign, 6, 103; screenings of propaganda, 106–7. *See also* cinemas; dance—films; *Delivering Goods on the Road* (*Songhuo lushang*); projectionists

First Auto Works: establishment of, 203–4; recruitment of workers from, to build Second Auto Works, 205–6, 209

First Front, 202, *203*

First Machine-Building Ministry, 204–5, 207

Fitzpatrick, Sheila, 149, 159

Five-Antis Campaign (1952). *See* Three-Antis and Five-Antis Campaigns (1951–52)

folk-national handicraft. *See* handicrafts and handicraft skills—folk-national

food: Beijing's habits during the Qing, 162; consumption of, in Shaanxi, 187–89; flow of, during the Transformation, 167–73; impact of policies on Beijing's "foodscape," 14–15, 165–66; items with lowest customs duties, 142; meat consumed during the Qing, 165; rationing of, and household registration, 4, 5, 164; in relief packages from Hong Kong, 130–31, 131–33, *134*, 135–37, *136*, 140–42, *141*, 226, 228; temporary ration coupons for "compatriots" (*tongbao*), 129. *See also* Donglaishun; famine; grain; Liubiju (Pickled Vegetable Store)

"Four Simultaneities" policy, 211

France: design principles of, 70; training of Chinese professional designers in, 67

Freud, Sigmund: on sacrifice as a form of substitution, 224–25; on the uncanny, 220, 230

fuel: from agricultural biomass (grain stalks), 192; bamboo as a source of, 20; as a material for socialist construction, 9, 15; shortages of cooking oil, 139; women's labor as substitute for biomass shortages, 196–97

Fujian, bamboo goods and furniture from, 22, 28, 29, 30

Fujian Natural Sciences Research Association, 29

Fujian Normal College, 28, 29

furniture: bamboo, from Fujian, 22, 28, 29, 30; bamboo, from Sichuan, 22; bamboo sofa chairs created for Mao Zedong and Zhou Enlai, 30; designs of, from Ming and Qing dynasties, 23; distributed by work units, 1; massification of bamboo, 10, 27–29; in rural households, 191–92

Fuzhou Bamboo Craft Experimental Factory (Fuzhou Zhucai Gongyi Shiyanchang): establishment of, 28; knowledge about bamboo work disseminated by, 28–29; as a model story, 31, 35

Fuzhou Provincial Light Industry Bureau, 28

Gao Yishui: bamboo sofa chairs created for Mao Zedong and Zhou Enlai, 30; and Fuzhou Bamboo Craft Experimental College, 28–29

Ge Kejian, 76

gender: commodities and, in Western semiotic system, 185–86; and raw materials prepared for consumption, 186. *See also Delivering Goods on the Road* (*Songhuo lushang*); women

Germany: foreign goods in, 126; Intershops in, 120; Plaste as achievement of the GDR, 21–22, 36n7; troops from, in Soviet World War II films, 112

Gerritsen, Anne, 7

Gerth, Karl, 231n4, 232n13; on commodities and status in socialist China, 186

Girard, René, 224–25

Goscilo, Helena, 149

grain: agricultural biomass from stalks of, 192; average consumption of, during the Qing, 164; commodity (*shangpin liang*), 194; husked, allocation of, 183, 186; impact of collectivization on, 179,

grain (*continued*)
186–87; "scissors pricing" of, by the state, 195; shortages of, in Shanghai (1960), 5; urban-rural gap reflected in allocations of, 5
Great Hall of the People, 24, 71
Great Leap Forward (1958–62): brickmaking during, 11, 53–55, *54*; cinema as propaganda during, 106, 114–15; famine and privation following, 3, 4, 5, 125; outside objects sent to mainland China during, 125, 133, *134*, *136*, 140–42, *141*, 226, 228; and propaganda murals, 78; reports about commodities during, 227
Guangdong: visitors to Hong Kong from, 127–28
Guangzhou: and border controls, 128; committees to welcome Hong Kong and Macau "compatriots" (*tongbao*), 129; confiscated goods originating from, 132; guidebooks for visitors to, 130; industrialization of, 42; red brick production in, 42
Guanzhong. *See* Shaanxi–Guanzhong region
Gunning, Tom, on aesthetic de-familiarization, 224, 232n10

handicrafts and handicraft skills: and CCP organization of handcraft families, 178; contribution of, to socialist construction, 27; and design knowledge, 11, 27–29; and Ministry of Light Industry, 68–69, 75–76; produced by women's labor, 65, 189–91, 196. *See also* Central Academy of Craft and Design; Zhang Shuiquan
—folk-national: during Anti-Rightist Campaign, 76; featured in *Decoration* (Zhuangshi), 77–78, *78*; and industrial production of folk craft, 27–30; and nation-building movements, 64; socialist material culture embedded within, 11, 22–27, 34–35, 65
Haraway, Donna Jeanne, 85
Hebei, Three Sisters Movie Team in, 105, *105*, 113
Hershatter, Gail, on "campaign time," 4

Ho, Christine I., 222
Ho, Denise Y., 221, 226, 228, 231n7
Hong Kong: border controls with China, 132; boundaries extended, 127; in Chinese propaganda, 128, 140; customs regulations outlined in *Xinwanbao*, 130; economic growth of, 179; migration from China to, 127–28; outside objects sent to mainland China from, 125, 131–33, *134*, *136*, 140–42, *141*, 226, 228; small packets sent to China from, 133–37; travel to China from, for Chinese New Year (1956), 128, 129–31
Hou Li, on industrialization without urbanization, 201
household registration system (*hukou*), 4, 5, 164
housing: assignments by work units, 5; bamboo used for, 20; brick construction of, 52; decommodification of urban, 185; factory construction prioritized over, 207–8, 225; national conference in Shanghai (1958), 51; and "produce first and live later" slogan, 201; rural, 191; scarcity of new, 16. *See also* architecture
Hubei. *See* Second Auto Works (the Works); Zhang Shuiquan
Hubei Hall, furniture for, 24
Hubei Provincial Industry and Agricultural Exhibition, 24
Hundred Flowers Campaign (1956–57): architectural production during, 52; handicraft production during, 76; relaxed political atmosphere of, 168, 176; urban-rural flow of agricultural products during, 168
Hungary, 75, 230
Hutheesing, Rajia, on brickmaking in China, 46

Japan: building tradition in, 45; film lecturers (*benshis*) in, 112; folk craft (*mingei*) movement in, 64; modernist developments in, 67; occupation of Hong Kong by, 127; Pang Xunqin's studies of design in, 67, 69; power generators and projectors produced in, 104. *See also* Second Sino-Japanese War (1937–45)

Jeyasingh, Shobana, 84–85
Jiang Qing, model works (*yangbanxi*) by, 106

Kahn, Louis, 44
knowledge: and architectural methods of production, 57; "exchange meetings" (*jingyan jiaoliu hui*) for sharing, 48; and Fuzhou Bamboo Craft Experimental Factory, 28–29; of handicraft design, 11, 27–29; and "how-to" manuals about bamboo, 31–32; perceptual vs. rational in Mao's *On Practice*, 11–12
Kong Qingde, 207–8
Korean-style folk dance, 90, 101n39
Korean War, 128, 163, 204
Kornai, János, 148–49

land reform, 3, 4, 70, 94, 187
Larkin, Brian, on Nigeria's media infrastructure, 108
Lei Guiyuan, 69–70, 75
Li, Jie, 158, 223–24
Liang Qichao, 40
Liang Sicheng, 40–41, 52
Lin Biao, 200, 212
Lin Jianqing, 28–30
Litzinger, Ralph A., 159n1
Liu Jiakun: Suzhou Imperial Kiln Ruins Park and Museum designed by, 59
Liubiju (Pickled Vegetable Store): establishment of, 168–69; products from, before Socialist Transformation, 169–71; "socialist commerce" exemplified by, 161, 172–75, 177–79
Long March, self-sacrifice as a theme of, 105, 228
Loos, Alfred, 65–66
Lowenstein, Matthew, 196

Macau: migration from China to, 138; outside objects sent to mainland China from, 125, 133–38; travel to China from, for Chinese New Year (1956), 129–31
Madokoro, Laura, 128
Mao era: bricks and brickmaking during, 43, 56; country's material landscape in, 2, 52; outside objects and, 125–27, 132–33, 140–41, 226, 228; shortages associated with, 1–3, 13–16, 57, 139, 227; two stages of, 4. *See also* Cultural Revolution (1966–76); Great Leap Forward (1958–62); Hundred Flowers Campaign (1956–57); reform era; slogans; socialist construction (*shehuizhuyi jianshe*); Socialist Transformation (Shehuizhuyi Gaizao; 1956); Third Front campaign; Three-Antis and Five-Antis Campaigns (1951–52)
Mao Zedong, 30, *41*, 161; bamboo sofa chair crafted for, 30; on construction process, 51; *Little Red Books*, 110; in newsreels and propaganda films, 107, 110; *On Contradiction* (Maodun lun), 3; *On Practice* (Shijian lun), 9–10, 11–12; quotes from, 110, 185; and Second Auto Works, 203, 209, 210–11. *See also* slogans
Maoist asceticism. *See* asceticism
Marx and Marxism: and bourgeois values, 151–52; on capitalist societies as collection of commodities, 184, 219; on material conditions and social relations, 6, 7, 219–21, 226; on social and physical environments, 85, 98
massification (*dazhonghua*): bamboo as a material for, 21–22, 24–28, 34–35, 37–38n34, 221; Pang Xunqin on design and, 72–74; objects and workers as agents, 26, 27–28
material contradictions: of bamboo objects, 10; in China's socialist market economy, 231; of Chinese socialist experiences, 8, 229–30; commodities and gender, 185–86; and consumption vs. commodity fetishism, 148, 219–21, 227–31; food distribution under state ownership, 167–68; introduced as an idea, 3; Mao's addressing of, 230–31; and mailed goods, 13, 125, 139–42; of Mother He's consumption practices, 154–56, 228; of outside objects sent to mainland China, 125–26, 132–33, 226; and "overseas connections" (*haiwai guanxi*), 126, 137; and "red and expert" prototype (*you hong you zhuan*), 151–52; of sacrifice, 228. *See also* urban-rural divide
material culture and materiality: defined, 7; "physicality" cinema, 102–3, 118–19;

material culture and materiality (*continued*)
    socialist construction illuminated by, 2, 7–11
Meisner, Maurice, on Chinese socialist ascetic values, 151
Meyskens, Covell F., 225
Miller, Daniel, 7
Ming dynasty (1368–1644): brickmaking during, 43; brocade patterns of, 74; furniture designs of, 23
Ministry of Construction, 50–51
Ministry of Culture, 68–69, 76
Ministry of Foreign Trade, on packages from Hong Kong and Macau, 135
Ministry of Light Industry, 68–69, 75–76
Ministry of Metallurgy, 204
minority groups. *See* ethnic minority groups
models: bamboo as, 21–22, 24–26, 34–35, 221; bricks as, 40–41, 44–46, 57, 222; local heroes as, 112–13, 115; nativist, of artistic design and training, 11, 58, 69–72, 76–78; objects and workers as political agents and, 23–26, 37–38n34, 221–22; projectionists as, 116; rammed earth construction as, 55–56
Mother He (He Dama). *See Delivering Goods on the Road* (*Songhuo lushang*)
Mukerji, Chandra, 79

National Goods Movement, 67
Nationalist Government: vs. CCP's success, 3; confiscation of enterprises owned by, 161; and food parcel airdrops, 141; Guomindang, 201, 202. *See also* Chiang Kai-shek
Naughton, Barry, on economic growth of Hong Kong and Taiwan, 179
New China: dance portrayal of lives of fishers in, 97; design studies in, 63–66, 69–70; new architecture proposed by Liang Sicheng for, 40–41; role of bricks and brickmaking in, 46–50, 58–59; role of materials in culture of, 10, 33–34, 70–71, 125; and steel, 52. *See also* People's Republic of China (PRC)
nianhua (New Year's prints), 158
North Korea: dance delegation from, 92; trade agreements with the PRC, 6

Organization of Design, The (Tu'an de zuzhi): compilation of, by Lei Guiyuan and Pang Xunqin, 69; peonies as a focus in, 73–74, *74*; print run of, 82n43
Oushakine, Serguei A., 13, 149
outside objects: anti-socialist agency acquired by, 126, 137, 140–41, 226; relief packages sent to mainland China as, 125–27, 131–33, *134*, 135–37, *136*, 140–42, *141*, 226, 228; in trade with Eastern bloc, 126, 129
overseas Chinese. *See* diaspora

packages: Hong Kong visitors bringing, 125, 135; "mailbag rush," 126–27, 137; mediation of propaganda by mailed goods, 12–13, 125, 139–42; relief, coordinated by China Travel Service, 126, *134*, 136, 138; relief, sent to mainland China in response to shortages, 125–27, 131–33, *134*, 135–37, *136*, 140–41, 140–42, *141*, 226, 228. *See also* outside objects
Pang Xunqin: Bauhaus buildings visited by, 81n36; and Central Academy of Craft and Design, 68–70; and Craft Research Studio, 67; criticism of work of, 76–77; on design as an object of mass culture, 72–73; *Problems of Design Research*, 70–72; travel to Eastern Europe by, 75. *See also Organization of Design, The* (Tu'an de zuzhi)
People's Republic of China (PRC): brickmaking technology exploited by, 46; design pedagogy during, 69–70; door gods replaced by socialist symbols in, 98; founding of, 1, 40; material conditions during, 3–7; Ministry of Culture, 68–69, 76; Ministry of Foreign Trade, 135; Ministry of Light Industry, 68–69, 75–76; Ministry of Metallurgy, 204; National Handicraft Exhibitions staged by, 75; regime of material governance established by the CCP, 20–21; significance of construction materials during, 41–43; socialist commerce in the 1950s, 178. *See also* New China; reform era; socialist construction (*shehuizhuyi jianshe*); work units (*danwei*)

production, mass. *See* massification (*dazhonghua*)
projectionists: acrobatic virtuosity of, 107; all-female movie teams, 104–5, *111*, 116, 118; bodily sacrifice of, 103, 104–6, 115–17; care of film reels by, 108–9, *109*, 119; films introduced by, 112, 114; material lives of, 117–18; and mediation between objects and bodies, 12, 102, 104, 118–19, 223; Three Sisters Movie Team from Hebei, 105, *105*, 113
propaganda: bamboo promoted in, 31; films, 102, 106–7; Hong Kong portrayed in, 128, 140; integration of, with socialist Chinese design, 67–68, 78; in material culture of urban China, 183, 185; and mediation by mailed goods, 12–13, 125, 139–42; and mediation by mobile projectionists, 102–3, 106, 109–10, *111*, 113–14, 119–20; during Second Sino-Japanese War, 67; simulacrum of abundance created through, 228
props (*daoju*). *See* dance—props (*daoju*)

Qin dynasty (221–206 BCE), imperial-era building treatises from, 43
Qing dynasty (1644–1911): Beijing's food habits during, 162; brickmaking during, 43, 45; feudal state represented by, 24; furniture designs from, 23; grain consumption during, 164; and industrialization, 45; Liubiju (Pickled Vegetable Store) founded during, 168–69; meat consumed during, 165; rise of consumer culture during, 1

railways: Chengdu-Wuhan railway plans, 205; construction of, 211–12; Kowloon-Canton Railway, 142; luggage inspection at Shenzhen Station, 125, 130; and Second Auto Works, 205
rammed earth: in construction during the Third Front campaign, 207, 211; as a revolutionary material, 42, 55–56
Rao Bin, 203–4, 205, 209, 212
rations and rationing: of cloth, 190; of consumer goods under socialism, 185; in context of scarcity, 132; coupons for registered visitors, 129–30; of electricity, 192; household registration system (*hukou*) linked to, 4, 5, 164
realism, socialist, 101n41, 158–59
Red Silk Dance (Hongchou wu), 88–90, *90*, *93*, 95
reform era: architectural production during, 10, 58; ideological reversal during, 226, 231; rise of markets during, 2
relief packages. *See under* packages
Republican period (1912–49): brick production during, 45; cinema brought to the countryside during, 103; design studies during, 66; "how-to" manuals on bamboo popular during, 31; material life during, 1–2, 21; and ornamental grammar, 80; vernacular modernism in, 72; Zhang Shuiquan's chairs during, 24
revolution: commodities inscribed with slogans of, 183; thrift and discipline extolled in slogans of, 151, 156, 201, 207, 225. *See also* Cultural Revolution; films and film production: revolutionary mobilization of; rammed earth: as a revolutionary material
Riello, Giorgio, 7
Rodchenko, Aleksandr, 219
Roskam, Cole, 222
rural-urban divide. *See* urban-rural divide
Ruskin, John, 65–66

sacrifice: bodily, demanded by scarcity, 119; consumption by top cadres without, 229; Long March as a model of, 105, 228; material contradictions of, 228; as substitution, 224–25
Saich, Tony, 209
Schoenhals, Michael, 3
"scissors pricing" by the state, 195
Second Auto Works (the Works): austere material conditions at, 207–8, 214; establishment of, 15, 200, 205, 212–14; and "Four Simultaneities" policy, 211; mobilization of workers for, 207, 211; as a product of a material regime, 200–201; site selection for, 205–6; suppression of information about, 202, 205, 215n10
Second Front, 202, *203*

Second Sino-Japanese War (1937–45): industrial planning during, 201; Mao's *On Contradiction* (Maodun lun) written during, 3; mass propaganda during, 67; rising nationalism of, 94; Zhang Shuiquan's chairs taken by Japanese officers during, 24–25

Shaanxi: access to commodities in, 15, 188–89; all-female movie team from, 116; durable consumer items in, 192; grain allocations in (1960), 5; housing construction in, 191; Third Front workers from, 15–16
—Guanzhong region, 187; energy consumption, 192; food consumption, 187–89; homespun (*tubu*) clothing worn in, 190; housing construction in, 191; hygiene in, 191

Shanghai: branded products from, in *Delivering*, 153–54; brick production in, 42–43, 45; China Travel Service's transmission of small packets sent to, 136, 138; grain shortages in (1960), 5; and imported foreign products, 132; national housing conference in, 51; open forums for representatives from work units, 57; and Republican-era vernacular modernism, 72; textile manufacturing in, 45, 67

Shanghai Auto Factory, 204

Shanghai Municipal Light Industry Research Institute, 75

Shanghai Number One Department Store: *Storm at the Counter* (Guitai fengbo) by workers at, 153; toothbrushes sold at, 132

Shen Fuwen, 67

Shenzhen: Chinese communist liberation of, 127; luggage inspection at Shenzhen Station, 125, 130; packages brought by Hong Kong visitors to, 125, 135; smuggling of products from Hong Kong to, 127

Shenzhen Commune, clothes worn by children in, 138

shortages: bamboo objects associated with, 10, 35n1; of cooking oil, 139; of cotton and wool, 139; material conditions of Mao era associated with, 1–3, 13–16, 57, 139, 227; relief packages sent to mainland China in response to, 125–27, 131–33, *134*, 135–37, *136*, 140–41, 140–42, *141*, 226, 228. *See also* austerity; rations and rationing; sacrifice

Sichuan, bamboo goods and furniture from, 22

slogans: "First build the factory and afterward housing," 207; "love machines as your life," 108; "produce first and live later," 201; socialist commodities inscribed with, 183, 185; thrift and discipline extolled in, 151, 156, 201, 207, 225; "two-story houses, electric light, and telephones" (*loushang louxia, diandeng dianhua*), 40–41; in verbal messaging in the countryside, 185

Smith, Brian K., 228

socialist asceticism. *See* asceticism

socialist construction (*shehuizhuyi jianshe*): and bamboo as a "hinge material," 21–23; bamboo as a material for, 9, 21, 24–26, 32–35, 221; bricks and brickmaking in, 46–50, 58–59; handcrafted work's contribution to, 27; and labor mobilization in the countryside, 189; and material landscape of the Mao era, 2, 7–11; and mobilization of film crews, 106, 153; and photo essays, 146–48

socialist realism, 158–59

Socialist Transformation (Shehuizhuyi Gaizao; 1956): announcement of, 167; and cultural identity, 161, 167–68, 179; and Donglaishun, 161, 176–77; duration of, 161; and Liubiju, 161, 168–75; urban-rural flow of agricultural products during, 167–73

Sofer, Andrew, on theater props, 223

Sohn-Rethel, Alfred, 186–87, 197n10

Soviet State Folk Dance Ensemble, 93

Soviet Union: border clashes with China, 15, 200–201, 210–11; capitalist resurgence in, 202; China's building technologies compared with, 50–51; as China's model, 6, 50; industrial enterprise model of, for factories, 207, 211; Lenin and Trotsky on cotton textiles, 189, 193; power generators and projectors imported to China from, 104; shortages and postwar austerity measures, 13–14,

149; Sino-Soviet split, 6, 7, 200, 202; socialist realism, 158–59; Stalin Automobile Plant, 204; Torgsin stores in, 120. *See also* Stalin, Joseph; Stalin era
Spuybroek, Lars, on matter and ornament, 66
Stalin, Joseph: on commodities and their production, 193, 194; military preparations of, 202, 213
Stalin Automobile Plant, 204
Stalin era: consumerism and consumer goods during, 149, 194; Stalinist engineers, 73
steel: association with capitalistic waste and excess, 52; backyard furnaces, 10, 53–54; as connecting the PRC to present and future, 21; high-rise, 58; I beam, 41–42; as a new material, 21; spirit of, in New China, 52
Su Changyou, model construction practices of, 46–47, *48*, 52
Sun, Peidong, on commodities and status, 186

Taiwan: entry permits issued for Hong Kong, 128; outside objects sent to mainland China from, 140; rapid economic growth, 179
taste, mass, 72–73, 75, 76
Taylor, Frederick Winslow, and construction techniques, 44, 47
Ten Great Buildings Campaign, 53
Third Front, 202, *203*
Third Front campaign: industrialization of China's interior sparked by, 202, 212; rammed-earth construction used during, 207, 211; suppression of information about, 202, 205, 215n10; threat of invasion leading to, 15, 200–201. *See also* Second Auto Works (the Works)
Three-Antis and Five-Antis Campaigns (1951–52): border controls with China during, 132; and material concerns, 4, 163, 175; thought reform during, 70; travel between Hong Kong and China during, 129
Tianjin: industrialization of, 43; material conditions in, during Cultural Revolution, 1–2, 5, 16; ocean fish from, 165

Tianjin People's Arts Publishing House, 24, 25
Tibetans, 104
toy-making: *Bamboo Animal Toys* (*Zhuzhi dongwu wanju*) and, 32, *33*; by women, 65; by Zhang Shuiquan, 24
tradition: and Beijing's food culture, 174–79; door gods replaced by socialist symbols, 98; modernization vs. persistence of, 2; portrayals in Chinese propaganda, 128; reanimation of native and ethnic, 64; and storytelling style evoked by film projectionists, 109, 110, 112–13, 119. *See also* bamboo; bricks and brickmaking; handicrafts and handicraft skills
Transformation. *See* Socialist Transformation (*Shehuizhuyi Gaizao*; 1956)
travel: to China for Chinese New Year (1956), 128, 129–31; clothing guidelines for visiting China, 130–31; between Hong Kong and China during the Three-Antis and Five-Antis Campaigns (1951–52), 129; of Lei Guiyuan to Eastern Europe, 75. *See also* China Travel Service
Treatise on Architectural Methods or State Building Standards (*Yingzao fashi*; 1103 CE), 43

United Front, 138
United Nations High Commission for Refugees, 128
urban-rural divide: access to commodities, 5, 8, 15, 16, 183–85, 193–97; commodity exchange, 184–86, 193–94, 229; experiences of owning bamboo objects, 23, 35; experiences of urban projectionists in the countryside, 118; flow of agricultural products, 167–73; and market regulation, 226–27, 229–30, 232n13; and mass campaigns, 4–6, 210; mediating role of dance props in, 93–98; and production of basic necessities, 5, 66; role of trial performances (*guanmo huiyan*) in bridging, 86, 95–96; rural women's unpaid labor, 196–97, 230; sent-down youths (*zhiqing*), 107–8, 116, 117–18; Zhang Shuiquan as a model of, 26–27

van der Rohe, Mies, 44
Verdery, Katherine, 149
Vietnam: brick's importance in, 60n8; Tonkin Gulf incident, 202, 215n11; trade agreements with the PRC, 6; US military presence in, 200

"Wall Reform" (Qiangti Gaige) Movement (1973–76), 57
Wang Anyi, *A Tale from the Cultural Revolution*, 107–8
Wang Wei, 58
Wang Xun, 73, 81–82n40
Watson, Sam, 49
Weber, Max, 151
Weins, Thomas, 198n24
Wemheuer, Felix, 208–9
Wilcox, Emily, 223
women: all-female movie teams, 104–6, 111, 116, 118; handicrafts produced by labor of, 65; rural, textile work of, 189–91, 196; rural, unpaid labor of, 196–97, 230; scarcity of female projectionists, 117; Three Sisters Movie Team from Hebei, 105, *105*, 113. See also *Delivering Goods on the Road* (*Songhuo lushang*)
work points, 5, 191
Works, the. *See* Second Auto Works (the Works)
work units (*danwei*): contribution to the First Auto Works, 204; and Handicraft Bureau, 73; household possessions distributed by, 1, 2, 5, 16, 191; housing assignments associated with, 5; ignored in organization of construction teams, 47; under Ministry of Light Industry, 75–76; Pang Xunqin's participation in, 70; rural women's unpaid labor contrasted with, 196; sharing knowledge between, 47–48; Wuxue Town bamboo goods cooperative as, 24
Wright, Frank Lloyd, on bricks, 44
Wu Lao: design approached by, 71; travel to Eastern Europe, 75

Xinjiang: papercut patterns from, 70; sidewalk paving in, *54*

Yan'an: emergence of technoscience in, 201; Lu Xun Academy of Art in, 67; *yangge* dance from, 94–95, 96, 97–98
Yang Fudong, 58
yangge dance, 94–95, 96, 97–98
Yu, Hua, 227

Zhang Shuiquan: ability to "serve the people" with teaching, 25, 26; as a labor model, 23–27, 29, 30–31, 35
Zhang Wentian, *41*
Zhongguo minzu minjian wu jicheng, 101n51
Zhou Enlai, *41*, 57, 161; bamboo sofa chair crafted for, 30; construction of the Works supported by, 210–11
Zhu De, 40
Zubrzycki, Geneviève, on "national sensorium," 79

www.ingramcontent.com/pod-product-compliance
Lightning Source LLC
Chambersburg PA
CBHW030616230426
43661CB00053B/2020